T0330034

Developments in Organizational Politics

Developments in Organizational Politics

How Political Dynamics Affect Employee
Performance in Modern Work Sites

Eran Vigoda

Senior Lecturer of Organizational Behavior and Public Administration, University of Haifa, Israel

Edward Elgar

Cheltenham, UK • Northampton, MA, USA

© Eran Vigoda 2003

All rights reserved. No part of this publication may be reproduced, stored in a retrieval system or transmitted in any form or by any means, electronic, mechanical or photocopying, recording, or otherwise without the prior permission of the publisher.

Published by
Edward Elgar Publishing Limited
Glensanda House
Montpellier Parade
Cheltenham
Glos GL50 1UA
UK

Edward Elgar Publishing, Inc.
136 West Street
Suite 202
Northampton
Massachusetts 01060
USA

A catalogue record for this book
is available from the British Library

Library of Congress Cataloguing in Publication Data

Vigoda, Eran, 1966–
    Developments in organizational politics : how political dynamics affect employee performance in modern worksites / Eran Vigoda.
        p.cm
    1. Office politics. 2. Organizational behavior. 3. Bureaucracy. 4. Interpersonal relations. 5. Work environment. 6. Job satisfaction. 7. Work—Psychological aspects. 8. Employee morale. 9. Labor Productivity. 10. Performance. I. Title.

    HF5386.5.V54 2003
    302.3'5—dc21

                                                            2003049042

ISBN 1 84376 397 4

Printed and bound in Great Britain by MPG Books Ltd, Bodmin, Cornwall

Contents

Figures

Tables

Preface

Why would anyone invest time and energy wading through a research-oriented volume that is interested in the amorphous phenomena of power, influence and politics in the workplace? To those who ask such a question I would say, politics in organizations is as crucial as doing the job itself and is as important as politics outside organizations. It has a massive impact on our well-being as employees, managers and stakeholders in organizations. I would even venture to say that increasing one's knowledge in the field often spells the difference between staying with an organization or leaving it, being promoted or being left behind, or winning or losing in competitive situations.

Take universities as an example. When people from within the academic system are asked to characterize their work, they tend to use various superlatives. Some emphasize the autonomy of such a career, others argue that being in the forefront of knowledge creation is the most exciting thing, and others mention the pleasure of teaching, educating and transferring knowledge to the next generation. When asked to become more critical they tend to mention the demanding nature of such a job, the slow promotion and tenure procedures and the agonies of publishing. I, however, see the academic arena in a totally different light. In my position as an academic I have seen, recognized and experienced how political universities can be. I thus believe today that from the point of view of everyone who is involved in such systems, or in others like them, internal politics is as important as producing quality research and as influential as performing in a professional manner on the job.

But let us get back to a more academic discussion. I was first introduced to the topic of organizational politics during my graduate studies in the late 1990s. Organizational politics was evolving at that time as a promising research field that related two of my major fields of interest; the study of human politics and the understanding of modern organizations. With time I found that it encapsulated much more than that. It integrated knowledge from various other disciplines in the social sciences such as political science, sociology, psychology, management and public administration. It reflected a unique domain in organizational studies and brought some fresh thinking into conservative approaches that had dominated the managerial literature. Its interdisciplinary orientation was firm and, most importantly, empirical studies in the field were few and far between. Hence the secrets of interpersonal political manoeuvres and their meaning for organizational members in general, and for me as an academic in a very 'political' environment, promised to be a fascinating field of study.

Nonetheless I soon found myself struggling with the difficulties of designing such empirical studies. Almost everyone around me believed that organizational politics were an inherent part of worksite dynamics but few people could operatively define it or put it in a measurable framework. Consequently my curiosity and motivation to study this phenomenon more effectively grew and intensified. Supported by the advice, experience and wisdom of my mentor at that time, Professor Aaron Cohen, I started putting together pieces of conceptual and empirical knowledge and conducted my own experiments and studies.

This book is in fact a partial summary of my efforts in recent years. Its prime goal is to suggest a comprehensive model that may prove useful in further investigations of organizational politics. The model is aimed at overcoming some of the difficulties in the study of organizational politics such as (1) better defining this arena, (2) using clear, reliable and valid measures, and (3) uncovering antecedents as well as possible reactions to workplace politics. The main purpose of the book is to test the potential impact of organizational politics on attitudes, orientations, behavioral intentions, and the actual performance of employees. As will be demonstrated in each one of the various chapters, organizational politics generally refers to the power relations and influence processes between individuals or groups in the internal or external organizational environment. However, the book focuses on interpersonal politics inside organizations and is based on my continuing investigation of these dynamics from a positivist approach. Similarly it draws on material from other works in various cultures that have also tried to present a useful framework for the study of the field. The seminal works by Kipnis et al. (1980) and Ferris et al. (1989) as well as many others that followed, have offered some conceptual, empirical, and methodological platforms that were used extensively in my studies. Consequently all the studies presented here rely on my previous writings and accumulated knowledge and experience. However, I believe that brought together in the format of a comprehensive book, they offer substantially added value by integrating various questions, methods and approaches that explore· the meaning of politics, power and influence relations in organizations in greater depth. Hence in my view the book makes at least five main contributions to the study of organizational politics in modern worksites:

1.   The book focuses on *aspects of intra-organizational politics* that take place in a variety of ways between organizational members, be they managers at different levels or employees. By so doing it tries to make a

clear distinction between politics inside and outside organizations and the impact of interpersonal relations on the horizontal, vertical, and diagonal lines.

2. The majority of the studies that are presented here deal with internal politics in *public administration systems*. Very few studies have addressed these issues in other non-profit bodies or private sector firms. As will be demonstrated in several chapters, there is a significant lack of knowledge about internal politics in bureaucracies that are closely attached to the classical political system. However all studies and ideas are also highly relevant for *private and business oriented firms*.

3. The studies included in this book were, for the most part, conducted in *one cultural environment*, which makes them a useful collection of data comparable with other cultural findings, most of which come from the North American culture. The Israeli setting was a source for most of the data but, using a unique British data set, one chapter also illuminates how cultural factors can prove useful in the study of workplace politics.

4. All of the studies included in this volume are predicated on the belief that *actual organizational politics substantially differ from perceived organizational politics*. I argue that actual organizational politics needs to be treated separately and independently from the more common variable that the literature measures using the perceptions of organizational politics scale (POPS). As will be explained in numerous places throughout this book, I have adopted the cognitive approach toward organizational politics that is common in contemporary literature. This approach was introduced by Lewin (1936), who argued that people respond to their perceptions of reality, not to reality itself. Similarly it was assumed that as a pervasive and illusive organizational phenomenon, organizational politics is best represented by what people think of it rather than by what it actually means. Nonetheless, the book has tried to present the two competing approaches toward organizational politics. Each one of them is analysed in depth and moreover some conceptual links are suggested to try to put the two theories together. However, in keeping with other scholarly writing, the perceptual approach has been emphasized in this book.

5. Finally, all of the studies in this book are strongly oriented toward a better understanding of the relationship between organizational politics and employees' performance. One of the main themes is that the investigation of organizational politics inside public systems and among public employees must focus on two areas – the structural and the functional.

   (a) Structurally speaking, the public sector interacts intensively with national political systems and operates as the formal enforcer of public policy. The strong interactions between these two mechanisms create a natural habitat for the emergence of political behaviors in public organizations and among their members. It is assumed that the political attitudes and behavior of individuals in public organizations are somehow affected by political activities that occur in the nearby environment. This mutual interaction is expected to reveal intra-organizational political processes.

(b) Functionally speaking, the uniqueness of public and non-profit organizations causes some serious methodological difficulties in evaluating their effectiveness and efficiency. Management theory has proposed only a few explanations for changes in the personal and general performance in such systems. This cluster of studies, presented here, generally claims that under some conditions political behavior and the perceptions of politics inside public organizations may help explain changes in employees' attitudes toward the workplace as well as their behavioral intentions and actual performance. It is important, though, to note that this is not expected to be a major contribution compared with other well-known factors such as motivation or participation in decision making. Nevertheless, it is expected to explain a significant part of the variance in employee performance in addition to what has already been explained by the other factors. The research model as followed here is designed to theoretically support and empirically test these claims.

Hence, our inquiry into organizational politics is in fact part of a more extensive quest for better explanations for organizational outputs and outcomes, especially in the public sector. This sector suffers from criticism regarding the intervention of political considerations in administrative processes. Many political scientists and public administration scholars have mentioned the close relationship between political systems and mechanisms and administrative operations as a core obstacle to better results in the public sector. While the democratic nature of modern states necessitates political control of civil servants' actions, critics often point to the negative impact of political behavior on public administration systems. This question has received extensive attention in the literature, yet this attention has only rarely been translated into empirical studies utilizing measurable methods and tools. The studies included here make an attempt to deal with this issue systematically, using behavioral methods that are available in the wider managerial literature. The reader will judge how successful they are.

Furthermore, the book criticizes the normative approaches in management theory that view organizational politics as an illegitimate use of power which is aimed at acquiring informal influence over others. As such, organizational politics is associated with a variety of negative actions that are harmful and dangerous from the organizational point of view. Alternatively, this book illuminates a complementary approach according to which organizational politics is part of the organizational reality and therefore has positive aspects as well. These aspects depend mainly on each organization's members' expectations and match with the workplace. Thus, the studies brought together in this book develop this approach theoretically and test it empirically.

Perhaps the greatest advantage of this book for scholars and students of organizational behavior and political behavior is the integrative model suggested for the inquiry into organizational politics. The model may be treated as an extension of the classical work by Ferris et al. (1989) and is based on three major factors, each of which leads to separate research areas:

1. the characteristics of organizational politics;
2. the antecedents of organizational politics;
3. the effect of organizational politics on employee behavioral intentions and actual performance.

The first area deals with the characteristics of organizational politics. I will focus the discussion on two dominant approaches in the field. The first approach deals with organizational politics as a set of influence tactics and actual behaviors. The second places more emphasis on the individual's understanding of the political game in organizations. Similarly, organizational politics may be treated in one of two ways: (1) in a *behavioral framework*, that is as a pattern of influential activities of organizational members which aim to maximize interests and goals; or (2) in a *cognitive framework*, that is as the employees' understanding of politics and its meaning in the organizational environment, elsewhere defined as perceptions of organizational politics.

The second area posits three groups of antecedents to perceptions of organizational politics: (1) intra-organizational, structural and situational understanding; (2) actual political behavior; and (3) personal and personality constructs. While the effects of personal and intra-organizational factors on organizational politics have been mentioned in previous studies, the effect of actual political behavior on perceptions of politics has seldom been investigated. Thus I hope to break new ground in linking employees' influential activities and their construction and reconstruction of organizational reality in terms of perceived politics, fairness, and equity in one's work environment.

Beyond these two exciting topics perhaps the most influential and significant one is whether organizational politics contributes to the explanation of employees' behavioral intentions and performance in the workplace. As the book demonstrates, management literature often discusses aspects of overall organizational performance as well as individual performance, due to their importance and contribution to modern society. Management theory has treated the issue of performance in different ways, yet it seems that the political approach has been relatively overlooked and has remained comparatively underdeveloped. Thus this book is trying to establish a politics–performance correlation in a more explicit way than has previous research.

Consequently the research model I have used consists of three main parts. The first deals with different influence tactics that together comprise the organizational politics scale and additionally suggest a variety of antecedents of organizational politics. The second part explores the correlation between organizational politics and perceptions of organizational politics through two mediating variables: (1) the extent of employees' Met Expectations (ME) and (2) the level of Person–Organization Fit (POF). According to my view, these variables set the conditions that determine whether organizational politics may result in positive or negative employee behavior. The third part develops a potential link between all of the independent variables, including actual organizational politics and perceptions of politics and a set of organizational outcomes. Naturally, from this point on, more attention is given to the study of politics perceptions. Hirschman's (1970) theory of Exit, Voice, Loyalty, and Neglect (EVLN) is used as a solid basis for the examination of employees' performance, together with in-role performance and organizational citizenship behavior (OCB). Special attention is given to stress-related outcomes of organizational politics such as stress, strain, burnout, and reported aggressive behavior in the workplace.

THE FRAMEWORK OF THE BOOK

The book is divided into eight parts. In addition to introductory and summary sections, most of the empirical data is analysed and discussed in six core chapters. Each chapter is based on a separate study or data analysis targeted at providing some support for the general research model. All presentations are made systematically in the following order:

1. A theoretical overview of the relevant research questions and background on previous studies that have dealt with similar or related topics.
2. A model and hypotheses section. The model outlines the explanatory arguments and a specific set of hypotheses as part of the more general

theoretical concepts that are presented in the introductory chapter. The hypotheses are arranged in sequential order and are designated by a string comprised of an H (for hypothesis), the letters a–e (for Studies 1–5 respectively; Study 6 does not include specific hypotheses), and a number indicating the intra-chapter order of hypotheses. For example, Hb3 represents Hypothesis number 3 of the second (b) study.

3. A description of the study and the results that provide information on the samples used, the statistical strategy and the main results. This section usually includes a set of accompanying tables or figures used to validate the solidity of the statistical methods employed to support the hypotheses.

4. A discussion and summary section that elaborates on the meaning and implications of the specific results. This section is aimed at providing a critical analysis of the study's findings in light of previous knowledge and any other existing empirical evidence taken from other cultures or work environments.

The core studies included in Chapters 1 to 6 are based on original published and unpublished materials by the author that have been reworked to cohere with the general theme of the book. These include papers in several influential journals such as the *Journal of Vocational Behavior*, *Public Personnel Management*, *Journal of Business Research*, *Journal of Organizational Behavior*, and *Human Relations*.

As one may also note, the research model suggested in the introductory chapter is quite complicated and includes a variety of variables. Therefore, the process of forming and testing the arguments via hypotheses is carried out gradually and in several sequential phases. Each study presented here is part of the gradual development of the general model. The various studies consist of several data sets, most of them taken from the public sector but others from the private and the voluntary sectors as well (see study 4: A, B, C, Chapter 4). For reasons of clarity and simplicity I have decided to separate the description of the measurements from the conceptual and analytical ones. Readers who are interested in the procedure and measures used in these studies can find them in appendix 1. Generally speaking, the model relied on a longitudinal design and a three-phase data collection. Note, however, that not every study employed data from all three points in time. In addition some of the studies used other data sources that were not longitudinal.

The book ends with a summary, synthesis and critical discussion of the findings as presented in each of the studies. The goal of this section is to offer a comprehensive and up-to-date set of results that integrate well with our theoretical framework. The summary chapter also suggests how theory in the field can be developed further. I present several suggestions that may help scholars interested in organizational politics determine where the gaps and missing links in the study of this discipline lie.

TARGET READERS

This book is intended as an analytical summary of a decade's worth of study of topics in organizational politics. It is characterized by a positivist, empirical approach. Such an empirical analysis of original data sources may be best used by scholars in various fields in the behavioral and social sciences such as organizational behavior, management and business, occupational psychology, and sociology or political science. The book's focus on the internal politics of organization makes it a useful tool for public and private administration scholars looking for better explanations of the bureaucratic environments of large federal, state, and local authorities as well as other business firms.

The prime readers of this book are thus expected to come from the professional ranks; the academia and the research and development arena in social sciences. However the book also provides a wealth of information that may prove useful for other audiences. For example, the theoretical sections of the book, particularly the introductory chapters, the summary, and the conceptual framing of each of the studies presented will be enlightening for graduate students in the social sciences seeking a better understanding of intra-organizational dynamics, the development of conflicts in organizations, and the nature of power influence and authority in various worksites. In addition some highly skilled professionals may find the book's description of power relations among individuals and groups helpful in the running of their organizations. Finally the book, with its strong academic and empirical orientation, delineates some important current developments in an area that is both obscure and misunderstood but which holds great potential for those who are interested in the nexus between management and politics.

Introduction to the study of organizational politics

THE STATE OF THE DISCIPLINE

Organizational politics represents a unique domain of interpersonal relations in the workplace. Its main characteristics are the readiness of people to use power in their efforts to influence others and secure their own interests or, alternatively, avoid negative outcomes within the organization (Bozeman et al., 1996). In recent decades organizational politics has become a topic of prime importance in management literature. In the late 1950s Lasswell claimed that politics is important since it represents the secret of 'who gets what, when, and how' in a social system (Lasswell, 1958). However, until the 1970s politics in organizations received little or no attention. Only with the recognition that, as in the national arena, organizations too have to deal with conflicts, resource sharing processes, and power struggles among their members and units has organizational politics begun to attract growing attention. In the late 1970s some studies established a theoretical framework for the inquiry into the role of politics in the workplace (Bacharach and Lawler, 1980; Mayes and Allen, 1977; Mintzberg, 1983; Pfeffer, 1981).

Drawing on these studies, Pfeffer (1992:8) argued that organizations, particularly large ones, are like governments in that they are fundamentally political entities. To understand them one needs to understand organizational politics, just as to understand governments one needs to understand governmental politics. With the rapidly growing interest in organizational politics the phenomenon is being discussed from a variety of perspectives. For example, some studies have tried to typologize the various influence tactics found in the workplace (for example, Kipnis et al., 1980) while others have used a theory of organizational conflict to explain power struggles and influence tactics (for example, Putnam, 1995). Most of these studies have focused on the nature and expressions of organizational politics and have done it using a negative perspective that concentrates on equating organizational politics with the dark side of human behavior, such as manipulation, coercive influence, or other subversive and semi-legal actions (for example, Ferris and King, 1991; Mintzberg, 1983, 1989). Yet few have used a balanced approach to determine the effects of organizational politics

1

on employees' attitudes, behavior and performance in the workplace. The relationship between organizational politics and organizational outcomes is important because every member of an organization has power and exercises it in a unique way to benefit himself/herself in his/her work environment. Power and politics have at least some effect on every member of an organization and thus on the entire organizational unit. Therefore many scholars have argued that the relationship between organizational politics and organizational outcomes is an important one that deserves further inquiry (Bozeman et al., 1996; Ferris and Kacmar, 1992; Kacmar and Carlson, 1994).

This chapter reviews contemporary theory on organizational politics and suggests some explanations for the relationship between organizational politics and employee performance. Therefore it is essential first to establish a clear and balanced conceptualization of and perspective on organizational politics and its nature.

POLITICAL BEHAVIOR AND ORGANIZATIONAL POLITICS

Organizational politics is a complex, pervasive and sometimes even ambiguous phenomenon. Its ambiguity derives from two distinct factors. On the one hand our natural feeling is that we know exactly what organizational politics means because we have to deal with it in everyday life. However, when you ask someone to clearly define organizational politics it is likely that you will not get two answers that are the same or even similar. Moreover there is some confusion concerning proximate terms which very often arise together when politics and especially organizational politics is discussed (for example, conflict, influence, force, authority, power, and so on). The most commonly used and definitely one of the most important terms in this connection is *power*. Politics is sometimes mistakenly considered synonymous with power, perhaps because both are significant factors of human behavior that affect one's ability to accomplish and secure goals and interests in a social system. Russell (1938) claimed that power expresses the capacity of individuals to produce intended and foreseen effects on others. Politics depends on power, and power is distributed unequally among members of the organization. Therefore whoever holds some power in the organization occasionally uses it to influence others. In other words, power is a social resource aimed at obtaining influence, which is a social process, and both are initiators of politics. Since power is considered a special case of the exercise of influence (Wrong, 1979:21), it would be much more accurate to discuss *influence* when one wants to study the nature of political processes in organizations.

Moreover, to better understand the meaning of organizational politics it may be useful to treat it as part of the general field of political behavior. People's political behavior raises a series of major questions that throughout the years have led to various research studies. These questions are centred on a number of issues of interest, including: What is political behavior? Can it be differentiated from other behavior types and, if so, in what way? Can one provide an exact definition of such behavior and can it also be classified and its various aspects identified? What brings people to act or not act in a manner of behavior that is termed 'political' and can such behavior be measured at all? Are there certain factors that influence such behavior more than others and to what extent?; Can political behavior be controlled somehow and, if so, how and to what extent? How is political behavior expressed and what are the differences, if there are any, between these different expressions?

For example, various studies have attempted to support empirically the claim that there is a connection between political behavior in organizations and political behavior in the extra-organizational sphere. The studies by Cohen and Vigoda (1999; 2000) have found a relationship between political behaviors and citizenship orientations in the workplace and in the national and communal environments. Their studies relied on an earlier work by Peterson (1990:177–197) who claimed that it is possible to find unique aspects of political behavior in the workplace. He maintains that the workplace serves as an agent of political socialization (p. 177), and among the various aspects which influence the arise of political behavior in general he mentions:

1. *Job autonomy*: the more independence the employee has in performing his duties, the more adept he will become at the employment of influence for the purpose of promoting his goals and the more responsible for the results of his activity he will be.
2. *Input into decisions*: involvement and cooperation in decision making will give the employee a feeling of connection to the organization, a sense of responsibility for its proper functioning, and a willingness to invest in keeping the organization competitive. Therefore there is a better chance of enhancing the political behavior which attempts to maximize organizational and personal goals and to reach achievements through influencing others so that they will assist in the realization of the individual's and the organization's goals.
3. *Job satisfaction*: the more satisfied an employee is, the more he trusts the organization and the processes in it and the less alienated from his job he is. The satisfaction he feels at work leads him to maintain the status quo,

while the lack of satisfaction may lead individuals to act in order to influence and change decisions in the organization.

4. *Occupational status and prestige*: are connected with milder political opinions, a greater willingness to express opinions, protest and actively promote preferred ideas. When the employee has high professional status and prestige he is also in charge of assets that require support and protection. He does not seek any major changes in his environment and uses his highly developed political proficiency to maintain his personal assets.

5. *Work relations*: close relations between the individual and others in the workplace lead to the permeation of views between these individuals with some of the members adopting the others' perceptions, political attitudes and behaviors.

6. *Unionization*: may lead to the spill over of ideas, behaviors, and political activity habits from the workplace into the national political system and vice versa. People who tend to be involved and active in employees' committees gain proficiencies that are simple to use even outside the organization, and so a mutual interaction between politics in the work sphere and outside it is formed.

The interest in relating general political attitudes and behaviors with organizational politics led to the abundance of studies conducted mainly by political scientists and political sociologists, among whom are Almond and Verba (1963), Campbell (1960, 1962), Dahl (1957, 1963), Lasswell (1958), Milbrath (1977, 1981), Nie et al. (1979), Pateman (1970), Verba and Nie (1972), Emerson (1962, 1972) and others. These researchers launched investigations in many different directions but most of them discussed national, local and governmental aspects of political behavior. Political behavior at the national and local levels expresses the willingness of the individual to participate in some manner in social processes which determine the power distribution within the state, impact the governing bodies and their elected representatives, and influence the way in which national assets are distributed. Most of the studies discussed the analysis of voters' behavior, their opinions and their influence on national systems and on public mechanisms (Asher, 1984; Campbell, 1960, 1962), identifying and defining the various kinds of political behaviors exhibited by those in high positions, members of parliament and public service personnel (for example, Bacharach, 1967; Goldenberg and Traugott, 1984), as well as those shaping the policies and performances of political parties and government departments (for example, Cook, 1977).

However, the discussion of political behavior sometimes went beyond the discussion of governmental political issues in order to probe the political aspect of daily human behavior in fields such as politics and humour, politics in sports and culture, politics inside the family, politics and religion, politics and the media (Molm, 1997; Peterson, 1990; Schwartz, 1974). Such studies stressed the basic human components of the employment of force or power meant to influence the environment in order to change processes or structures in social frameworks that are not necessarily state oriented. These studies also explored the different factors that shape human political behavior, both in the field of government and in the arenas noted above. The findings of these studies contributed to the classification of the factors into a number of general groups:

1. social and personal/sociological factors (for example, socialization, group influences, socio-economic status and demographic factors such as education, age, and place of residence);
2. personality/psychological influences (for example, an ability to process information, locus of control, self-confidence, ego, a desire for power, Machiavellianism, a tendency to dogmatism, a level of self-appreciation, and personal needs);
3. socio-political influences (for example, governmental policy, the government's ideological approach, the performance of various governmental bodies, the behavior of leaders and of parties, and the occurrence of exceptional external events such as security crises or significant social and economic processes);
4. concrete background and situational conditions (for example, what are the purposes and goals of the political activity? whom is it addressing? what is its timing? to what degree is it supported or rejected?).

POLITICAL BEHAVIOR AT WORK: MACRO AND MICRO ASPECTS

The influence factors mentioned and the questions that they raise have led to an interest in another scientific area of research, dedicated to the study of politics in its organizational context. Like the classic aspects of national and governmental politics, organizational politics basically represents the behavior of an individual looking to influence others for the purpose of promoting particular goals and interests in the work environment.

Most of the attention in the early studies was initially focused on macro politics (Allison, 1969; Kaufman, 1964; Pandarus, 1973; Zaleznik, 1970). A macro politics analysis usually focuses on the entire organization or on some central units within it and examines the relations among them, as well as the relations between them and the social and political system in the country. For example, Wildavski (1966) analysed processes of budgeting in general, and public budgeting specifically, in terms borrowed from the world of political behavior and thus articulated the important influence of this behavior on the system's products in the private and public sectors. With regard to public administration and policy Wamsley and Zald (1973) defined organizational politics as the process and the structure of the use of authority and force to advance the main goals, directions and parameters of organizational economics. It seems that this definition is more suitable for the analysis of politics at the higher organizational levels where the decisions about policy and its implementation are discussed. Indeed, Wamsley and Zald's study refers mainly to public organizations but does not reflect political processes at more basic organizational levels such as at the interpersonal and intergroup level.

Throughout the years the phenomenon has also been examined as micro politics, and various studies have focused on the complex structure of power, force, and influence relations within work organizations and among its members. In contrast to the macro politics analysis, the micro politics studies deal with the individual, his standing, perceptions and behavior in small groups. Samuel (1990:57) maintains that in order to understand the processes of power and politics within organizations 'it is more useful to focus on the level of analysis of inter-personal relations and processes'. On this level they are easier to diagnose and study analytically, but are basically very similar to the interactions that occur at the group or inter-organizational level. In the political micro-organizational context, Peterson (1990:47) mentions the Hornell studies which show that people tend to view the workplace as a much more political environment than religious groups, fraternal clubs, cultural organizations or even the family.

Other micro politics studies have focused on the influence tactics employed by the organization's members that create the inter-organizational political game (for example, Judge and Bretz, 1994; Kipnis et al., 1980). There was a significant increase in these studies at the end of the 1970s and the beginning of the 1980s (for example, Allen et al., 1979; Bacharach and Lawler, 1980; Benson and Hornsby, 1988), and in specific studies there was a reference to both the macro and the micro levels together (for example, Frost and Egri, 1991). On the one hand there was an interest in examining such processes because they represented an additional level of political human behavior not specifically understood in the behavioral disciplines and in political science. On the other hand the importance of such behavior and its contribution to the advancement of theoretical and practical knowledge in organizational, public management, and administration theory was understood.

It is important to note that the main theoretical basis for the need to study work organizations from a political perspective and on the micro-organizational level can be found in the work of researchers such as Emerson (1962, 1972) and Molm (1997:4). These researchers claimed that a social exchange system based on power and force occurs on different levels, and the players in it can be individuals, groups or organizations acting inside a familial structure, in the work environment, in international relations, and so on. Other researchers, such as Dahl (1970) and Pateman (1970) presented two points that connect the world of work with the world outside it regarding anything to do with political activity.

1. When employees are more aware of what is happening around them at work and can influence decisions and activities in the organization or solve problems that arise in the organization, they become more proficient in the political process of distributing organizational assets. This proficiency may serve them later on in the national context and in national political activities. This process is called a 'spillover effect' or an 'education function' or a 'participatory predisposition.'
2. The individual's involvement in what is happening in the work sphere strengthens his identification with the group and accordingly raises his level of involvement with and his desire to influence what is happening locally and nationally. The enhancement of identification contributes to the increase in the employee's sense of connection to the workplace, to his social environment in general, and to the world outside the work environment itself. It is important, however, to note that the direction of the spillover suggested by Dahl and Pateman moves from within the work environment into the world outside the work environment. In their most recent study Brady et al. (1995) supported this view and made a connection between the various assets a person has at his disposal, such as time, money, civic skills, and socioeconomic status and political activity in the workplace and in other organizations.

Sobel (1993) also strengthens this view, and his findings show that on the one hand, in accordance with the spillover theory, employees' participation in processes taking place in the workplace is a significant factor for political participation outside the workplace. On the other hand, he claims that an opposite connection is also very likely. A spillover from the general political sphere into the organization may also occur when employees' performances are influenced by factors that stem from political activity outside the workplace such as political participation and efficiency.

While the theoretical framework for the study of organizational politics on the micro level began to take shape approximately two decades ago, many believe that it is not yet sufficiently broad or well developed (see, for example, Cropanzano et al., 1997; Drory and Romm, 1990). An important area that has been largely ignored is the relation between organizational politics and employees' performance, a hole in our knowledge that is apparent from the remarkable lack of empirical studies in this field. There are various reasons for the small number of such studies.

1. For many years the development of organizational theories focused on certain factors that seem to have a better potential than others for explaining behavior in general and employees' performance specifically. Among these factors were motivation to work, cooperation in decision making, autonomy in the job position, commitment to the organization, and personal factors. Surprisingly, components of organizational politics are rarely mentioned in these explanations (for example, Spector, 1986; Wagner and Gooding, 1987).
2. The study of employees' performance and system products has expanded in recent decades largely due to a significant growth in consumption, in international trade, and in public demand for better products and services. The rising economic competition both in the national and in the international arenas has led the scientific world to search for new factors that influence the deterioration of a product's quality or service and that cause a reduction in production qualities, all for the purpose of finding efficient remedies and reasonable solutions for them. Only in the past few years have political components inside and outside the organizations been suggested as a reason for changes in production (Klingner, 1982; Pavett and Lau, 1983).
3. The study of political behavior is a complex field with significant methodological challenges. There is a real difficulty in collecting data regarding the political nature of human behavior because usually there is a fear of reporting it or no awareness of its existence. This difficulty leads to a certain reticence among researchers, thus limiting the attempts at conducting empirical studies based on original field data.

Until now these main reasons have limited the scope of research into issues of political behavior in organizations. Therefore one of the important challenges facing this study is elucidating the central aspects of organizational politics on the micro level, including its various causes, expressions and implications.

THE CONCEPTUAL BOUNDARIES OF INTRA-ORGANIZATIONAL POLITICS

Organizational politics is usually associated with phenomena such as power struggles, conflicts over the sources of power and influence, and planned and directed attempts to actualize warring interests in the workplace. Indeed, the political approach to the study of organizations and the understanding of the structure of relations, activities, and decisions made in them focuses to a large degree on the natural differences which exist among the various parts of the organization and on the numerous and sometimes conflicting interests of its members (Allison, 1971; Cyert and March, 1963; March, 1962). Although other approaches to the study of organizations, such as the rational choice approach, bureaucratic models, and decision process models, are significantly different from the political approach both in their basic assumptions and in the explanations they provide for organizational processes (for further reading see, Pfeffer, 1981:1–32) – they all assume that the struggle over interests significantly influences organizational life.

Since the end of the 1960s and the beginning of the 1970s several definitions for organizational politics have been developed. Wildavski (1966) claimed that the budgeting process most accurately represents the centre of the political phenomenon in organizations as it expresses a conflict that ends both in the organizational assets' distribution and in the products of organizational policy. Harvey and Mills (1970) also argued that organizational politics expresses activities that aim to influence the organizational assets' distribution system and, accordingly, Pettigrew (1973) defined the political process in organizations as the setting of goals, the demand for assets, and the gaining of support in order to achieve them. Mintzberg (1983) maintained that organizational politics expresses the illegitimate and informal use of force and therefore the phenomenon as a whole exceeds the social consensus and the norms of the organization. In her most recent book, Hardy (1995:xii–xxiv) also claimed that the accepted approach in current literature views organizational politics as an illegitimate aspect of the use of force in an organization, a claim I tend to agree with. However, the definition of organizational politics exclusively as a process involving conflict or as a process that is always illegitimate and socially unacceptable is too narrow a definition. There are political behaviors that do not involve either of the two. For example, attempts to influence through persuasion do not necessarily express conflict and yet do make use of legitimate assets in order to promote certain interests of the person employing them. The employees are usually aware of the existence of organizational politics and influence and even make use of them when necessary. Organizations usually do not actively invoke formal or informal sanctions against those who employ influence in various manners, and there are many influence tactics which are common, acceptable and expressed daily in every organization.

Indeed an objective discussion of organizational politics is required as it is an acceptable, common and socially functional phenomenon. Such a comprehensive discussion of the different definitions of organizational politics is given by Mayes and Allen (1977). In their opinion, the understanding of political processes in organizations must be based on some basic assumptions:

1. Political behavior takes place in different levels of the organization.
2. Not all behaviors in the organization are political.
3. Political processes in the organization can be analysed in objective terms.
4. Political processes in the organization are unique, and their analysis requires the development of an autonomous conceptual and theoretical system.

Mayes and Allen (1977) also argue that an accurate definition of organizational politics must conform to three main criteria. First, it must reflect both the micro-organizational level and the macro-organizational level. Therefore they attach great importance to the approach of Martin and Sims (1974) and Burns (1961) who maintain that organizational politics refers to the control, force, and influence relations between members of the organization themselves vis-à-vis the organization and as an organization vis-à-vis various extra-organizational systems. Second, each definition of organizational politics must relate to behaviors other than those concerned with the distribution of assets in the organization. Third, each definition has to distinguish between political behaviors and behaviors which are not political. Therefore organizational politics is defined by Mayes and Allen (1977:675) as a dynamic process of influence which results in organizational products exceeding the simple performance of job tasks, or in a more detailed manner as 'the management of influence meant to achieve acceptable goals which are not sanctioned by the organization or alternatively, an influence meant to achieve unacceptable goals which are sanctioned by the organization through acceptable influence means'. This complex definition conforms to the three criteria defined earlier and even differentiates influence means (tactics) from influence goals (strategies), which is important for an analysis of the political process as a whole.

Over the years the approach that stressed influence tactics as a central component of organizational politics has gained the most favor. For example, Izraeli (1975) examined the significance of organizational politics employed by managers in the middle ranks, describing it as the actual use of influence tactics. Kipnis et al. (1980:440) differentiated organizational politics expressing inter-organizational influence processes in various directions from the influence employed by managers toward their subordinates that expressed aspects of leadership. Frost and Egri (1991) referred to organizational politics as a process of influence meant to achieve goals that takes place as Surface Politics or as Deep Politics. More recent acceptable definitions of organizational politics have been offered by Parker et al. (1995) and by Ferris et al. (1989; 1989a), who stated that this phenomenon represents directed social influence processes where a planned and strategic behavior aimed at the maximization of short- or long-term interests of the individual is expressed.

Cropanzano et al. (1997) see organizational politics as a term that implies unsupportive behavior as it usually represents activity in a competitive system. In their study they differentiate 'wide' definitions of organizational politics from 'limited' ones and argue that the definition of Ferris et al. (1989) is a limited and specific definition of the term that loads it with connotations that are usually negative. In this context organizational politics can be expressed, for example, in the behavior of managers who are making use of the organization's performance evaluation mechanisms in order to promote themselves or in order to assist people whom they favor. According to Cropanzano et al., wide definitions relate to organizational politics as the general process of employing influence through the use of power, force, and authority assets in the organization (for example, Pfeffer, 1981). The advantage of such a definition is that it allows for a balanced discussion of this phenomenon, a discussion that examines both its negative and its positive influences.

Kipnis et al. (1980) define organizational politics in a broader manner through the interpersonal influence tactics that are employed in the workplace. This kind of broad definition, on which I will elaborate later in this chapter, runs the risk of widening the scope of the discussion too much and may lead to a blurring of the real boundaries of political behavior in the organization. However, such a definition may contribute to the development of a more balanced discussion of the phenomenon, one that faithfully represents its various aspects and expressions. Politics is not necessarily a negative term implying illegitimate behavior. When discussing the use of force and influence in the national arena the term 'politics' allows researchers to objectively express a social phenomenon (behavioral or bureaucratic) describing the force and influence relations in the state. Similarly, there is no need for the term 'organizational politics' to be loaded with negative meanings. Rather it should serve organizational and management theory researchers as an analytical tool and a natural term which contributes to the analysis and examination of organizational force and influence relations and their influence on organizational products.

SOURCES AND DIRECTIONS OF ORGANIZATIONAL POLITICS

For some years organizational politics was perceived as behavior largely confined to top executives or as processes by which managers influenced their subordinates (top-down influence) (for example, French and Raven, 1959; Kanter, 1979). It became clear rather quickly, however, that organizational politics also involves other organization members and can be executed in additional directions, such as employees influencing managers (upward influence), employees influencing each other, or mutual influence among interest groups, aimed at affecting the decision-making process (Pettigrew, 1973). The participants in the intra-organizational political game are categorized into several influence groups which include managers such as chief executive officers (CEOs) or line managers, and employees such as operators, analysts of the techo-structure, or administrative and support staff. An inter-organizational analysis of organizational politics involves even more players. Among them one can find clients of the organization, suppliers, other organizations, and even political, economic, and cultural systems in the extra-organizational environment (Mintzberg, 1983).

Discussing organizational politics as a process of mutual influence among all the participants mentioned above leads to the conclusion that organizational politics can be derived from formal as well as informal power or position (Mintzberg, 1983). Supervisors can use cohesive tactics (for example, sanctions, upward appeal, blocking) toward subordinates in order to force them to act in a certain way. They have some legitimate power and authority to do so, but they are not the only ones who can use influence at work. Subordinates as well can influence supervisors or co-workers by the same cohesive tactics. Those influence tactics are neither formal nor illegitimate, although they are part of the overall political game. However, both supervisors and subordinates can use other non-cohesive influence tactics that do not require any legitimacy or authority at all (for example, assertiveness, ingratiation, exchange). In fact, not everyone in the organization holds authority or formal power, but every member of the organization has some informal power that allows him to exert influence to further his interests. Accordingly, organizational politics can be categorized in a number of ways, as shown in Figure I.1:

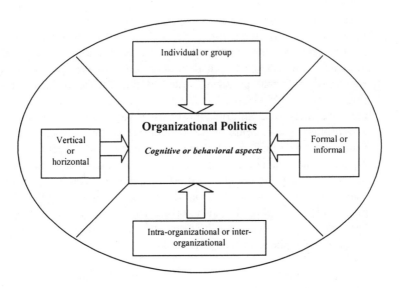

Figure I.1   Sources and directions of organizational politics

1. as an influence process executed by *individuals* or by a whole *group*;
2. as a *vertical* or *horizontal* influence process. Vertical politics expresses influence relations between supervisors and their employees while horizontal politics expresses influence relations inside a hierarchical level such as among co-workers or managers and themselves;
3. as a process with some *formal* as well as *informal* aspects. Formal politics expresses the implementation of legal and authorized power to influence others while informal politics refers to the use of different sources of informal power in order to pressure or influence others (French and Raven, 1959). Usually those who do not hold formal power are more likely to use informal power whenever it is necessary; and
4. As an *interorganizational* or *intra-organizational* phenomenon. Politics inside organizations includes only the relationships between formal organizational members while a broader definition of organizational politics includes the complex variety of extra-organizational members. This book concentrates on individual and group politics in an organization, its formal and informal aspects, and its vertical and horizontal expressions. Thus, it covers some important dimensions of the entire political phenomenon in the workplace.

The research in the field of political organizational behavior may also be classified into two main types: (1) theoretical research frameworks which have laid the conceptual and ideological basis for this field, and (2) empirical research frameworks which have taken theoretical ideas and examined them in actuality. At this stage it seems that our understanding of the knowledge currently existing regarding organizational political behavior would profit from a short review of seminal studies in both areas. This review will clarify the place of our study in the research on the organizational politics phenomenon and its contribution to it.

Previous Theoretical Frameworks for the Study of Organizational Politics

Since the beginning of the 1980s certain attempts at the construction of broad theoretical frameworks to examine the interorganizational politics phenomenon were made. Such basic theoretical frameworks were suggested by Bachrach and Lawler (1980), Pfeffer (1992, 1981) and Mintzberg (1983, 1989). The questions raised by the researchers dealt with the rise of conflicts in the organization, their development and their results, the functionality of the organizational political system, and the expressions of the use of power, force, authority, and ideology in order to create influence in the organizational environment. In order to achieve a balanced analysis of organizational politics and its characteristics the main concepts related to this field should first be identified and defined properly.

Power, Force, Influence and Authority are generally recognized as basic concepts in this field. These terms are also central in the study of politics on the extra-organizational level (Bluhm, 1971; Dahl, 1963; Lasswell, 1958). Lasswell (1958:13) states that politics centre on those employing influence on the one hand and on those influenced by it on the other. Dahl (1963) argues that a political system comprises mutual human relations in which Power, Force, Influence and Authority are significantly involved. Bluhm (1971) shows that politics is a social process in which contradictions, agreements and the use of force are involved in the making of decisions. It seems that most of these decisions are directly or indirectly related to the distribution of assets and properties that the group has at its disposal.

One of the first interactional differentiations between Power and Force was made by Parsons (1956b, 1956a). Parsons conceives of a system as a unit which is larger than the sum of all its components, and he therefore stresses the systematic interactions that transform the organization into more than a collection of individuals (the Synergetic Theory). The activities of individuals in the organization are usually directed toward others in the system and are designed to advance the individuals' interests and satisfy their needs. All these goals are realized through organizational interactions and the use of influence.

It is also customary to differentiate the employment of power from the employment of force. Power comprises the total of the current and potential assets that are at an individual's or at another social unit's disposal. The bases of power were extensively detailed in the study by French and Raven (1959) and include a physical, economic, value-related, informational, and charismatic basis. The use of force, on the other hand, expresses a real activity that makes use of the potential power bases and turns them into a real sanction. In most cases the use of power precedes the use of force, as it is cheaper and sometimes quicker in achieving results. The purpose of using power, force, or authority is to influence a certain target. According to Whetten and Cameron (1991:297) social power turns into influence when it is employed on a person for the purpose of changing his behavior. This opinion is accepted by most researchers. Therefore influence expresses politics in actuality better than similar terms such as power or force.

The conventional definition of the term "influence" maintains that the ability of side A to change the behavior of side B without side B's initial consent and without using sanctions is the actualization of power which expresses the influence of A on B (for example, Pfeffer, 1981). In this regard, *force* is the need to use a means of enforcement and certain sanctions in order to force B to act in accordance with A's wishes after A's use of power alone has failed to create influence. On the other hand *authority* is the legitimate privilege to employ force, an authority derived largely from the job definition of the authoritative party (Dahl, 1957). Influence is expressed, therefore, in all three cases: following the actualization of power, following the use of force when it turns into coercion or compulsion, and in the use of legitimate authority. Samuel (1990:160–168) argues that people's ability to influence is derived from the assets at their disposal. Influence can be achieved by convincing, explaining, preaching, conniving, deterring, deceiving, and by other means. The process of influencing the organization's goals, structures, and activity formats plunges the individuals and the groups into a competition that may be likened to a political game which takes place in a political arena with its own game rules. Samuel and Zelditch (1989) specify the components of political behavior in organizations while focusing on the complex social relations underlying the power and dependency between employees that are expressed through influence tactics.

We generally think of influence as a more objective term than power, which carries with it a certain negative connotation. Therefore, the term influence may be considered a clearer and more balanced expression of political processes in organizations or in other social units. The differentiation of influence, force, power, and other related terms has been made in the past by many researchers among whom are Weber (1947), Machanic (1962), Blau (1964), Kaplan (1964) and Dahl (1957, 1963, 1970). It may be assumed that all members of the organization have a certain degree of influence on others in the workplace but not all of them have formal authority or the ability to exert force. A central component of organizational politics is, therefore, the skill, ability, and desire to make use of influence in order to promote goals (Ferris et al., 1989, 1989a).

One of the first studies that promoted our understanding of influence in organizations and developed a theoretical system to discuss it was that of Bacharach and Lawler (1980). In their book they present a comprehensive comparison of opposing views about the meaning of organizational politics and define the terms that comprise it. In the process they also examine various forms of influence, force, and power, as well as their components and motivations for employing them. They describe the relationship between power and influence and the difference between them and provide a definition for the term 'force.' The basis of the differentiation on which the two base their approach lays in their definition of force as a phenomenon with a 'finite' value rather than a 'non-finite' value. Those who understand force as a term with a finite value relate to the struggle over force as a 'Zero-Sum Game.' Among those one may find Marxists such as Mills (1959) who maintains that the force exerted by side A necessarily diminishes the force available to side B. At the other end of the spectrum are the functionalists such as Parsons (1956a, 1956b) who understand force as a 'Non-Zero-Sum Game'. Parsons argues therefore that side A can exert force without diminishing that of side B.

Bacharach and Lawler (1980) deal with interorganizational political activity using the tools supplied by the Exchange Theory (Blau, 1964; Emerson, 1962, 1972). According to them organizational political activity includes various structures and forms such as internal coalitions and interest or pressure groups that employ a variety of influence tactics while at the same time using power and force to achieve their goals. Bacharach and Lawler's study is distinguished by its conceptual clarity and insightful differentiation between similar terms such as power, force, influence, and authority. However, aside from its theoretical and conceptual importance it does have certain limitations. Its main limitations lie in its focus on aspects of *bargaining* between organizational units while neglecting the discussion of other influence tactics such as persuasion, manipulation, ingratiation, or the actual use of force on the basis of authority or even when authority is lacking. In addition, their study focuses on the group as the central analysis unit for the study of organizational politics because in their opinion: (1) it serves as the main supplier of 'force mobility', and (2) its large number of members protects them from threats (p. 8). On the other hand, the focus on the group precludes a comprehensive discussion of the important and autonomous political activity of the individual as having his own goals and interests that are sometimes opposed to those of the group.

Throughout the years increasing attention has been paid to the group's function as one of the most important factors which moulds the processes of employing influence in organizations, and which, as such, has a special function in times of conflict. The group helps to shape the individual's opinions and attitudes toward his environment. It is a source of pressure on the individual, and it sometimes encourages him to undertake a certain activity. It assists in the receiving, processing, analysing, and transferring of information, and it is therefore closely related to internal influence processes (Mocoas, 1995). However the main weakness of a group analysis from a sociological perspective lies in the insufficient attention given to the use of politics by the individual in an organization as an autonomous individual, with desires, principles, and goals of his own, which are sometimes different from those of his social surroundings. This does not mean that the importance of the social effect on organizational influence processes should be disregarded, but in my opinion it is also important to examine the relative weight of personal politics and its implications for the perception of work in the eyes of the individual. The individual is the basic unit of which each group is comprised. Sometimes a certain person has a significant influence on the direction a whole group takes, and this influence is especially strong if he or she has significant formal or informal authority or power. In addition, political activity in organizations does not always take place in groups. Different people have individual interests, and sometimes they act in order to actualize them without including others in the process (for example, when there is no broad agreement on the goals, or when the process holds rewards that are significant only to the individual). The organization, as a much more intimate unit than the state, for example, contains within it, besides group activities, a significant number of autonomous activities conducted by individuals for the purpose of advancing their own goals and interests. Great importance is, therefore, attached to the analysis of political processes in the organization from the individual's perspective, that is, a micro analysis.

Other studies that have contributed significantly to the theory behind the study of organizational politics are those of Mintzberg (1983) and Pfeffer (1981, 1992). Mintzberg (1983) focused on the practical aspect of interorganizational politics in the daily life of managers and employees. Pfeffer described how organizational politics influence organizational culture, effectiveness, and efficiency. However, this description is largely theoretical and is not really tested empirically. Mintzberg outlines a broad area for discussion, describing characteristics and components of interorganizational and extra-organizational power dynamics. His main argument is that the political component of personal relations in organizations and outside of them to a large degree determines the potential of organizations to achieve their goals. According to his evaluation, the existence of interest-based political activity in every human structure is an indisputable fact. However, when such behavior leads to interorganizational conflicts, acute struggles, and friction between the organization's members, the system's balance is destabilized and the common interests are harmed. This means that organizational politics always exist, that they have a degree of functionality for the organization but that when they exceed certain boundaries they can harm employees' performance, the organization's efficiency and effectiveness, and the ability of the organization to successfully compete with its rivals. This attitude is also supported by Tosi (1992).

The discussion by Mintzberg (1983) is divided into interorganizational influence processes and extra-organizational influence processes, which together comprise the political power game in the organization. In his opinion, internal influencers should be distinguished from external influencers. The distinction between them is quite clear: 'The internal influencers are the full-time employees who use voice, those people charged with making the decision and taking the actions on a permanent, regular basis; it is they who determine the outcomes, which express the goals pursued by the organization. The external influencers are non-employees who use their bases of influence to try to affect the behavior of the employees' (Mintzberg, 1983:26). In the external power game the organization as a whole usually deals as one unit with influences from the environment that stem from various interested bodies (suppliers, clients, stockholders), from other organizations and from the political, social, and economic systems within the country and outside it.

There are six influence groups that play a part in the internal power game:

1. the CEO – chief executive officers headed by the organization's chief;
2. the operators – the employees who manufacture the products or services in actuality;
3. the line managers – who communicate both with the employees and with the chief executive officers;
4. the analysts of the techno-structure – planning, research, and supervision staff;
5. the support staff – administration staff;
6. ideology – the common beliefs and perceptions of the other groups that distinguish the specific organization from other organizations.

All these groups have different amounts of force, power, and influence. Mintzberg (1983) sums it up by stating that organizational politics is 'individual or group behavior that is informal, ostensibly parochial, typically divisive, and above all, in the technical sense, illegitimate – sanctioned neither by formal authority, accepted ideology, nor certified expertise (though it may exploit any one of these)' (p. 172). Despite his nod to organizational politics as a necessary phenomenon that is sometimes functional for the organization, the gist of Mintzberg's arguments implies a clearly negative attitude toward organizational politics. As mentioned earlier, such an attitude characterizes most researchers' attitudes to this phenomenon. Like Bacharach and Lawler (1980), Mintzberg focuses on the political activity of groups while neglecting to some degree the discussion of the autonomous political activity of the individual.

Another approach which serves as a theoretical background and basis for a discussion of political issues in organizations is related to the perception of the organization as a social system frequently beset by conflict. Various studies, mine included, regard conflict as an unavoidable and highly significant aspect of the workplace (Baron, 1984; Fisher, 1993; Katz and Kahn, 1966; Perrow, 1979). Conflicts in organizations often stem from a divergence between the values and goals of the organization's members. Conflicts occur on several levels, among them the interpersonal level (for example, among employees, and between employees and their managers), the interprofessional or interpositional level (for example, among sales and service personnel and clients), among different groups in the organization, or among different organizations. The aim of the conflicts is to influence the distribution of assets in the organization in a certain direction that is consistent with the interests and aims of one side or another.

In accordance with the work of Papa and Canary (1995) our discussion deals with the interpersonal level of conflict and does not involve other aspects of conflict, the understanding of which is important but distracts from the current focus of the discussion. Although conflict expresses a forceful clash aimed at achieving influence, the term 'conflict' is not central to the current study. The broad definition employed here in referring to organizational politics sees conflict relations as another aspect of the political phenomenon in general, not necessarily the centre of discussion. Organizational politics are definitely present in situations of conflict, but in many cases exist in the absence of actual conflict, for example, when one achieves a goal through ingratiation. Organizational politics do not necessarily involve situations of conflict, but often there is a connection between the two, evident when the attempts of an individual to promote goals leads to a visible and direct conflict with whomever opposes him and disagreements which were previously hidden are brought to the fore in some way or another. Conflict is a situation of struggle that is not necessary in an organization, yet it is an inseparable part of it, just as in relations between states military conflict is considered part of the policy process.

In summary, most of the researchers and studies mentioned have stressed the term 'influence' as a central component and maybe the best common denominator of the organizational politics phenomenon. Therefore the current book focuses on the employment of influence in the organization and among its members. The term 'influence' will be examined comparatively as a way of understanding employees' output in the organization. Despite the major contribution of all the studies mentioned thus far to the study of this field, they are not sufficient on their own. These theories need to be tested empirically. Indeed in recent years a number of studies have done just that, so it would be appropriate at this point to broaden the scope of our discussion to include several of them.

Earlier Empirical Frameworks for the Study of Organizational Politics

The empirical studies conducted up until now on the micro-organizational political aspect have studied the political activity and behavior of employees, focusing on the various assets at their disposal (Hills and Mahoney, 1978; Pfeffer and Salancik, 1974; Salancik and Pfeffer, 1974) or examining the influences of organizational politics on managers and their management style (Pfeffer and Moore, 1980; Salancik and Pfeffer, 1974). Other studies have examined the relations and mutual influences between employees and their superiors in organizations, the relations between professional committees and the management, the impact on employees' influence of integrating them in decision-making processes in the organization, the influence of the organization's members on policy making, as well as the factors that influence the individual and lead him to behave in a more 'political' manner in the workplace. A major part of these studies focused on the *perception of politics* and not on the direct processes of the use of organizational influence. Most of the studies in this field have been conducted only in recent years (for example, Allen et al., 1979; Drory and Romm, 1988; Ferris et al., 1989, 1989a, 1991, 1992; Kumar and Ghadilly, 1989; Peterson, 1990). It is important to note that currently it is customary to distinguish the perception of organizational politics by the organization's members from the actual existence of political behavior. Although some connection between the two is expected, various studies have proven that there is a gap between the group's and the individual's perception of their relative power and the degree of the group members' influence on their actual performance (for example, Bottger, 1984). An important model examining the perception of organizational politics is suggested by Ferris et al. (1989) and developed by Ferris and Kacmar (1992). This model is at the heart of this book and is presented in Figure I.2. It includes both the factors that influence the perception of organizational politics by the employees and its impact on organizational performance.

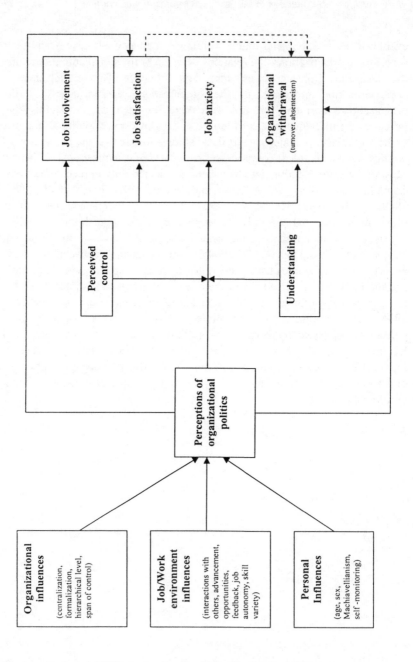

Source: Ferris et al. (1989), reprinted by permission from Lawrence Erlbaum

Figure I.2   The Ferris et al. model of perceptions of organizational politics

POSITIVE AND NEGATIVE ASPECTS OF ORGANIZATIONAL POLITICS

A comprehensive overview of the scientific literature dealing with the organizational politics phenomenon creates the initial impression that this is a negative phenomenon by definition, one that harms the organization and its members. However, this impression is generally formed when the researchers take a narrow approach to defining organizational politics. Block (1988:5) states that, 'Politics in organizations is like sex was in the 1950s – we knew it was going on, but nobody would really tell us about it. The same with politics – we know it is woven in the fabric of our work, but to get reliable information about it is next to impossible.' Moreover, Block argues that, 'If I told you you were a very political person, you would take it either as an insult or at best as a mixed blessing.'

Kanter (1979:166) argues that the terms power, force, and politics together create a whole whose general context is far from positive: 'Its connotations tend to be more negative than positive, and it has multiple meanings.' Organizational politics is often tied up with terms such as cunning, manipulations, subversion, mutual degradation, or the achievement of goals in improper ways (Drory and Beaty, 1991; Ferris and King, 1991; Moorhead and Griffin, 1989). As was mentioned earlier, Mintzberg (1989:238) stresses the negative side of organizational politics when he argues that organizational politics reflect illegitimate force relations between the organization's members. He contrasts organizational politics with 'authority,' which implies a legitimate force. Gummer (1990) strengthens the approach, maintaining that force has a negative connotation and in comparison with other terms is regarded as a very negative term in American culture.

Indeed, various studies have examined the harmful effects of political behavior on employees' performance levels (Eisenhardt and Bourgeois, 1988). This behavior has negative aspects such as ingratiatory conduct (Liden and Mitchell, 1988), which lead to a rise in the stress and pressure at work (Ferris et al., 1996; Frost and Egri, 1991; Matuszek et al., 1995), to unfairness in evaluating employees' performance (Tziner et al., 1996) and to the formation of negative attitudes toward work among employees with different statuses (Drory, 1993). The image arising from these studies corresponds largely to the perceptions of the organizations' members themselves with regard to this phenomenon. A study conducted by Gandz and Murray (1980) found that employees usually consider organizational politics to be an unfair, evil, irrational, and unhealthy behavior. These findings were later supported by the study conducted by Voyer (1994).

However, many of the organizations' members also believe that political behavior is necessary in many cases, especially if someone has an interest in advancing in the organization and becoming acknowledged by his co-workers and employers as a good employee or as a talented manager. Indeed a more careful examination of the term organizational politics reveals that this phenomenon has a multitude of meanings and one cannot absolutely decide that it necessarily expresses negative and harmful behavior. Political behavior is a human and natural phenomenon that serves a certain personal and social function. Whetten and Cameron (1991:278) argue, for example, that politics and force are marks of a personal ability to change and contribute to the environment by using a variety of assets aimed at improving products at work. People who have force, power, and influence can shape their environment according to their own will, while others who do not make use of these assets remain unsatisfied and ungratified (Putnam, 1995).

May (1972) strengthens a classic argument arising from studies conducted in the 1950s and 1960s, which maintains that organizational conflicts that involve the forceful aspect of organizational politics sometimes have an aspect that is positive and functional for the organization. Conflicts create balance between those who have force and those who lack it, improve the organization's flexibility and ability to deal with a changing environment, prevent stagnation of the organizational units, sometimes promote growth and rejuvenation, prevent group-thinking and enrich decision-making processes (Bacharach and Lawler, 1980; Pfeffer, 1981). Ferris and King (1991) found that the use of influence in the organization is positively related to the managers' positive attitude toward his employees, that is, the more an employee uses influence in the organization, the better employee he is perceived to be and the more his performance is appreciated. Organizational politics is sometimes perceived as a legitimate *fight response* in times of crisis or when conflicts arise in the organization. Such conditions are usually characterized by the centralization of essential information and by flexibility with regard to activity methods (Hirschman, 1970; Ryan, 1989).

A balanced attitude toward organizational politics is exemplified by Kumar and Ghadially (1989) who argue that politics can harm the organization but that the organization may also profit from it. Among the negative impacts the two mention a risk of losing power and status, hostility from others, an internal feeling of guilt, and reduced performance levels. Among the positive impacts of organizational politics they mention career advancement, recognition and respect from others, enhancement of personal power, realization of personal goals and organizational goals, a feeling of achievement, the nurturing of the ego, self-control and self-realization. Randolph (1985) also strengthens the claim that organizational politics has many positive aspects. In his view it is an additional mechanism that members of the organization can utilize in the workplace to promote a variety of goals.

It seems, then, that the scientific approach to the study of political processes in the organization must be balanced. Such research should carefully examine the conditions under which organizational politics is harmful for the organization and/or its surroundings and, on the other hand, the conditions under which it becomes a functional component that has a positive influence on organizations and their employees. Drory (1993:69) argued that organizational politics is an aspect of behavior in the workplace that is so deeply rooted in human nature and in the organizational structure that its negative effects cannot be completely prevented. Pfeffer (1992) maintains that although nuclear, medical, biological or genetic knowledge may be put to harmful use, the existence of such knowledge may not be prevented. All that is left to be done is learn its characteristics so as to make intelligent use of it and educate others to be careful with it. The existence of organizational politics may not be prevented either, and there will surely be those who will make evil and harmful use of it. Therefore empirical studies should attempt to find the conditions under which the influence of organizational politics is negative, or, alternatively, when it is positive.

ORGANIZATIONAL POLITICS IN PUBLIC ADMINISTRATION

The examination of organizational politics and the connection it has with employees' performance in public administration is not a simple task. There are many differences between private and public organizations. Most of the differences are related to political issues and to the problems on the social agenda, both of which require a comprehensive treatment (Vasu et al., 1990:1–4, 6). An enlightening comparison between public and private organizations may be found in the works of many researchers (for example, Dye, 1995; McKevitt, 1998; Murray, 1975; Reiney, 1991, and others). Murray (1975) sums up this comparison as the dichotomy between the profit goals of private organizations versus the service goals of public organizations. The differences center on five main points:

1. *Criteria for the goal realization.* In a private organization there are purely economic considerations. In a public organization, there are blurred considerations meant to ultimately achieve consensus among the various population components.
2. *The degree of activity and values level.* In a private organization there are simple activities and a limited emphasis on values. In a public

organization there are value-based and complex activities that serve the interests of different and sometimes opposing groups. Such activities result in extensive extra-organizational and interorganizational politics.

3. *Law.* A private organization may act within any framework that is not against the law. A public organization abides exclusively by the letter of the law.
4. *Exposure and auditing.* A private organization is less exposed to auditing because of alternatives available to the client. A public organization can be subjected to a long list of auditors and supervising bodies.
5. *Dependence upon the system.* A private organization is free from politization. A public organization is often impacted by, and must always be cognisant of, politics.

The main difference between private organizations and public organizations stems from the latter's relationship with the state and the government and their dependence upon taxpayers' money and national assets that come from the state's budget. Therefore the nature of their dealings within the organizational environment is different from that of private organizations. Private organizations act in a market dominated by the laws of supply and demand, while public organizations are not usually subjected to such game rules. It is easier to measure organizational efficiency in economic terms in bodies which are economically oriented and for whom profitability is the reason for existence. A private organization that over time does not make a profit and does not prove economically viable cannot continue to function. However, things are different in the public system. This system is designed to spend money that has been collected from the public through various taxes and fees. Despite the change in trends over the last few years (exposure to competitive processes, privatization, and the examination of public services in the light of more stringent private sector criteria) the public service is not yet sufficiently economically oriented to compete under 'free market' conditions. Therefore, it is more difficult to measure success or efficiency in public systems through profitability factors or through other economic indicators, and alternative criteria and analytical tools should be found. Perhaps these tools should be based on the examination of goal achievement in terms of policy implementation, the degree of support they gain from the public, their ability to cope with potential competitors, and the degree of legitimacy they gain among their employees. Another aspect worthy of attention is the study of the behavioral aspects of employees' performance within these systems.

This book focuses on the examination of organizational politics and its influence on employees' performance within public systems for two main reasons:

1. By their very nature public organizations are intimately tied to political and governmental systems. Many are familiar with the problematic question of political nominations in public administration, the complexity of the internal rewards and promotion processes in such bureaucratic systems, and the tense relations at times between the politically appointed rank and file and the professional ranks of the public servants. Political issues of influence relations take on a special character within public systems. The link between the political and the professional ranks potentially increases the degree of employees' friction with many kinds of influence processes. In addition, the public administration systems generally provide better job security for its employees than does the private sector. Organizations that provide a higher level of job security are expected to be characterized by a higher level of political activity both internally and externally, as a major part of the attention at work is directed to activities which are not directly related to manufacturing, production, or the supply of service but to less central activities such as the political power game.

2. The task of studying organizational performance in the public systems is very important as it has implications beyond the issue of organizational efficiency proper. The public systems are financed by the taxpayers who in many regards are equivalent to both the stockholders and the clients in the private sector. Complaints regarding the tremendous amount of internal politics that exists within public structures and impedes their efficiency are often raised both by the public and by the public sector's employees themselves. For example, Cropanzano et al. (1997) argue that political organizations direct many assets toward internal power and influence struggles, assets which are usually used at the expense of actual production or human relations in the organization. In addition public organizations are usually large bureaucratic bodies. Studies that have been conducted in the past show that managers estimated that organizational politics exist in such bodies to a much greater degree than in small organizations and have a more negative effect on them (Madison et al., 1980). The implications of malfunctions in public mechanisms are expressed both on the operative level of the service afforded to the public and on the ethical level of the improper manner of spending public money. It seems that organizational politics exists in private as well as in public organizations, but while its implications in the private sector are usually limited to the question of the business firm's survival, in the public sector it is the ability to perform duties that have an influence on the entire population. This fact alone underscores the need for an in-depth examination of the political phenomenon, especially in the public sector.

The current existing knowledge in the field of organizational politics in the public sector is relatively small. Pfeffer (1992) mentions two main points that emphasize the importance of discussing organizational politics within the public sector:

1. *The degree of agreement on organizational goals among the organization's members.* Organizational politics reflect, among other things, a lack of agreement and clarity among the organization's members, especially with regard to the collective goals. While the activity boundaries in the private sector are relatively well defined and clear, there is a certain blurring with regard to the activity and involvement boundaries of a public institution in the individual's life. The goal of the private and the business sectors is to provide products that are as high quality, attractive, and numerous as possible. The public sector also seeks to provide quality service but its scope of operation is frequently questioned. What is the range of education, health, employment, and social support services with which the state should provide its citizens? Therefore the relative lack of clarity about the public sector's aims and the internal disagreement regarding them may provide fertile ground for the development of internal organizational politics.

2. *The scope of the external pressure.* When external pressure that focuses the competition on extra-organizational goals is exerted on the organization, we expect to see a reduction in internal organizational politics and an increase in inter-organizational politics. The degree of external competition in the private sector is higher than that in the public sector, and it is logical that organizational politics in the former arena will be more focused outside the organization. Although recently many of the world's nations have introduced a significant level of competition into the public sector as well (many public bodies and mechanisms have to justify their mere existence by the comparison between their performances and those of their competitors in the private sector in the fields of employment, health, education, and even security), this competition is still not similar to what is happening in the private sector. Therefore this explanation strengthens the expectation that we will find more internal politics at play in the public sector than in the private one.

For all of these reasons the study of organizational politics in public administration should prove a fascinating topic. The need for this analysis becomes even more important when the centre of discussion focuses on issues of organizational performance. The main difficulty facing those who wish to evaluate organizational performance in the public sector is the need to examine a 'service' and not an actual product. As the ultimate 'product' of most public systems is public service, a study of organizational performance must relate to it, and this is where the main problem lies. It is relatively difficult to evaluate public service in an objective manner using hard data about the product's quantity, quality, and utility in addressing needs. Such a problem does not exist in private organizations that provide actual products. The efficiency of a private organization that produces, for example, personal computers will be assessed according to the number of computers it produced, their quality as measured according to some technical standard, the supply time to the clients, and the profit made. In contrast it is difficult to objectively measure the quality of service afforded to the citizen by the local council, the efficiency of its delivery, and the relative price that the citizen pays for the service. This difficulty poses an ambitious challenge for many researchers who are trying to identify additional factors that influence the performance of public organizations. The current book addresses this challenge to some degree and posits the question of organizational politics as a potential factor that influences employees' performance in the public sector. The differences presented thus far between public and private organizations have led me to distinguish between the two sectors and to focus on the public sector in this book. The role of the micro aspects of organizational politics in public administration has received scant examination, especially regarding its impact on performance. It will be enlightening to broaden our knowledge in this field and to lay the foundation for further research in it.

TOWARD A DEFINITION OF ORGANIZATIONAL POLITICS

Politics is thus a widespread phenomenon in organizations, one that deserves more attention and empirical examination (for example, Gandz and Murray, 1980; Mayes and Allen, 1977; Mintzberg, 1983; Pfeffer, 1981, 1992). The importance of organizational politics lies in its potential consequences and effect on work outcomes. Theoretical arguments suggest that politics often interferes with normal organizational processes (for example, decision making, promotion, and rewards), and damages productivity and performance on individual and organizational levels. Empirical attempts to support this notion have proved equivocal. Some studies found a negative relationship of organizational politics to job attitudes or stress-related responses (for example, Drory, 1993; Ferris et al., 1996a, 1996b). More recent works have suggested that politics enhances withdrawal behaviors and turnover intentions (for example, Bozeman et al., 1996; Cropanzano et al., 1997), but others found no such relationship (for example, Parker et al., 1995). All of these studies overlooked the relationship between organizational politics and other possible work outcomes, such as direct negligent behavior and actual job performance.

Organizations are social entities that involve a struggle for resources, personal conflicts, and a variety of influence tactics executed by individuals and groups to obtain benefits and goals in different ways (Molm, 1997). Estimating the political climate of a work unit is a complex task but it is crucial for a better understanding of organizations. Organizational politics is usually defined as behavior strategically designed to maximize self-interests (Ferris et al., 1989) and it therefore contradicts the collective organizational goals or the interests of other individuals. This perspective reflects a generally negative image of organizational politics in the eyes of most organization members. Gandz and Murray (1980) and Madison et al. (1980) observed that when individuals were asked to describe workplace politics they typically listed self-serving and manipulative activities that are not perceived positively. Studies that developed this conception (for example, Drory, 1993; Ferris and Kacmar, 1992) found that organizational politics was perceived as self-serving behavior by employees to achieve self-interests, advantages, and benefits at the expense of others and as sometimes contrary to the interests of the entire organization or work unit. This behavior was frequently associated with manipulation, defamation, subversion, and illegitimate ways of overusing power to attain one's objectives.

Ferris et al. (1989) suggested the concept of *perception* of organizational politics (Perception of Organizational Politics Scale – POPS) as a good measure of organizational politics. Kacmar and Ferris (1991:193–4) and Ferris and Kacmar (1992:93) argued that the higher the perceptions of politics are in the eyes of an organization member, the lower in that person's eyes is the level of justice, equity, and fairness. More recent studies (Ferris et al., 1996b; Folger et al., 1992) have used the theory of procedural justice to argue that organizational politics is related to the efficiency of human resource systems and to decision-making processes. Lack of minimal justice and fairness in these systems was found as a main cause of higher perceptions of organizational politics and therefore of hampered organizational outcomes. All these studies relied on Kurt Lewin's (1936) argument that people respond to their perceptions of reality, not to reality itself. Likewise politics in organizations should be understood in terms of what people think of it rather than what it actually represents. Studies thus proposed that perceptions of justice and fairness reflect a political climate in the workplace and may also be related to a variety of work outcomes. These ideas were extensively advocated by Ferris, Kacmar, and their colleagues in numerous studies (Ferris et al., 1996a, 1996b; Ferris et al., 1994; Ferris and Kacmar, 1992; Ferris et al., 1991; Kacmar and Ferris, 1991).

Hence organizational politics has been given many definitions, some so wide-ranging that they no longer describe politics as the core activity, others so narrow that they include only those activities that are illegal or undesirable from the viewpoint of the organization (for example, manipulation, ingratiation, or going over the head of one's supervisor). Researchers have defined organizational politics as ways to get ahead in an organization (Wallace and Szilagyi, 1982:181), as dynamic processes of influence that produce organizationally relevant outcomes beyond the simple performance of job tasks, or as the management of influence to obtain ends not sanctioned by the organization, or to obtain sanctioned ends through non-sanctioned influence means (Mayes and Allen, 1977:675). Pfeffer (1981:4–5) defined organizational politics as those activities carried out by people to acquire, enhance, and use power and other resources to obtain their preferred outcomes in a situation where there is uncertainty or disagreement. Ferris et al. (1989) suggested that organizational politics is a social influence process in which behavior is strategically designed to maximize short-term or long-term self-interest, which is either consistent with, or at the expense of, others' interests.

One thing is central to all these and other definitions, namely the use of influence tactics as the major component of political behavior. Bacharach and Lawler (1980:154) defined influence tactics as behaviors that can change power relations, while Kipnis et al. (1980) identified influence tactics as a basic component of organizational politics. In their study, organizational politics is defined as the ways in which people at work influence their colleagues and superiors to obtain personal benefits or to satisfy organizational goals. Basically the approach taken in this book follows the definitions of Ferris, Kacmar, and their colleagues as well as Kipnis et al. Thus organizational politics is built upon *intra-organizational influence tactics used by organization members to promote self-interests or organizational goals in different ways.* Alternatively I will argue that for practical and methodological reasons most studies have followed the road paved by Ferris, Kacmar, and their colleagues and focused on perceptions of organizational politics rather than on actual influence tactics.

THE BEHAVIORAL APPROACH AND THE FOCUS ON INTERPERSONAL INFLUENCE TACTICS

As mentioned above, one common view treats organizational politics as based on different influence tactics that represent organizational members' ability to achieve and safeguard their own interests. In order to operatively conceptualize organizational politics some studies have taken a behavioral approach and explored and typologized the influence tactics employees resort to in their work environment. While this study has not focused on the variety of possible influence tactics that one may use in the workplace, it is important to summarize some of them in order to provide a theoretical grounding for further research.

Wayne and Ferris (1990) have identified three types of influence tactics according to the target at which they are aimed: (1) supervisors-focused tactics, (2) job-focused tactics, and (3) self-focused tactics. Judge and Bretz (1994) argued that there are two main influence tactics: (1) ingratiation, a supervisors-focused tactic, which can be defined as influence behavior attempts that are intended to increase liking by, or similarity to, a target individual, and (2) self-promotion, which is the act of highlighting one's personal accomplishments, characteristics, or qualities in order to present oneself in the most favorable manner.

Although one of the earliest studies in this context, the research of Kipnis et al. (1980) remains the most precise, detailed and often-quoted analysis. Kipnis et al. outlined eight influence tactics that have proven important in illuminating the operative use of organizational politics: *Assertiveness, Ingratiation, Rationality, Sanctions, Exchange, Upward-Appeal, Blocking,* and *Coalition.* Table I.1 presents a summary of these factors and exemplary items that may be useful in measuring them. In this figure the items represent statements that reflect various methods of influencing others. Respondents are usually requested to indicate how frequently they use a specific tactic for influencing others. In addition, Table I.2 provides an extended set of such influence tactics as well as their definitions, culled from other studies that followed the Kipnis et al. (1980) taxonomy. These studies and their effect on the scholarly thinking in the field will be discussed throughout the various chapters of the book. They created what we define as a revised set of influence tactics as follows: *Rational Persuasion, Inspirational Appeals, Consultation, Ingratiation, Personal Appeals, Exchange, Coalition, Legitimating, Assertiveness, Pressure, Sanctions, Upward-Appeal,* and *Blocking.* Appendix 3 suggests three sets of questionnaires aimed at measuring employees' influence tactics toward other organizational members. The questionnaires are based on the taxonomy of Kipnis et al. (1980) and the studies that followed it, and represent one way of operationalizing organizational politics in modern worksites.

Table I.1   Original set of political behaviors by influence tactics

Influence tactics – (Actual Organizational Politics)		Representative forms of behavior used by employees toward others
1.	Assertiveness	(a)	Kept checking up on him or her
		(b)	Simply ordering him or her to do what was asked
2.	Ingratiation	(a)	Telling someone, Only you have the brains and talent to do this
		(b)	Inflating the importance of what is needed to be done
3.	Rationality	(a)	Presenting information that supports the point
		(b)	Writing a detailed plan that justifies the ideas
4.	Sanctions	(a)	Giving no salary increase or bonus
		(b)	Threatening one's job security
5.	Exchange	(a)	Telling someone, If you do this for me I will do something for you
		(b)	Reminding him/her of past favors that I did for them
6.	Upward-Appeal	(a)	Filing a report about the other person with higher-ups (for example my superior)
		(b)	Sending him/her to my superior
7.	Blocking	(a)	Threatening to notify an outside agency if he/she did not give in to my request
		(b)	Threatening to stop working with him or her until he or she gave in
8.	Coalition	(a)	Obtaining the support of my subordinates to back up requests
		(b)	Making him/her come to a formal conference at which I made my request

Source: Kipnis et al. (1980).

Table I.2   Revised set of political behaviors by influence tactics

Tactic	Definition
1. Rational Persuasion	Using logical arguments and facts to persuade another that a desired result will occur
2. Inspirational Appeals	Arousing enthusiasm by appealing to another's values, ideals, and aspirations, or by increasing the other's self-confidence
3. Consultation	Asking for participation in decision making or planning a change when the other's support and assistance are desired; showing willingness to modify a proposal to deal with the other's concerns and suggestions
4. Ingratiation	Using praise, flattery, and friendly or helpful behavior to get the other in a good mood or to think favorably of you; acting humbly and making the other person feel important
5. Personal Appeals	Appealing to the other's feelings of loyalty and friendship toward you when asking for something
6. Exchange	Offering an exchange of positive benefits or offering to make a personal sacrifice, indicating willingness to reciprocate at a later time, or promising a share of the benefits if the other helps accomplish a task
7. Coalition	Using the assistance of others or noting their support to persuade the other to comply with the desired goal
8. Legitimating	Pointing out one's authority to make a request, or reiterating that it is consistent with organizational policies, rules, practices, or traditions
9. Assertiveness	Demanding, ordering, and setting deadlines
10. Pressure	Seeking compliance by using demands, threats, frequent checking, or persistent reminders
11. Sanctions	Preventing or threatening to prevent benefits such as salary increases or job security
12. Upward-Appeal	Causing additional pressure to conform by invoking the influence of higher levels in the organization such as making a formal appeal to higher levels or obtaining their informal support
13. Blocking	Attempting to stop the other from carrying out an action by activities such as engaging in a work slowdown or threatening to stop working with someone

Notwithstanding its importance, the study of Kipnis et al. (1980) did not consider the possibility that the various influential behaviors presented above vary in relation with organizational characteristics, organizational size, sectoral orientation (for example, public or private), or organizational culture. According to the contingency theory people will adjust their tactics to the type of environment, the participants who take part in the political game, the type of interface they use, or other conditions. Still, the typology of these influence tactics may contribute to a better operationalization of organizational politics and should be used in further theoretical studies or empirical examinations of the field.

THE COGNITIVE APPROACH AND THE VALUE OF PERCEPTIONS OF ORGANIZATIONAL POLITICS

The cognitive approach is however more realistic in terms of handling political behaviors. This approach focuses on perceptions of organizational politics that represent the degree to which employees view their work environment as political in nature (Kacmar and Ferris, 1991; Ferris and Kacmar, 1992). Most of the behaviors associated with political perceptions have some negative meaning (for example, favouritism, not merit, gets people ahead, supervisor only looks as if she/he helps others, co-workers lend a hand if they get something out of it, people left because hard work was not enough to get ahead). In recent years POPS has become a common measure used in studies dealing with political phenomena at work (Ferris and Kacmar, 1992; Kacmar and Carlson, 1994; Kacmar and Ferris, 1991). It examines perceptions such as:

1. How much favoritism is established in the organization?
2. What is the relative power and dominance of internal influence groups in the intra-organizational game?
3. Is there fair reward sharing in the organization (do only those who work hard receive rewards)?
4. Does the organization stand for a fair and just promotion policy?
5. Is there room in the organization for honest and frank people; do they really have a fair chance in influencing the decision-making process, compared with others?

Putting it another way, perceptions of politics represent the level at which the organization is perceived as unfair or unjust. When organizational fairness is high, the whole workplace appears to be less political, and vice versa. As mentioned by Ferris and Kacmar (1992), perceptions of politics is a major component of organizational politics and therefore it should be an inherent part of every exploratory model that discusses this phenomena. Whenever a political act is performed by someone in the organization, it can end in success or failure. According to the present model, political perceptions are largely determined by the extent to which employees use effective influence tactics resulting in successful outcomes.

ANTECEDENTS OF ORGANIZATIONAL POLITICS

The studies of Ferris et al. (1989, 1989a) and Ferris and Kacmar (1992) provide a good starting-point for analysing the antecedents of organizational politics. However, because the focus of this book is on the impact of workplace politics on organizational performance I will touch on the core elements of this approach only briefly. According to the above studies and others that have followed, the use of politics fluctuates with three main groups of variables: (1) personal and personality variables (for example, age, gender, Machiavellianism, self-monitoring), (2) job/work variables (for example, job autonomy, job variety, feedback, advancement opportunity, interactions with others), and (3) organizational variables (for example, centralization, formalization, hierarchical level, span of control). Over time other variables were also added to these three main groups, including job satisfaction, organizational commitment, and extra-organizational variables such as general political behavior and community involvement outside organizations. Nonetheless, virtually no studies have shown a causal relationship between theses variables and organizational politics. For example, while it is a common view that more educated individuals will be more engaged in workplace politics, this claim has never gained wide support in empirical studies. As will also be demonstrated in this book, job satisfaction and organizational commitment are usually correlated with perceptions of organizational politics, but here again no study has supported a direct relationship between the two variables. Finally, the emergence of organizational politics may also be affected by other conditions such as the professional sector to which the organization belongs, environmental conditions of stability or instability, stress and tension in the workplace, or the specific problems that call for managerial decisions. However, the question of which variables are most significant remains an open one.

OUTCOMES AND CONSEQUENCES OF ORGANIZATIONAL POLITICS

A clear definition of organizational politics and articulated assumptions about its nature provides a strong basis for further discussions about its outcomes and implications. As noted by Bozeman et al. (1996), there is a substantial lack of literature and empirical evidence concerning this issue. During the late 1990s some progress was made in this direction yet, as the studies in this book demonstrate, there is still a long way to go. A basic question is *how might organizational politics and employee performance be related to each other*? It may also turn out to be the most important question for managers looking to understand and control this phenomenon and turn it into a useful tool in day-to-day activity.

The scientific evidence concerning the relationship between organizational politics and employees' performance not only leaves much to be desired but in many ways it is even contradictory. Most studies conducted to date have paid little or no attention to it and, even among those that have, there is substantive disagreement concerning the nature and the strength of this relationship. As mentioned before, organizational politics commonly connotes negative behavior, and the possibility that it can yield positive outcomes (for example, enhanced performance) is seldom raised.

Some studies have attempted to partly support a negative relationship between organizational politics and employees' performance. For example, Eisenhardt and Bourgeois (1988) found that organizational politics negatively impacts a firm's performance, Ferris and King (1991) argued that the use of politics by employees leads supervisors to rate them more favorably even though they do not always deserve it, and Kumar and Ghadially (1989) mentioned reduced employee performance as a harmful outcome of organizational politics. Ferris and Kacmar (1992) and Parker et al. (1995) proposed and partially supported a negative relationship between the perception of politics and different organizational outcomes. That none of these studies was able to empirically support a direct negative relationship between organizational politics and employees' performance suggests that the relationship, if it exists, is far more complex. My argument is that organizational politics might affect employees' performance, but only under certain conditions and through mediating and moderating variables. Moreover, under certain conditions more extensive use of politics may even cause better performance.

Accordingly, a balanced conceptualization of organizational politics leads to the establishment of a contingent approach toward the effect of organizational politics on employee performances. This relationship is expected to involve several elements. Two are quite new in regard to organizational politics (Met Expectations [ME] and Person–Organization Fit [POF]), while the third has already been mentioned in previous studies (Perception of Organizational Politics Scale [POPS]). The mutual relationships among these elements are described in a comprehensive model. This model is presented in Figure I.3, and it will guide our analysis and discussion in the next chapters.

EXPLORING THE MODEL

Organizational Politics and Employees' Performance

The research model presented in Figure I.3 suggests a new theoretical framework for the explanation of the relationship between organizational politics and employees' performance. This model involves individual as well as situational differences that facilitate the success of influence attempts (Schilit and Locke, 1982). My starting-point is that organizational politics is essential to securing one's varying interests and needs at the workplace. The effect of organizational politics on employees' performance is indirect and primarily depends on (1) the degree to which an employee's expectations are fulfilled, and (2) the fit between an employee and his or her work environment. While it appears rather natural to put pressure on someone else to make him or her do what one wants, it is the result of such pressure that determines what one thinks not only about this person, but especially about what he or she symbolizes or represents (for example, supervisors, subordinates, or co-workers).

For example, when an employee thinks that a salary raise is in order but this raise fails to materialize, he or she will most probably resort to some influence tactics to try and change the situation. This influence activity is a political behavior. Yet, only the results of this behavior will determine the employee's future attitudes toward the organizational system, as well as his or her performance. Important too is whether the results of organizational politics are successful or not. Results that from the employee's point of view are successful create the feeling of satisfaction, and therefore organizational politics is perceived as positive, useful and beneficial. On the other hand, when organizational politics proves ineffective it may result in a feeling of dissatisfaction with one's ability to achieve one's goals, alienation, or the perception that the organization treats one unjustly or unfairly.

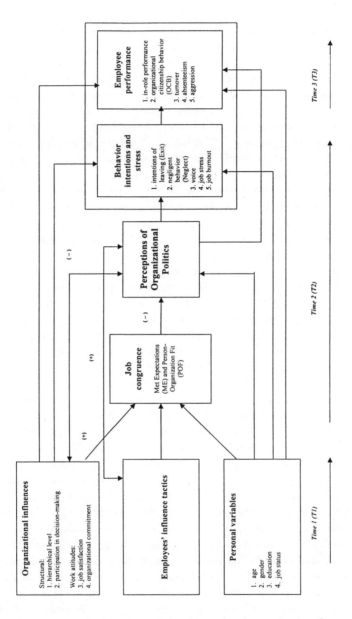

Figure I.3   A theoretical framework for the study of organizational politics and employee performance

The results of organizational politics can be measured by the employee's level of Met Expectations (ME). Since everyone has some expectations from his workplace, and politics is a tool through which these expectations can be accomplished, in many ways expectations express the effectiveness of organizational politics. This effectiveness is the gap between what we wish to obtain and what we actually receive in the workplace. Simultaneously the level of Met Expectations (ME) is not solely determined by one's political behavior in the organization. The basic fit between an employee and his or her work environment is also important because it expresses the adjustment of personal qualifications and personality factors to a certain work arena. The relationship between organizational politics and employee performance is expected to be mediated by the expectations and by the basic fit between person and organization (POF). The fit between a person and his or her environment is crucial for the emergence of reasonable expectations that will have a reasonable chance of being met.

Organizational politics, met expectations, and person–organization fit affect employees' perceptions of organizational politics that in turn impact how employees feel about justice and fairness in the workplace (Ferris and Kacmar, 1992). Perceptions of organizational politics are important for the way they reflect employees' attitudes toward actual politics. Though previous studies have already shed light on the importance of perceptions of organizational politics, its antecedents and effects on employees' performance (Ferris and Kacmar, 1992; Parker et al., 1995), none of them have examined the actual effectiveness of political behavior in the workplace or the relationship between actual political behavior and perceptions of political behavior. Theoretically I support the importance given to perceptions of organizational politics by Ferris and Kacmar (1992) and Kacmar and Carlson (1994). However, I also suggest discussing organizational politics from a broader point of view which includes the specific influence tactics used by all organizational members well as their perception of this behavior. The model further argues that person–organization fit is an important predictor of how effective the use of organizational politics will be. A strong fit improves the probability of achieving desirable results through organizational politics implementation. On the other hand a poor fit negatively affects the likelihood of desirable results from the use of organizational politics, because the lack of a basic fit between the employee and his or her work environment prevents the organization, as well as the employee, from achieving effective outcomes. Met expectations expresses the individual's fulfilled interests and goals. It is expected to be positively related to person–organization fit and in the long run to have some effect on attitudes toward the organization (such as perceptions of politics), attitudes toward the work itself, behavioural intentions, and actual performance at work.

Perceptions of Politics and Employees' Performance

The importance of dealing with performance using a political approach is twofold: (1) along with other variables that have been mentioned in the management literature such as motivation, ability and skills, it can help explain changes in individual and organizational performance; (2) it may contribute to the understanding of the political process inside organizations and their negative as well as positive outcomes. A recent study by Bozeman et al. (1996:3) argues that 'given the significant implications of organizational politics for individuals and organizations . . . the issue of how organizational politics affects each of these parties should be of interest to management scholars and practitioners alike.'

A perceptual approach that is usually taken toward the investigation of organizational politics has tried to deal with the question of the relationship between politics and employees' performance. However, as mentioned earlier, this approach usually views organizational politics as a negative and unwanted phenomenon. Thus, Ferris and Kacmar (1992) and Kacmar and Carlson (1994) suggested that perceptions held by individuals about politics in their work environment negatively influence the way they do their jobs, their feeling about the company, their boss, their co-workers, productivity, satisfaction, absenteeism, and their intention of leaving. Ferris and Kacmar (1992) have also argued that some potential outcomes of the perception of politics inside organizations are an intention to withdraw from the organization, low job involvement, high job anxiety, and low job satisfaction.

In the earlier work of Ferris et al. (1989), three potential outcomes were mentioned in this connection: (1) withdrawal from the organization; (2) remaining a member of the organization and becoming involved in politics, and (3) remaining a member of the organization but not becoming involved in politics. Mintzberg (1983) also mentioned these options, relating them to Hirschman's (1970) Exit, Voice, and Loyalty theory. Nevertheless, the relationship between organizational politics and organizational outcomes, especially on the micro level, remains unclear and no theory has yet been put forward to explain the actual mechanism of this relationship. Another goal of our model is to pinpoint the workings of this relationship.

What outcomes are relevant on the micro level of employee performance? Several measures should be mentioned here, and the most important ones are absenteeism, turnover, negligent behaviors, in-role performance and organizational citizenship behavior (OCB). Absenteeism (Bycio, 1992; Porter and Steers, 1973) and turnover (Pfeffer, 1991) are objective measures that have been found to relate negatively to job satisfaction and organizational commitment and positively to role ambiguity, conflict, and overload at work (Brooke and Price, 1989; Meyer et al., 1989; Shore and Martin, 1989). Ferris and Kacmar (1992) mentioned absenteeism and turnover as potential outcomes of perceptions of politics. In addition to these performance measures I suggest adding some other aspects of performance appraisal to the examination of organizational politics outcomes. For example, I find the objective evaluation of employees by their supervisors and Organizational Citizenship Behavior (OCB) to be the most reliable and promising ones. Indeed, they are used quite frequently to test employee performance at work (Huselid, 1995; Organ and Ryan, 1995; Tharenou, 1993). Note too that, of these two aspects, OCB has received considerable attention in management research during the past two decades. Yet few studies have examined the mutual effect of organizational politics, perceptions of politics, fit, and expectations on performance in the workplace. This field is unstudied and remains unclear.

1. Political behavior in organizations: between perceptions and implementations[1]

As indicated in the introduction to this book, organizational politics is a controversial concept. While there is no doubt that internal politics is a common phenomenon in every organization (for example Ferris and Kacmar, 1992; Ferris and King, 1991; Mintzberg, 1983; Pfeffer, 1992; Zhou and Ferris, 1995) very little is known about the nature and boundaries of such politics (Cropanzano et al., 1997; Kipnis et al., 1980; Mayes and Allen, 1977).

The introduction also mentioned two approaches to organizational politics that have dominated the literature. The first focuses on employees' influence tactics at work as the best expression of political behavior. This line of research proposes a variety of typologies for influence tactics as well as possible antecedents and consequences of different influence tactics (Allen et al., 1979; Brass, 1984; Burns, 1961; Cheng, 1983; Erez and Rim, 1982; Izraeli, 1975, 1987; Kipnis et al., 1980). The second approach is more recent and focuses on employees' subjective *perceptions* of organizational politics rather than on political behavior or influence tactics. As was suggested by Kacmar and Ferris (1991:193–4) and Kacmar and Carlson (1994:3), perceptions of organizational politics represent the degree to which respondents view their work environment as political in nature, promoting the self-interests of others, and thereby unjust and unfair from the individual's point of view. These studies proposed a scale for the measurement of political perceptions called the 'Perceptions of Organizational Politics Scale' (POPS). This approach was extensively tested by Ferris, Kacmar, and their colleagues in numerous studies (Ferris and Kacmar, 1992; Ferris et al., 1989, 1989a; Ferris et al., 1991; Ferris et al., 1994; Ferris et al., 1996; Kacmar and Carlson, 1994; Kacmar and Ferris, 1991).

Due to various reasons that have limited the empirical approach to organizational politics, most of the relatively few studies on organizational politics have concentrated on employees' perceptions of politics. In addition, while some research has discussed and examined actual political behavior, very little has tested the relationship between political behavior and perceptions of politics. This chapter argues that actual political behavior, such as employees' influence tactics, is an important component that should be integrated in any conceptual framework of organizational politics.

Actual political behavior differs conceptually from perceptions of politics. It is however causally related to perceptions, and the nature of this relationship is posited and tested here. Hence this chapter proposes and tests several sections of the conceptual model for the relationship between influence tactics and perceptions of organizational politics. It is argued that this relationship is mediated by factors representing the congruence between the individual and his or her work environment. The model is empirically tested by a longitudinal design, allowing meaningful conclusions about a causal relationship between actual influence tactics and perceptions of politics. Thus this chapter makes two important contributions – a model that can be tested relating political behavior to perceptions of politics and a longitudinal study that permits causal conclusions.

EXPLORING THE POLITICAL LANDSCAPE IN ORGANIZATIONS

Research on organizational politics has argued that politics is an important component in the workplace that needs further inquiry and examination (DuBrin, 1988; Drory and Romm, 1990; Mayes and Allen, 1977; Mintzberg, 1983; Parker et al., 1995; Pfeffer, 1981, 1992). Mayes and Allen (1977:675), for example, defined it as the management of influence to obtain ends not sanctioned by the organization or to obtain sanctioned ends through non-sanctioned influence means. Pfeffer (1981:7) defined organizational politics as actions undertaken to acquire, enhance, and use power to obtain preferred outcomes in situations with incompatible choices. Gray and Ariss (1985:707) suggested that organizational politics consists of intentional acts of influence undertaken by individuals or groups to enhance or protect their self-interest when conflicting courses of action are possible. All of these definitions refer to the existence of influence processes on the organizational macro or micro level. This study focuses on intra-organizational influence relationships, which has two main dimensions – political behavior and perceptions of politics (Cropanzano et al., 1997).

The first dimension sees organizational politics as part of a general set of social behaviors used as tools that can contribute to the basic functioning of the organization (Pfeffer, 1981). Accordingly organizational politics should be investigated through employees' influence tactics aimed at various goals that are self-focused as well as organizational-focused (Kipnis et al., 1980:440). While several studies have looked at politics and influence tactics in organizations (for example, DuBrin, 1978, 1988; French and Raven, 1959; Izraeli, 1975; Schein, 1977), Kipnis et al.'s study is of major importance for its theoretical perspective and empirical evidence.

Kipnis et al. (1980) view organizational politics as the way in which people at work influence their colleagues, subordinates, and superiors to obtain personal benefits or to satisfy organizational goals. This definition allows a balanced analysis of the phenomenon (Drory, 1993). The main goal of Kipnis et al.'s (1980) study was to identify the range and dimensions of tactics that people use at work, which ultimately were reduced to the eight categories presented in Table I.1: (1) assertiveness, (2) ingratiation, (3) rationality, (4) sanctions, (5) exchange, (6) upward appeal, (7) blocking, and (8) coalitions. These influence tactics accord closely with similar groupings of influence tactics presented in other studies (Erez and Rim, 1982; Erez et al., 1986; Yukl and Tracey, 1992). Note that all the scales used in these studies were based on employees' self-reports of actual influence tactics in their work environment.

The second dimension defines politics as behavior strategically designed to maximize employees' short-term or long-term self-interests (Ferris et al., 1989). This definition was adopted in many studies that tended to treat organizational politics as dysfunctional behavior in organizations (Cropanzano et al., 1997; Drory, 1993; Ferris and Kacmar, 1992; Ferris et al., 1989, 1996a, 1996b). According to this perspective, organizational politics is self-serving behavior by employees to gain self-interests, advantages, and benefits at the expense of others and sometimes contrary to the interests of the entire organization or work unit. In studies following this approach political behavior is represented by the individual's subjective perceptions of politics, not actual politics or influence tactics. Porter (1976), for example, argued that perceptions of organizational politics are important even if they are misperceptions of actual events. Gandz and Murray (1980) argued that organizational politics is a state of mind. Ferris et al. (1989) and Zhou and Ferris (1995) noted that this concept views organizational politics as basically a subjective perception that may or may not reflect objective reality. As I have mentioned earlier, the notion of the perception of organizational politics was extensively researched by Ferris et al. (1989), who developed a theoretical model of a new perspective of organizational politics based on Lewin's (1936) argument that people respond to their perceptions of reality, not to reality itself. Politics in organizations should similarly be understood in terms of what people think the politics is rather than what it actually is.

BETWEEN INFLUENCE TACTICS AND PERCEPTIONS OF POLITICS

Throughout the years some serious work has been done on influence tactics and on perceptions of politics. However, the relationship between the two has rarely been examined. Cropanzano et al. (1997) argued that 'both [approaches] are useful and a contribution can be made using either perspective, so long as researchers are clear about their definition' (p. 161). Other studies more specifically stressed the need to examine the relationship between actual political behavior and perceptions of organizational politics. For example, Ferris and Kacmar (1992:94) surmised a strong correspondence between employees' political behavior and the perception of politics in the organization because they represent similar phenomenon. Kacmar and Carlson (1994) and Ferris et al. (1989a) argued that because both factors describe the same organizational environment and culture they should be related. Some support for this relationship was found by Kumar and Ghadially (1989) who determined that employees' actual political behavior was related to feelings of alienation and interpersonal mistrust in the workplace.

All of these studies suggest that the two phenomena, political behavior and perceptions of politics, might be related, but little research has attempted to explore and to test the nature of this relationship. My study, reported in this chapter, was predicated on the assumption that actual political behavior and perceptions of politics should be positively related, as they are two dimensions of the political work environment. Still, an important question is the nature of their relationship. One possibility is that an individual's political behaviors may help formulate his perceptions of the work environment, or put another way, political behavior affects perceptions of organizational politics. Another option is that the individual's political perceptions may assist in determining actual political behaviors. Accordingly one's perceptions of politics should affect one's political behavior. I incline toward the first possibility. Below I argue that influence tactics aim at accomplishing certain goals for the individual who applies them. One's degree of success is demonstrated in one's met expectations and perceptions of fit with the organization and that success determines one's perceptions of politics. If this explanation is correct, the relationship between actual politics and the perception of politics is not direct but mediated by factors that represent fit with the organization, a notion advanced by Ferris and Kacmar (1992:112–13).

MODEL AND HYPOTHESES

The first empirical model in this book relates influence tactics and perceptions of organizational politics. This model is presented in Figure 1.1. As argued by Ferris et al. (1989) the perception of organizational politics can be affected by several constructs. My basic argument is that one of these constructs can be the actual political behavior of an employee. Hence perceptions of politics in the workplace might be determined after the employee has had the chance to be directly involved in political activity and to apply some influence tactics aimed at achieving particular goals. This political activity, which may also be impacted when observing what happens to others as they exercise influence tactics, is expected to affect one's perceptions of organizational politics. I also argue that the congruence between the individual and his or her work environment will mediate the relationship between employees' influence tactics and perceptions of politics. The rationale for this relationship is based on Cropanzano et al. (1997:163) and Hulin (1991), who argued that individuals are more likely to have a positive evaluation of an organization when their goals are met than when their aspirations are threatened.

The research model proposes employees' level of met expectations (ME) and person–organization fit (POF) to be the two variables that mediate the relationship between actual politics and perceptions of politics. As presented in the introductory chapter these are two well-established constructs reflecting the fit between an employee and his or her organization. Vroom (1964) and Blau (1964) argued that expectations significantly affect employees' motivation, perceptions, and performance in the workplace. The expectancy theory suggests that a better fit between individuals and their work environment enhances employees' met expectations. When one's personal characteristics and attitudes are close to those of the workplace a better fit between the employee and his or her organization is expected. The importance of fit and expectations in social life and their implications in the study of politics was further discussed by Molm (1997), according to whom actors in every social political system are motivated by the cost and benefits of their activities and the mutual political exchange relations with the environment (p. 4). Those who better fit the organization and succeed in fulfilling self-expectations will tend to develop positive perceptions toward their social environment. Molm's basic argument is reflected in the expected relationship between employees' influence tactics and met expectations and person–organization fit as can be seen in Figure 1.1. Thus I expected to find that:

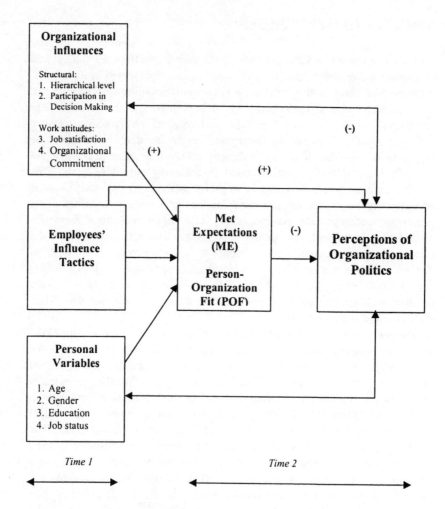

Figure 1.1 Influence tactics and perceptions of politics

Ha1. *The relationship between employees' influence tactics and perceptions of politics is mediated by employees' met expectations (ME) and person–organization fit (POF).*

As described above, I expected perceptions of politics in the workplace to be affected by employees' actual political behavior. Employees are involved in political activities and use a variety of influence tactics (Kipnis et al., 1980). Sometimes these tactics will result in what the individual defines as successful outcomes, and this in turn will lead to a high degree of met expectations or fit between the employee and the organization. Employees who have achieved their goals feel that their expectations have been met and perceive a close fit between themselves and the organization; also they perceive the organization as less political. They will probably attribute their success to factors other than politics, such as their own qualifications and level of performance at work. However, when influence tactics fail to achieve successful outcomes the individual will feel that his or her expectations have not been met, and feelings of disappointment, frustration, and alienation will result. When such feelings are created the emotional as well as the functional gap between a person and his or her organization widens. Consequently employees will tend to attribute their failure to achieve their goals to the political system of the organization rather than to their own failure (for example, in applying the wrong influence tactics or trying to achieve high-risk goals with little chance of success). In short, the above explanation leads to the following hypothesis:

Ha2. *Met expectations and person–organization fit are negatively related to perceptions of organizational politics.*

A PRELIMINARY EXAMINATION OF ANTECEDENTS TO ORGANIZATIONAL POLITICS: STRUCTURAL FACTORS, WORK ATTITUDES, AND PERSONAL INFLUENCES

The main goal of this chapter is to elaborate on the relationship between employee influence tactics (that is, actual political behavior) and employee perceptions of organizational politics. Nonetheless one cannot ignore compelling research evidence that other factors are strongly related to perceptions of organizational politics. A comprehensive approach would be to test the relationship between influence tactics and perceptions of organizational politics controlling for the common antecedents of perceptions of organizational politics as suggested by Ferris et al. (1989) and Kacmar et al. (1999). This approach would enable us to determine the contribution of influence tactics relative to that of other common antecedents. It is argued that influence tactics should be an important component in any model of politics in an organization. The best way to examine this argument is to test the relationship between employee influence tactics and perceptions of organizational politics together with other common predictors of perceptions of politics. If influence tactics are not significantly related to perceptions of organizational politics when other determinants are included in the model, then one of my basic arguments will not have empirical support, and vice versa. Following the original work by Ferris et al. (1989) as well as others who followed (that is, Ferris and Kacmar, 1992; Kacmar et al., 1999; Parker et al., 1995), it was expected that perceptions of organizational politics would be affected by structural factors, job/work factors and personal factors. Variables representing each of the three categories are included in the model as follows.

Organizational Structure Factors

Two variables were tested here: employees' hierarchical level and participation in decision making. It was expected that employees' hierarchical level and participation in decision making will affect perceptions of organizational politics negatively and in addition affect met expectations and person–organization fit positively. As for perceptions of organizational politics, a study by Ferris et al. (1996b) noted that lower-level employees tend to perceive their work environment as more political, perhaps because of their lack of involvement and control over various processes in the workplace. This argument was supported by Drory (1993) and Drory and Romm (1988) who found that, while supervisors are more involved in organizational politics, they also define it as a natural part of their job, so their perceptions of politics are low. Participation in decision making largely reflects the power distribution in organizations. More participative employees also have more influence over decisions and processes at work. This control might lead to a sense of fairness and justice, which is expected to result in low perceptions of politics in the workplace. Thus it was expected that employees' hierarchical level and participation in decision making would positively affect met expectations and person–organization fit because they represent integration into the workplace. By engaging in important activities such as decision-making processes or by working in high-level positions, employees express their identification with and acceptance of the organization's norms and values. As a result, the perceptual and functional gap between the individual and his or her organization narrows, expectations are more likely to materialize, and perceptions of organizational politics are more likely to diminish.

Ha3. *Employees' hierarchical level positively affects employees' met expectations (ME) and person–organization fit (POF) and negatively affects perceptions of organizational politics.*

Ha4. *Employees' participation in decision making positively affects employees' met expectations (ME) and person–organization fit (POF) and negatively affects perceptions of organizational politics.*

Job/Work Attitudes

The two constructs examined here were job satisfaction and organizational commitment. While the original model of Ferris et al. (1989) and subsequent studies paid much attention to job/work environment factors, little consideration has been given to job satisfaction and organizational commitment as predictors of perceptions of organizational politics. While other chapters in this book are more in line with the conventional causality described by Ferris et al. (1989), the present chapter considers the alternative possibility that job satisfaction and organizational commitment are actually predictors of perceptions of organizational politics. Accordingly high perceptions of organizational politics may be the result of negative work attitudes such as low job satisfaction and low organizational commitment.

The rationale for this relationship is based on the person–organization fit theory (Chatman, 1989; Porter et al., 1974; Schein, 1978; Tosi, 1992; Vroom, 1964) applied by Papa and Canary (1995) and Cropanzano et al. (1997). According to these studies, highly satisfied employees are expected to be a strong fit with the organization and are also expected to have better chances of fulfilling their expectations at work. When person–organization fit is strong and expectations are met, one feels that one has a fair chance of realizing one's essential interests in the workplace. One will perceive the organization as a work setting offering equal opportunities and as sensitive and responsive to the needs of every member; this attitude will eventually result in a low perception of politics. A similar rationale can be applied in the case of organizational commitment. High organizational commitment represents a desire to retain membership in the organization, belief in and acceptance of the values and goals of the organization and a willingness to exert effort on behalf of the organization (Porter et al., 1974). Therefore commitment results in a strong fit between the employees' individual values and attitudes and those of their organization (Chatman, 1989). High organizational commitment is expected to positively affect person–organization fit as well as employees' met expectations. On the other hand, it is expected to negatively affect employees' perceptions of politics, which reflect feelings of alienation, mistrust, and dissatisfaction with the organization's power distribution and with the ability to attain one's desired goals. Thus it was hypothesized that:

Ha5. *Job satisfaction positively affects employees' met expectations (ME) and person–organization fit (POF) and negatively affects perceptions of organizational politics.*

Ha6. *Organizational commitment positively affects employees' met expectations (ME) and person–organization fit (POF) and negatively affects perceptions of organizational politics.*

Personal Influences

In keeping with the Ferris et al. (1989) model, age, gender, education, and job status were also examined as control variables and potential predictors of perceptions of organizational politics. As reported by Ferris et al. (1996a, 1996b) previous research did not show consistent findings on a relationship between personal variables and perceptions of organizational politics. Therefore, no specific hypotheses were formulated here, and the personal variables were used more as control variables. However, a brief account of the rationale for selecting these four variables is warranted.

Gender and organizational politics
As for gender, some studies (for example, Ferris et al., 1989; Rosen, 1982) found that female employees perceive organizations as more political in nature than do male employees. Other studies argued that males tend to be more involved in organizational politics and regard the political processes as a natural and normative part of organizational life (Drory and Beaty, 1991).

Age and organizational politics
Mixed results are also reported for the relationship of age and perceptions of organizational politics. Some studies found it positive and some negative (Ferris and Kacmar, 1992; Gandz and Murray, 1980; Parker et al., 1995). Ferris et al. (1996a, 1996b) tended to agree with the notion that perceptions of politics decrease with and are tempered by age because anyone familiar with the realities of how organizations operate may be less prone to cognitively process, evaluate and interpret events as being political in nature. Met expectations and higher fit with the organization are more likely to be found among older employees, who are also more senior in the organization. Older employees are more familiar with the organization, depend on it more and accept it as a substantial part of their life.

Education and organizational politics

As for education, highly educated employees are expected to invest more effort in looking for jobs that better suit their personality and attitudes. Therefore their expectations are more likely to be met and their perceptions of organizational politics to be lower than those of less educated employees.

Job status and organizational politics

Permanent employees are usually those who have decided to stay with the organization for a long time. By providing them with permanency the organization basically shows them that they are among its core employees. Therefore they are expected to have a better fit with the work environment, have a higher level of met expectations and consequently fewer perceptions of politics.

As mentioned above, I proposed no specific directional hypotheses for the relationships between the personal variables and perceptions of organizational politics. These are included in the model following the recommendations of Ferris et al. (1989, 1996b) and Parker et al. (1995). Finally, as presented in Figure 1.1, I expected that:

Ha7. *Met expectations (ME) and person–organization fit (POF) mediate the relationship between structural variables, work attitudes, and personal influences and perceptions of organizational politics.*

STUDY 1 POLITICS PERCEPTIONS AND INFLUENCE TACTICS IN LOCAL AUTHORITIES

The empirical examination of the hypotheses presented in this chapter was based on an original study of public sector employees. The study was based on a two-phase survey of 411 employees in two local municipalities located in northern Israel. The survey was conducted between May 1996 and January 1997. I have distinguished three time phases. First, at T1 employees were asked to provide information about their influence tactics toward others in the work setting (supervisors, co-workers, subordinates), work attitudes (such as job satisfaction, organizational commitment), intentions of exit and neglect, and organizational/structural and personal variables. At T2, six months later, we returned to those who had completed the questionnaires at T1 and distributed a second survey including the variables, person–organization fit, met expectations, and perceptions of political scale. At T3, six months after T2, we returned to the employees' direct supervisors and asked them to provide detailed performance evaluations for each of the participants. Here we collected data on employees' in-role performance and on organizational citizenship behavior (OCB). The data collected at T3 were used in studies 2 and 3 only.

The decision to collect data for the second and third stages was made for two main reasons. First, I wanted to allow for the development of any possible behavior that might occur as a response to organizational politics. This is especially important for newcomers and recently tenured employees who need time to understand and adjust to a new organizational politics climate. According to Schein (1968, 1978), during the first stages of entering an organization employees experience political events only as bystanders. With time they actively enter into situations where their personal power and influence encounter other employees' ambitions. The consequences of such confrontations can be translated into positive or negative work outcomes. Second, the six-month interval took into account the organizations' needs and schedules and was a compromise with our requirements. Hence I decided on a longer period between the two stages for both practical and procedural reasons.

Participation in the entire research was voluntary, and employees were assured of full confidentiality in the data analysis. A total of 343 usable questionnaires (a return rate of 83.5 percent) at T1 and 303 questionnaires (a return rate of 88.3 percent) at T2 were used in the final analysis. Data analysis was performed on those who participated at T1 and T2, namely 303 employees comprising a return rate of 73.7 percent. A breakdown by occupation showed that 17 percent of the sample were blue-collar employees, 43 percent clerical and administrative workers, 20 percent high-tech workers, and 29 percent engineers, architects and other professionals; 56 percent of the sample were female, 77 percent were married, 89 percent had a full-time job and 33 percent were low-level or middle-level managers. Average age was 44.2 years (s.d. = 10.3); average tenure in the organizations was 11.8 years (s.d. = 8.6) and 32 percent of the respondents held a BA degree or higher. The demographic characteristics of the sample were quite similar to those of the total population in the two organizations that participated in the study: 57 percent females, 74 percent married, average age 45, average tenure in the organization 9 years and 31 percent with a BA degree or higher.

The main statistical analyses in this study were multiple and hierarchical regressions. To support the hypotheses regarding the mediated relationship among influence tactics, work attitudes, structural and personal variables, and perceptions of politics I followed Baron and Kenny (1986) and James and Brett (1984). According to them, a mediating relationship can be supported in one or more of the following methods: (1) regression analysis, (2) ANOVA or MANOVA, and (3) testing for interactions. Nevertheless, Baron and Kenny (1986) elaborated on the simplicity and the effectiveness of regression analysis compared with the limited test for mediation in other methods such as ANOVA. Accordingly, I applied the regression analysis method described by Baron and Kenny (1986:1177) to test for mediation. The process involves the following three regression equations. First, the mediator is regressed on the independent variable, whereby the independent variable must affect the mediator. Second, the dependent variable is regressed on the independent variable, whereby the independent variable must affect the dependent variable. Third, the dependent variable is regressed on both the independent variable and on the mediator, whereby the mediator must affect the dependent variable. If these conditions all hold in the predicted direction, then the effect of the independent variable on the dependent variable must be less in the third equation than in the second.

Table 1.1 presents descriptive statistics, intercorrelations, and reliabilities of the research variables. The measures displayed sound psychometric properties and the correlations among the independent variables were not high except for the relationship between organizational commitment and job satisfaction ($r = 0.56$; $p < 0.001$), which is very typical for these variables. These findings support the absence of multicollinearity between the research variables. The correlation matrix shows a positive relationship between employee's influence tactics that represent actual politics (OP) and the perceptions of organizational politics scale (POPS) ($r = 0.16$; $p < 0.01$). ME and POF were negatively related to perceptions of organizational politics, as was predicted by hypothesis Ha2 ($r = -0.52$; $p < 0.001$, $r = -0.47$; $p < 0.001$ respectively). Job satisfaction and organizational commitment positively affected ME ($r = 0.50$; $p < 0.001$, $r = 0.41$; $p < 0.001$ respectively) and POF ($r = 0.28$; $p < 0.001$, $r = 0.27$; $p < 0.001$ respectively) as was predicted in the first part of hypotheses Ha5 and Ha6. Thus the correlations provide some support for the research model.

Table 1.2 shows the result of two multiple regressions that were conducted following the first term for mediation of Baron and Kenny (1986) and were designed to measure a significant relationship between the mediator and the independent variable. In each of the equations the mediating variables (ME and POF) were regressed on the independent variables. The findings in Table 1.2 generally support the first term for mediation mentioned above. Significant relationships existed between the independent and dependent variables in both equations. The relationships were stronger for met expectation as a dependent variable than for person–organization fit. Influence tactics were strongly and significantly related to ME but not to POF. Thus a more appropriate conclusion is that ME was a good mediator while POF showed no mediating effect. The general conclusion is that the findings of Table 1.2 meet the first requirement for mediation as described by Baron and Kenny (1986). This requirement however holds for ME and not for POF. The findings of Table 1.2 provide no support for hypotheses Ha3 and Ha4. No significant relationships were found between the two mediators, ME and POF, and hierarchical level and participation in decision making. Organizational commitment and job satisfaction were strongly related to the two mediators, which partially supports hypotheses Ha5 and Ha6. It is also interesting that three personal variables (that is, gender, education, and job status) were related to person–organization fit while none related to met expectations.

Table 1.3 reports the data for the second and third requirements for mediation described by Baron and Kenny (1986), demonstrating the results of two multiple regressions. In the first equation perceptions of organizational politics were regressed on the independent variables with the exclusion of the effect of the assumed mediating factors (ME and POF), as suggested by Baron and Kenny (1986) in their second term for mediation. In the second equation of Table 1.3, perceptions of organizational politics were regressed on the independent and mediating variables by using a hierarchical regression method. This was done to estimate the relative contribution of the predicted mediating factors (ME and POF) to the explanation of perceptions of organizational politics. Although this estimation was not part of the research hypotheses, one should note the significant and relatively strong affect of ME and POF on perceptions of organizational politics. This finding supports the conceptual arguments of this study that expected strong relationships between person–organization fit and met expectations as mediating factors and the dependent variable, perceptions of organizational politics. This approach follows Ferris et al. (1996b) who also used the hierarchical regression method to test for mediation in a model of organizational politics. The mediating factors were entered into the equation in the first step, while all other independent variables were entered in the second step.

The second term for mediation requires that the independent variable(s) affect the dependent variable. The first equation in Table 1.3 shows clearly that this requirement was satisfied. Many of the independent variables were significantly related to perceptions of organizational politics, including influence tactics, the two work attitudes (organizational commitment and job satisfaction), and three of the personal variables. The effect of influence tactics on perceptions of organizational politics is worth noting in particular. Thus, the main conclusion from the findings of the first equation in Table 1.3 is that the second requirement for mediation has empirical support.

Some other notable findings of this equation are as follows. First, the findings do not support hypotheses Ha3 and Ha4, which expected a significant relationship between hierarchical level and participation in decision making and perceptions of organizational politics. Second, the findings do support hypotheses Ha5 and Ha6, which predicted that job satisfaction and organizational commitment would negatively affect perceptions of organizational politics. Third, although no hypotheses were formulated for the personal variables, the effects of gender, education, and job status on perceptions of organizational politics were significant. These findings show that women, less educated employees and more senior employees tended to perceive their work environment as more political (that is, high perceptions of organizational politics).

The second equation in Table 1.3 provides the information for the third requirement for mediation, namely regressing the dependent variable on both the independent variables and the mediators. Here I performed a two-step regression analysis, where in the first step the dependent variable was regressed on the mediators and in the second step the dependent variable was regressed on both the independent variables and the mediators. This two-step regression was proposed by Ferris et al. (1996b) to allow a more sensitive evaluation of the third condition for mediation: the mediators must affect the dependent variable, and, more importantly, the effect of the independent variables on the dependent variable must be less in the third equation (the two-step equation in Table 1.3) than in the second (the first equation in Table 1.3). The findings in Table 1.3 provide empirical support for the third condition of mediation. First, the data strongly support Ha2, which posited that employees' use of influence tactics would indirectly affect their perceptions of organizational politics. Most of the variance in perceptions of organizational politics was due to the effect of ME and POF ($R^2 = 34$ percent), while all other variables (including organizational politics) contributed only 4 percent to the total explained variance. Second, if we compare the contribution of the independent variables to the explained variance of perceptions of organizational politics when ME and POF were not controlled ($R^2 = 19$ percent) with the contribution when both ME and POF were controlled ($R^2 = 4$ percent) we can easily conclude that the third condition for mediation was met. The data in Table 1.3 support hypothesis Ha7 when we compare the first equation in Table 1.3 with the last one in the table, namely the one performed in step 2. The data clearly show that the effect of each of the independent variables, including employees' influence tactics, was less in the last regression equation than in the first regression of Table 1.3. For example, job satisfaction and organizational commitment, which had significant effects on perceptions of organizational politics in the first equation, demonstrated no significant effects in the last one when the two mediators were included in the equation. Two personal variables, gender and education, which were significant in the first equation of Table 1.3, became insignificant in the last one. Other variables such as influence tactics and job status remained significant, but their effects became much weaker when the two presumed mediators were included in the equation. This is demonstrated in the coefficients of these variables, which were lower in the last equation than in the first, the one without ME and POF. All of these findings are in line with the third condition for mediation of Baron and Kenny (1986). Note however that they basically hold for ME and not for POF because the former was not related to the independent variables as required in the first condition for mediation. Hence the findings in Table 1.3 support hypothesis Ha7 for the variable ME but not for the variable POF. ME was found to be a mediator of the relationship between all the independent variables and perceptions of organizational politics.

DISCUSSION AND SUMMARY

In this chapter an initial study was presented to examine whether and how employees' influence tactics affected perceptions of organizational politics. It also tested the effects of other determinants such as work attitudes and personal constructs on perceptions of politics. The results supported the positive effects of employees' influence tactics on perceptions of organizational politics. They also showed that this effect was mediated by employees' met expectations (ME). The mediating effect of person–organization fit (POF) was not supported largely because POF showed no relationship with influence tactics as can be seen in Table 1.2.

Moreover, ME mediated the effect of some work attitudes as well as some personal variables on perceptions of organizational politics. In many ways this chapter supported the notion that perceptions of organizational politics are affected by the success or failure of actual political behavior. The findings gave empirical support to the following process of politics in organizations, some parts of which were advanced in other research (for example, Ferris and King, 1991; Kumar and Ghadially, 1989; Randolph, 1985; Wayne et al., 1997). Organizational politics and employees' influence tactics function as tools by which the employee can progress in the organization. When actual politics contributes to the fulfillment of employees' expectations, perceptions of politics are reduced and the organization is perceived as just and fair. However, when individuals' expectations are not met, feelings of indignation against the organization arise, perceptions of politics become higher, and the entire work setting is perceived as unjust, unfair, and 'political' in nature.

Table 1.1 Descriptive statistics, reliabilities and intercorrelations among research variables for study 1 (reliabilities in parentheses)

Variables	Mean	S.D.	1	2	3	4	5	6	7	8	9	10	11
1. Perception of organizational politics (POPS)[b]	3.06	0.60	(0.77)										
2. Met expectations (ME)[b]	3.06	.067	-0.52***	(0.83)									
3. Person-organization fit (POF)[b]	3.35	.067	-0.47***	0.43***	(0.78)								
4. Organizational politics (OP)/ influence tactics[a]	1.74	0.46	0.16**	-0.14*	-0.05	(0.93)							
5. Job satisfaction[a]	3.53	0.67	-0.30***	0.50***	0.28***	-0.06	(0.77)						
6. Organizational commitment[a]	3.63	0.77	-0.26***	0.41***	0.27***	-0.07	0.58***	(0.88)					
7. Hierarchical level (1=managers)[a]	0.34	0.48	-0.02	0.06	-0.02	0.32***	0.14*	-0.02	-				
8. Participation in decision-making[a]	1.92	0.97	-0.04	0.11	0.02	0.38***	0.24***	0.05	0.48***	(0.85)			
9. Age[a]	44.34	10.23	-0.09	0.09	-0.01	0.02	0.07	0.10	0.24***	0.18**	-		
10. Gender (1=female)[a]	0.57	0.50	0.19***	-0.18**	-0.21***	-0.08	-0.20***	-0.20***	-0.13*	-0.17**	-0.29***	-	
11. Education[a]	2.71	1.42	-0.12*	0.04	0.09	0.08	0.04	-0.13*	0.10	-0.09	0.03	0.05	-
12. Job status (1=temporary)[a]	0.15	0.35	-0.17**	0.12*	0.08	-0.01	0.09	0.05	-0.20***	-0.16**	-0.31***	0.03	0.25***

Notes:
N=296-303 due to missing values
* $p \leq 0.05$ ** $p \leq 0.01$ *** $p \leq 0.001$
a= variables measured at time T1
b= variables measured at time T2

*Table 1.2   Findings of multiple regression analysis (standardized coefficients)
for the effect of independent variables on met expectations and person–
organization fit (t-test in parentheses) in study 1*

Variables	Met expectations (ME)	Person–organization fit (POF)
1. Organizational politics (OP)/ influence tactics	−0.15 (−2.69**)	−0.04 (−0.65)
Work attitudes		
2. Job satisfaction	0.35 (5.33***)	0.17 (2.39*)
3. Organizational commitment	0.19 (3.01**)	0.16 (2.24*)
Structural variables		
4. Hierarchical level (1 = managers)	0.04 (0.74)	−0.02 (−0.32)
5. Participation in decision making	0.04 (0.64)	−0.04 (−0.49)
Personal variables		
6. Age	0.04 (0.62)	−0.08 (−1.26)
7. Gender (1 = female)	−0.09 (−1.63)	−0.19 (−3.24***)
8. Education	0.04 (0.67)	0.12 (1.97*)
9. Job status (1 = temporary)	0.11 (1.88)	0.01 (0.14)
R^2	0.31	0.15
Adjusted R^2	0.29	0.12
F	13.66***	5.11***

Notes:
N = 296–303 due to missing values
* $p \leq 0.05$ ** $p \leq 0.01$ *** $p \leq 0.001$

Table 1.3   Findings of standard and hierarchical regression analysis (standardized coefficients) for the effect of independent variables on perceptions of organizational politics and the role of ME and POF as mediators (t-test in parentheses) in study 1

Variables	The effect of independent variables on POPS (ME and POF not included in equation)	The effect of independent variables on POPS controlling for ME and POF	
		Step 1	Step 2
1. Met expectations (ME)	–	−0.39 (−7.14***)	−0.33 (−5.35***)
2. Person–organization fit (POF)	–	−0.30 (−5.55***)	−0.29 (−5.16***)
3. Organizational politics (OP)/ influence tactics	0.19 (3.10**)	–	0.13 (2.34*)
Work attitudes			
4. Job satisfaction	−0.16 (−2.26*)	–	0.01 (0.07)
5. Organizational commitment	−0.14 (−1.97*)	–	0.03 (0.44)
Structural variables			
6. Hierarchical level (1 = managers)	−0.03 (−0.44)	–	−0.02 (−0.35)
7. Participation in decision making	−0.03 (−0.41)	–	−0.03 (−0.41)
Personal variables			
8. Age	−0.06 (−0.98)	–	0.07 (1.30)
9. Gender (1 = female)	0.15 (2.54**)	–	0.06 (1.21)
10. Education	−0.12 (−1.97*)	–	0 07 (−1.34)
11. Job status (1 = temporary)	−0.16 (−2.66**)	–	0 13 (2 31*)

The findings that are presented even at this stage hold beyond simple correlative relationships. Most of the data and conclusions on organizational politics have been based on cross-sectional designs that are too limited for any causal conclusions about the relationships among the variables. The longitudinal design in this study enabled us to draw causal conclusions about some of the relationships found here. While the model was based in part on an earlier model of perceptions of organizational politics suggested by Ferris et al. (1989), a contribution of these findings in this regard is that they allow us to re-examine some of the previous findings proposed and tested by Ferris et al. (1989) using a longitudinal design.

Another important contribution is the addition of employees' influence tactics, which represent individuals' actual political behavior (Kipnis et al., 1980), to the factors that need to be considered in organizational politics models. Most studies on organizational politics have used perceptions of politics as the main concept for the study of politics in organizations and have omitted actual political behavior from their models. Based on study 1 this chapter found that both constructs are important for understanding politics in organizations (Cropanzano et al., 1997). The research related behavioral and perceptual dimensions of politics and its findings support an indirect model in which ME mediates the relationship between political behavior and attitudes. The findings demonstrate the importance of ME for understanding politics in the workplace. However, in regard to POF the findings are mixed and do not support a mediating effect of this construct.

We found a high level of person–organization fit and met expectations to be positively and strongly correlated. Both represent congruence between the individual and the workplace but only ME mediated the relationship between influence tactics and perceptions of politics. This finding highlights the importance of expectations in the work environment as a factor that enhances positive reactions and attitudes toward the organization. POF was found to have a more direct effect on perceptions of politics and may be included in further studies as part of the job/work influences on political perceptions (Ferris and Kacmar, 1992). As noted by O'Reilly et al. (1991), a good fit results in positive work-related outcomes. Those who have a better fit with the organization are socially and politically supported by the organization's members and systems (Bretz and Judge, 1994) and thus tend to have lower levels of perceptions of politics.

Some of the relationships found here also relate work attitudes and structural and personal variables to perceptions of organizational politics and are similar to those found in other studies. For example other studies also found political perceptions to be negatively related to job satisfaction (Ferris and Kacmar, 1992; Ferris et al., 1996b; Zhou and Ferris, 1995) and organizational commitment (Drory, 1993; Cropanzano et al., 1997). Yet while these studies could only conclude that the variables were related, the present longitudinal design enabled me to determine a casual relationship in which job satisfaction and organizational commitment affected perceptions of organizational politics. I found no evidence for the effect of structural variables on perceptions of organizational politics. However, some support was found for the effect of gender and education on perceptions of organizational politics, while age was not related to them. Women workers and less educated workers tended to perceive the workplace as more political compared with men and more educated employees. These findings are in line with the studies of Ferris and Kacmar (1992) and Ferris et al. (1996b). The findings presented in this chapter also support the hypotheses regarding the effects of job satisfaction and organizational commitment on perceptions of organizational politics, ME and POF. As noted earlier, this study predicted that both variables would positively affect ME and POF and negatively affect perceptions of organizational politics. In line with hypothesis Ha1 ME mediated the relationship among work attitudes (for example, job satisfaction and organizational commitment), personal variables (for example, gender, education, and job status) and perceptions of organizational politics. While the Ferris et al. (1989) model mentioned the important effect of job/work influences on perceptions of organizational politics it disregarded the potential contribution of work attitudes to the explanation of organizational political perceptions. The first study thus enriches the set of antecedents that may affect political perceptions.

However, these initial findings did not support some of the expectations regarding the effects of structural variables on ME, POF, and perceptions of organizational politics, suggested by Ferris et al. (1989, 1996a, 1996b), Drory (1993), Drory and Romm (1988) and Bretz and Judge (1994). Participation in decision making showed no relationship with perceptions of organizational politics. These findings further contradict previous results of Ferris et al. (1996a, 1996b) who found a negative relationship between centralization and perceptions of organizational politics. My speculation is that participation in decision making is a less important predictor of perceptions of organizational politics when considered with other work attitudes in the same equation. Another explanation for this somewhat surprising finding is the specific setting of this study that was conducted among employees with relatively low levels of participation (Mean = 1.92; SD = 0.97).

While other studies found that hierarchical level was related to perceptions of organizational politics (for example, Ferris et al., 1996b), I found no such relationship. An implication of this finding may be that under certain conditions perceptions of organizational politics are subject to change at all levels of the organization. Another possible explanation may be found in the study of Parker et al. (1995). They found a non-linear relationship between employees' hierarchical level and perceptions of organizational politics. The findings indicated that the relationship was affected by employees' type of occupation (clerical, engineers, project managers, and so on). Since in study 1 I did not include participants' occupation among the independent variables, I was able to test only the general linear relationship between structural variables and perceptions of organizational politics. This may be the reason for the lack here of significant relationships between structural variables and perceptions of organizational politics. Moreover, the findings of study 1 may indicate that structural factors are less important in explaining perceptions of politics, as well as person–organization fit and expectations, than job/work attitudes, actual political behavior, and other personal constructs (Parker et al., 1995:903).

The fact that study 1 was not conducted in a North American setting constitutes another possible explanation for the results. Most studies on organizational politics have been performed in that environment and thus a cross-cultural comparison has not been possible until now. Study 1 provides evidence from another culture for similar relationships between organizational politics and a set of work attitudes, structural and personal variables that were suggested by Ferris et al. (1989). These findings promote the idea that the basic model of Ferris et al. can be applied in other cultures and thus enhances the possibility of trans-cultural implications.

Finally, several limitations of study 1 should be mentioned. First, the fact that major constructs of the study were self-reported raises a potential problem of source bias or general method variance. Therefore the findings must be interpreted cautiously. Despite the fact that data was collected at two different time points one should notice that the mediating variables and the dependent variable were all measured at the same time (T2). Perhaps the failure to support a mediating effect of POF on the relationship between influence tactics and perceptions of organizational politics was partly due to this fact. While the intercorrelations among the measures were not very high and decrease the possibility of common method error, this option cannot be totally ignored. A possible strategy to overcome this potential bias is to adopt a technique that separates the measurement of dependent and independent variables. Future studies may use this recommendation as a guide for better models in the study of organizational politics. Yet one should note that because the multivariate analysis considered the simultaneous effects of all variables, the extent of this problem was reduced. The use of a behavioural-dependent variable based on information provided by the supervisors also reduced the potential for common method error because not all the data in this study were collected from the same source.

Second, despite the longitudinal design, one may argue that an interval of six months between T1 and T2 may not be sufficient if one seeks to more strongly support the relationships as described by the research hypotheses. For example, this time span may be too short for employees' influence tactics to affect ME and POF. Nevertheless, the fact that a six-month interval yielded some significant and interesting findings that are in line with the theoretical arguments is encouraging and deserves more attention as well as further development and empirical examination. Future studies should also look for similar relationships to those suggested in the present model, but perhaps should consider using a longer interval or more phases of data collection, thus allowing for more striking results and trends to emerge. Using this strategy may also overcome the limitation of common method variance between the mediating and the independent variables. A longer period of time between measurements will probably contribute to minimizing this possibility and create more robust measures.

Despite these limitations, the findings of study 1 have demonstrated the usefulness of concepts such as employees' influence tactics, ME, and POF to our understanding of the process of organizational politics. As suggested by Ferris et al. (1996b:262), 'there is a vast area of social and political dynamics in organizations that remains largely unexplored'. The following chapters in this book will try to respond to this challenge.

NOTE

1. Some parts of this chapter are based on Vigoda and Cohen (2002) 'Influence tactics and perceptions of organizational politics: A longitudinal study' *Journal of Business Research*, 55, 4, 311-24. Copyright with permission from Elsevier Science.

2. Organizational politics, job attitudes, and work outcomes[1]

In the previous chapters I have suggested a variety of definitions for organizational politics and possible reactions to it on the intra-organizational level. Most if not all of these definitions have suggested that organizational politics can result in negative or destructive work outcomes. However, empirical efforts to support this proposition have been inconclusive. As mentioned in the previous chapter Parker et al. (1995) found that organizational politics was not related to job satisfaction, loyalty, senior management effectiveness or endorsements of positive organization values. Nevertheless they found that respondents who perceived more politics in the organization also tended to see the organization as less supportive of innovation. Ferris et al. (1989) mentioned three potential responses to such a situation: increased job anxiety, decreased job satisfaction, and withdrawal from the organization. Later studies confirmed some of these relationships. Still, the most salient association was between perceptions of organizational politics and job attitudes.

For example Drory (1993) found that perceptions of politics were negatively related to job satisfaction and organizational commitment. He found that organizational politics had a potentially damaging effect on lower-status employees but no negative effect on higher-status employees. He speculated that lower-status employees, who lacked a stable power base and effective means of influence, perceived organizational politics as a source of frustration and reacted to a climate of politics by displaying increasingly negative attitudes toward the organization (pp. 68–69). Bozeman et al. (1996) elaborated on the effect of the perception of organizational politics on several work outcomes. No direct effects were revealed in this two-study investigation, yet some interactive relationships were found among the perception of politics, feelings of self-efficacy, and the outcome variables. Specifically, the relationship between organizational politics, job satisfaction, organizational commitment, turnover intentions, and job stress was moderated by the variable job self-efficacy. The relationship was stronger for individuals with high job self-efficacy rather than with low. Hence in this chapter I examine the possibility that both organizational politics and job attitudes will be useful in explaining other work outcomes such as employees' intentions to leave (exit) and tendencies to ignore job duties (neglect). I further propose that employees' performance may decline in response to high levels of perceived organizational politics.

STUDIES ON ORGANIZATIONAL POLITICS IN THE PUBLIC SECTOR

Few studies have examined issues related to organizational politics in the public sector. At first glance several studies appear to have done so, but in fact they were conducted mainly at universities (for example, Christiansen et al., 1997; Ferris et al., 1996a, 1996b; Welsh and Slusher, 1986) or they used mixed samples of private and semi-public agencies like hospitals and government-owned industries (for example, Drory, 1993; Ferris and Kacmar, 1992; Kumar and Ghadially, 1989). Also, most studies of organizational politics refer to the North American private sector (for example, Bozeman et al., 1996; Cropanzano et al., 1997; Hochwarter et al., 1997; Wayne et al., 1997). With the exception of Parker et al. (1995) no study has examined the effect of perceived organizational politics on work outcomes among public sector employees who serve the general public (for example, governmental agencies or local municipalities). Patterns of employment and service in public organizations substantially differ from those of private or semi-public systems. In most countries the wages of public servants are lower than those of private-sector employees, promotion is slower and rewards are generally not related to work outcomes (Rainey, 1991). On the other hand public organizations usually offer a stable work environment, higher job security and some the challenge of serving a large and heterogeneous population. Hence the possible unique effect of internal politics on public agencies and public servants is still unclear and deserves more attention.

POSSIBLE RESULTS OF ORGANIZATIONAL POLITICS

As suggested in the previous chapters, a comprehensive framework of antecedents and responses to perceptions of organizational politics was advanced by Ferris et al. (1989). The present theoretical conception relies on their work and tries to extend it in several ways. Figure 2.1 presents another section of our general model for the examination of the relationship among organizational politics, job attitudes and several work outcomes. First, it fosters the idea that organizational politics reflects perceptions of procedural justice, fairness and equity in one's work environment, so it may be related to

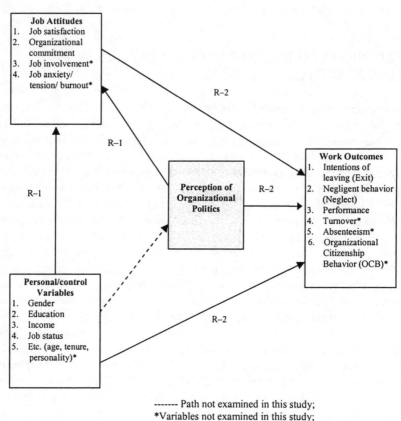

Job Attitudes
1. Job satisfaction
2. Organizational commitment
3. Job involvement*
4. Job anxiety/ tension/ burnout*

R–2

R–1

R–1

Perception of Organizational Politics

R–2

Personal/control Variables
1. Gender
2. Education
3. Income
4. Job status
5. Etc. (age, tenure, personality)*

R–2

Work Outcomes
1. Intentions of leaving (Exit)
2. Negligent behavior (Neglect)
3. Performance
4. Turnover*
5. Absenteeism*
6. Organizational Citizenship Behavior (OCB)*

------- Path not examined in this study;
*Variables not examined in this study;
R–1 = Multiple Standard Regression;
R–2 = Multiple Hierarchical Regression.

Figure 2.1   Perceptions of organizational politics, job attitudes, and work outcomes

job attitudes. Second, the model anticipates that both politics and job attitudes have an effect on employees' behavioral intentions and job performance. This idea also draws substance from extensive literature that relates workplace justice to job attitudes and to a variety of work outcomes such as career development, and formal and informal job performance (for example, Blau et al., 1993; Farh et al., 1990; Fitzgerald and Rounds, 1989; Moorman, 1991; Morrow et al., 1990; Niehoff and Moorman, 1993; Scandura, 1997).

The first part of the model refers to the possible relationship between perceptions of organizational politics and job attitudes. Drory (1993) suggested that the events comprising organizational politics naturally occur within the social arena of the organization. Consequently perceptions of fairness stemming from internal politics will be primarily reflected in one's attitudes to elements one considers responsible for the political climate. As mentioned in the opening chapters these components may be supervisors, co-workers, and other factors in the organization that together generate overall job satisfaction. Previous studies have suggested a relationship between constructs of procedural justice (for example, time since last promotion or time since last appraisal) and the perception of politics (Ferris et al., 1996b). A political organizational climate may suppress unfair and unjust activities that are easily observed by employees. When an employee feels deprived and unfairly treated because of political considerations, he or she will be inclined to initially react by reducing the activities he or she undertakes voluntarily and his or her attachment to the organization. These spontaneous attitudes and reactions are not directly controlled by the organization and are expected to change more easily in response to disappointment with the workplace. One of the most studied aspects in this regard is organizational commitment. According to Mowday et al. (1979) this variable is fundamental in determining job attitudes. It comprises involvement in and identification with the organization, and it is greatly affected by job satisfaction and overall organizational climate.

Recent studies have followed these arguments and incline to a more empirical examination of the politics–job attitudes relationship. Ferris et al. (1996b; 1998) found that the perception of organizational politics was negatively related to job satisfaction. Bozeman et al. (1996) supported this finding and in addition found that the perception of politics was negatively related to organizational commitment. In keeping with these studies I expected to find that a perceived political atmosphere in public agencies would first result in negative job attitudes. Hence public employees with high perceptions of organizational politics will tend to show lower levels of job satisfaction and organizational commitment than other employees. Based on the results presented in the previous chapter I therefore suggest that the relationship between political perceptions and job satisfaction as well as the relationship between political perceptions and organizational commitment is actually bi-directional (see the general theoretical framework in Figure I.3). While job satisfaction and organizational commitment may affect perceptions of organizational politics, they may also be affected by it in return. Therefore hypothesis Hb1 was formulated to re-test this elementary relationship in a more conservative way, and it suggests that:

Hb1. *Perception of organizational politics will be negatively related to job satisfaction and organizational commitment.*

ORGANIZATIONAL POLITICS AND HIRSCHMAN'S EVLN THEORY

The second part of the model in this chapter examined the relationship between the perception of organizational politics, job attitudes, behavioral intentions, and job performance. It is widely accepted in organizational behavior theory that job attitudes may lead to behavioral intentions and in time to actual behaviors. For example Drory (1993) suggested that a change in job attitudes might be regarded as the immediate reaction to organizational politics, potentially signaling more negative responses by employees in the long run. To better understand the effect of organizational politics on work outcomes it may prove useful to employ the Exit, Voice, Loyalty, and Neglect (EVLN) theory created by Albert Hirschman (1970). This theory is relevant because it suggested the option of exit (leaving the organization) as a possible negative reaction to decline in organizations. This behavior differs substantially from the active destructive reaction of neglect and from other, more constructive responses such as voice (intention to stay and fight for one's beliefs and occupational goals) and loyalty (willingness to adjust and comply with the current environment). Ferris and Kacmar (1992) proposed several responses to organizational politics that 'appear similar in nature to Hirschman's (1970) exit, loyalty and voice' (p. 97). Cropanzano et al. (1997) suggested that employees who view the organization as political in nature, unjust, or responsive only to the aspirations of the powerful members may be encouraged to leave it physically and also psychologically. Organizational politics can cause the disengagement or psychological withdrawal of individuals. Employees may be physically present at the workplace but their minds are elsewhere. Still, empirical studies provide only marginal support for this idea (for example, Bozeman et al., 1996).

Examinations of Hirschman's framework (for example, Farrell and Rusbult, 1992; Rusbult and Lowery, 1985) elaborated on another negative reaction to instability and unfairness at work. This option, called neglect, represents an alternative whereby the individual stays in the organization but expresses dissatisfaction by unproductive activity or even harmful behavior. For example, employees may put less effort into their work, delay the completion of certain assignments without justification, or show no creativity and initiative even though they are capable of it. Other forms of neglect may reflect little consideration for citizens'/clients' needs or carelessness in using organizational property. Neglect is considered a more negative/passive response because of its covert image and potential long-term damage to the organization. An employee may remain with the organization but neglect his or her essential duties and assignments when he or she has no other job alternatives or wishes to punish the organization for being unfair (Farrell and Rusbult, 1992). Aspects of such behavior were found among employees in an American federal agency (Rusbult and Lowery, 1985). These findings may suggest that negligent behavior serves as an operative alternative for public personnel who feel abused by internal politics but still would not choose actually to leave the organization for a variety of reasons. Symptoms of psychological withdrawal, like continuous daydreaming or chatting to co-workers about nonwork-related subjects (for example, internal politics?), have much in common with negligent behavior (Hulin, 1991). Note that negligent behavior may also reflect misbehavior or activities that damage the organization, not always because of overtly vicious intentions but sometimes through irresponsibility or sloppiness stemming from reduced attachment to the organization or lack of identification with it (Vardi and Wiener, 1996). Misbehavior can thus be driven by high levels of organizational politics that lead to job dissatisfaction and low organizational commitment.

Ferris et al. (1998) applied the ideas of Hirschman (1970) to support a theory of reactions to organizational politics. They found that organizational politics might result in negative repercussions such as low job satisfaction, high levels of neglect, or intention to exit. That is, when some organizational members misuse politics to achieve self-interests and thereby violate basic norms of fairness and justice the effect on co-workers is inevitable. Employees who see themselves as injured by such power-seeking activities may react in several ways. One response may be an intention to leave the organization. An alternative is to stay, but to reciprocate with negligent behavior. Hence I expected that organizational politics would be positively related to destructive work outcomes such as exit and neglect. The second hypothesis in this chapter is thus:

Hb2. *Perception of organizational politics will be positively related to employees' intentions of exit and neglect.*

A negative relationship is further expected between the perception of organizational politics and job performance. To my knowledge, with the exception of Hochwarter et al.'s (1997) study, this relationship has not been examined so far. If internal politics is related to job attitudes and thereby to intentions to exit and neglect, there is a sound rationale for the belief that actual performance by employees will also be affected. Previous studies have found a relationship between intention to turnover and job performance (for example, Mossholder et al., 1988). Other studies have used both variables as important work outcomes that are related to the emotional state of an individual (Wright and Cropanzano, 1998). This state (for example, job anxiety, job tension, burnout) was found to correlate with feelings of fairness and justice in the work environment as caused by the political behavior of others (for example, Bozeman et al., 1996; Ferris et al., 1996a, 1996b). When individuals are consciously planning to leave the organizations their minds and energies are focused on other available job options. They are also more exposed to job and occupation stressors and therefore tend to be less focused on their job duties. All of these factors may cause a decline in job performance. Hence the third hypothesis in this chapter is:

Hb3. *Perception of politics will be negatively related to employees' performance.*

The perception of organizational politics should make a unique contribution to the explanation of the three work outcomes mentioned above, beyond the explanations offered by job attitudes and other personal variables. Drawing on the early works of Ferris et al. (1989, 1989a) I presumed that the perception of organizational politics is distinct from other job-related attitudes and should be analyzed as an independent construct.

The personal variables were integrated into the model for control purposes but also for a more substantial reason. Previous studies have mentioned personal and personality factors as important determinants of organizational politics. The basic argument in the studies of Ferris, Kacmar, and their colleagues was that personal as well as personality characteristics of employees better explain the emergence of perceptions of organizational politics. Several studies supported the notion that individuals with different educational, income, seniority, and hierarchical levels, as well as male and female employees, will perceive politics in different ways. For example, Ferris et al. (1996a) found differences between white women and white men when they examined the moderating effect of understanding on the relationship between co-workers' political behavior and employees' reactions. Drory (1993) found that the association between political climate and negative job attitudes was stronger for employees of lower status than for those of higher status. An additional explanation for the relationship between personal/personality variables and organizational politics derives from the theory of person–organization fit (Blau, 1987; Bretz and Judge, 1994; Meir and Hasson, 1982; Smart et al., 1986; Spokane, 1985). These studies provided evidence that when employees fit their work environment better they also show improved job attitudes, had more career success and were more likely to stay in the organization. Coping more effectively with a given political atmosphere reflects a better person–organization fit. Hence employees who fit better with their organization may have more positive attitudes to their job and to the workplace. Such employees will not develop feelings of alienation, disappointment, mistrust, or other negative job attitudes and are expected to show improved work outcomes. All of these considerations led to the fourth hypothesis in this chapter:

Hb4. *Perception of organizational politics will contribute to the explanation of work outcomes over and above the contribution of other job attitudes and personal variables.*

STUDY 2   ORGANIZATIONAL POLITICS, JOB ATTITUDES, AND WORK OUTCOMES OF LOCAL GOVERNMENT EMPLOYEES

The sample for study 2 was similar to the sample used in study 1. However, unlike the former, this study distinguished only two time phases. The data collected at the original T1 and T2 were combined to test the more conventional general relationship between job attitudes and perceptions of politics. Thus the first time phase in this study represents information about employees' work attitudes, perceptions of organizational politics, intentions of exit and neglect, and organizational/structural and personal variables. The second time phase represents information collected from the employees' direct supervisors who were asked to provide detailed in-role performance evaluations for each of the participants. Altogether, 22 supervisors participated in the second stage, each providing between 12 and 17 performance evaluations. However, unlike study 1, this one made no causal implications.

The research hypotheses were tested by multiple standard and hierarchical regressions. To test hypothesis Hb1 I regressed job satisfaction and organizational commitment on perception of politics and the personal variables. Hypotheses Hb2, Hb3, and Hb4 were tested by three multiple hierarchical regressions. Here, intentions of exit, neglect, and job performance were regressed on perception of organizational politics, job satisfaction, organizational commitment, and the personal variables. The variables were entered into the equations in three steps. This was done to examine the individual contribution of each construct in the model to the explanation of the work outcomes.

Table 2.1 presents descriptive statistics, intercorrelations and reliabilities of the research variables. All measures displayed good reliabilities and good psychometric properties. Perception of organizational politics was positively correlated with job satisfaction and organizational commitment ($r = -0.30$; $p < 0.001$ and $r = -0.26$; $p < 0.001$ respectively). It also showed a positive correlation with intentions of exit and neglect ($r = 0.29$; $p < 0.001$ and $r = 0.27$; $p < 0.001$ respectively). Furthermore, perception of politics was negatively correlated with performance evaluations as reported by supervisors ($r = -0.14$; $p < 0.05$).

Table 2.2 displays the results of two multiple regressions. Both regression models show that perception of organizational politics was negatively related to job attitudes after controlling for several personal variables. The relationship between perception of organizational politics and job satisfaction ($r = -0.27$; $p < 0.001$) was slightly stronger than the relationship between perceptions of organizational politics and organizational commitment ($r = -0.24$; $p < 0.001$). While part-time employees and those with higher incomes were more satisfied at work, male employees and those with a lower education level showed more organizational commitment. Perception of organizational politics and the personal-control variables explained 13.6 percent of the variance in job satisfaction and 11.6 percent of the variance in organizational commitment. These findings support hypothesis Hb1, which argued that organizational politics is negatively related to job satisfaction and organizational commitment.

Table 2.3 shows the results of three multiple hierarchical regressions. In each regression model the personal variables were entered first in order to control for the other variables. Job attitudes were entered in the second step of each equation while the third step added the primary variable, perception of organizational politics. This variable was added last in order to estimate the additional explained variance contributed by this construct above and beyond other variables. In the first regression model intentions of exit were negatively related to job satisfaction and organizational commitment ($\beta = -0.23$; $p < 0.001$ and $\beta = -0.29$; $p < 0.001$ respectively). These variables made the highest contribution to the explained variance in the equation (19.8 percent). Perception of organizational politics was positively related with intentions of exit ($\beta = 0.19$; $p < 0.001$). Note that this variable raised the explained variance by an additional 3.2 percent and brought the total value of variance in the final equation to 26.1 percent.

In the second regression, job satisfaction showed a negative relationship with negligent behavior ($\beta = -0.19$; $p < 0.01$). However the perception of organizational politics was positively related to neglect ($\beta = 0.15$; $p = 0.001$) and contributed 12.6 percent to the explained variance in the final equation. This value was higher than the combined explained variance of both job satisfaction and the personal/control variables together (9.2 percent). It set the total explained variance of neglect after the third step at 14.7 percent. The findings reported so far supported hypothesis Hb2 for intentions of exit and were even more solid for the neglect variable. Thus employees who viewed the workplace as political in nature were more likely than other employees to develop intentions of exit and negligent behaviors.

The third equation examined the relationship among job attitudes, perception of organizational politics and employees' performance. None of the job attitudes showed a relationship with performance. Nevertheless, perception of organizational politics was negatively related to employees' performance ($\beta = -0.13$; $p = 0.05$). Hence employees with lower perceptions of organizational politics tended to perform better than those with high perceptions. Three of the personal/control variables also demonstrated a significant relationship with performance. Individuals with a low educational level, a higher income, and a part-time job were described by supervisors as employees with better performance. These findings strongly supported hypothesis Hb3 regarding the intentions of exit and neglect variables. They more modestly supported this hypothesis for the performance variable. Hence the findings further demonstrate that the perception of organizational politics may play a significant role in predicting employees' performance, beyond the effect of other job attitudes.

The regression models discussed so far also supported hypothesis Hb4. In each of the hierarchical regression models the perception of organizational politics made a significant contribution to the explanation of the dependent variable. This contribution varied from 3.2 percent for intentions of exit, to 3.6 percent for performance, and up to 12.6 percent for neglect. Perceptions of organizational politics was strongly related to negligent behavior and to a lesser extent to intentions of exit. Employees' performance was negatively related to perception of organizational politics yet this relationship was not very strong. It is important to mention that intentions of exit were better explained by job attitudes and the perception of organizational politics than were the other two work outcomes ($R^2 = 26.1$ percent). Performance had the lowest level of explained variance among the three work outcomes examined here ($R^2 = 5.9$ percent).

Among the personal variables gender was found to have a significant relationship with neglect, as women employees demonstrated lower levels of negligent behavior ($\beta = 0.20$; $p < 0.01$). More highly educated employees were more likely to consider leaving the organization ($\beta = 0.13$; $p < 0.05$) but were less likely to exhibit neglect behaviors or negative impacts on their performance ($\beta = -0.14$; $p < 0.05$ and $\beta = -0.16$; $p < 0.05$ respectively). Income was negatively related to intentions of exit and neglect ($\beta = -0.16$; $p < 0.01$ and $\beta = -0.15$; $p < 0.05$ respectively) and positively related to performance ($\beta = 0.17$; $p < 0.05$). Supervisors also reported better performance by part-time employees than by full-time ones ($\beta = 0.13$; $p < 0.05$).

The model in this chapter reflects a potential mediating effect of job attitudes on the relationship between the independent and dependent variables. Although I did not posit specific hypotheses for such a mediating effect it is an important finding worthy of further consideration. Table 2.4 presents a test of mediation. To support a mediating relationship I followed the studies of Baron and Kenny (1986) and James and Brett (1984). As may be observed, job attitudes mediate the relationship between organizational politics and intentions of exit and neglect. First, the zero-order correlations between perceptions of politics and job attitudes are significant ($r = -0.30$; $p < 0.001$ for job satisfaction and $r = -0.26$; $p < 0.001$ for organizational commitment: see Table 2.1). Second, as Table 2.4 proves, with the exception of performance, job attitudes and work outcomes were also significantly correlated. Job satisfaction was negatively related to exit and neglect ($r = -0.40$; $p < 0.001$ and $r = -0.25$; $p < .01$ respectively). Organizational commitment was negatively related to exit and neglect ($r = -0.41$; $p < 0.001$ and $r = -0.19$; $p < 0.001$ respectively). Finally, when perceptions of organizational politics were controlled these correlations diminished considerably, as the major criterion for mediation requires (Baron and Kenny, 1986:1177). Job satisfaction was related to exit and neglect ($\beta = -0.19$; $p < 0.01$ and $\beta = -0.14$; $p < 0.05$ respectively). Organizational commitment was related to exit ($\beta = -0.27$; $p < 0.001$) and was not related to neglect. No support was found for a mediating effect of job attitudes on the relationship between organizational politics and performance.

Table 2.1   Descriptive statistics, reliabilities, and intercorrelations among research variables (reliabilities in parentheses) for study 2

Variables	Mean	S.D.	1	2	3	4	5	6	7	8	9
Organizational politics (OP)											
1. Perception of organizational politics (POPS) [a]	3.06	0.60	(0.77)								
Job attitudes											
2. Job satisfaction [b]	3.54	.067	-0.30***	(0.77)							
3. Organizational commitment [a]	3.64	0.77	-0.26***	0.58***	(0.88)						
Work outcomes											
4. Intentions of exit [a]	2.07	.085	.029***	-0.40***	-0.41***	(0.84)					
5. Neglect [a]	1.88	0.64	0.27***	-0.25***	-0.19***	0.52***	(0.67)				
6. Performance [c]	4.19	0.65	-0.14*	0.10	0.09	-0.21***	-0.26***	(0.92)			
Control variables											
7. Gender (female)	0.56	0.50	0.19***	-0.15**	-0.18***	0.08	-0.07	-0.04	–		
8. Education	2.71	1.43	-0.12*	0.05	-0.13*	0.07	-0.05	-0.08	.04	–	
9. Income	2.58	1.04	-0.04	0.14*	-0.07	-0.09	-0.06	0.07	-0.29***	0.39***	–
10. Job status (part-time job)	0.11	0.31	-0.07	0.11*	0.06	-0.03	-0.06	0.10	-0.25***	-0.02	-0.30***

Notes:
N = 296–303 due to missing values
* p ≤ 0.05   ** p ≤ 0.01   *** p ≤ 0.001
Scale anchors: a   1 = Strongly disagree to 5 = Strongly agree;
b   1 = Very dissatisfied to 5 = Very satisfied;
c   1 = Never or almost never to 5 = Always or almost always

Table 2.2   Findings of multiple regression analysis (standardized coefficients) for the relationship of organizational politics and job attitudes (t test in parentheses) for study 2

Variable	Job satisfaction	Organizational commitment
Control variables		
1. Gender (female)	−0.09 (−1.48)	−0.16 (−2.60**)
2. Education	−0.05 (−0.83)	−0.13 (−2.14*)
3. Income	0.17 (2.70**)	−0.05 (−0.83)
4. Job status (part-time job)	0.16 (2.74**)	−0.06 (1.09)
Organizational Politics (OP)		
5. Perception of organizational politics (POPS)	−0.27 (−4.79***)	−0.24 (−4.20***)
R^2	0.136	0.116
Adjusted R^2	0.121	0.100
F	9.07***	7.60***

Notes:

N = 296–303 due to missing values

* $p \leq 0.05$ ** $p \leq 0.01$ *** $p \leq 0.001$

Table 2.3   Findings of multiple hierarchical regression analysis (standardized coefficients) for the effect of organizational politics and job attitudes on work outcomes (t-test in parentheses) for study 2

Variable	Step	Exit			Neglect			Performance		
		1	2	3	1	2	3	1	2	3
Control variables										
1. Gender (female)		0.05 (0.82)	-0.05 (-.85)	-0.08 (-1.49)	-0.09 (-1.52)	-0.15 (-2.39*)	-0.20 (-3.20**)	-0.03 (-.47)	-0.01 (-0.18)	0.01 (0.20)
2. Education		0.13 (2.05*)	0.10 (1.78)	0.13 (2.34*)	0.11 (1.76)	0.10 (1.62)	-0.14 (2.34*)	-0.14 (-2.21*)	-0.14 (-2.12*)	-0.16 (-2.44**)
3. Income		-0.16 (-2.29*)	-0.14 (-2.24*)	-0.16 (-2.54**)	-0.15 (-2.20*)	-0.13 (-1.89)	-0.15 (-2.26*)	0.16 (2.36*)	0.16 (2.27*)	0.17 (2.43*)
4. Job status (part-time job)		-0.09 (-1.45)	-0.02 (-0.33)	-0.01 (-0.11)	-0.08 (-1.26)	-0.03 (-0.51)	-0.01 (-0.24)	0.15 (2.43*)	0.14 (2.19*)	0.13 (2.06*)
Job attitudes										
5. Job satisfaction			-0.23 (-3.507***)	-0.19 (-2.93**)		-0.19 (-2.70**)	-0.14 (-2.02*)		0.04 (0.53)	0.01 (0.17)
6. Organizational commitment			-0.29 (-4.46***)	-0.27 (-4.15***)		-0.11 (-1.51)	-0.07 (-1.09)		0.05 (0.73)	0.04 (0.51)
Organizational politics (OP)										
7 Perception of organizational politics (POPS)				0.19 (3.47***)			0.25 (4.26***)			-0.13 (-2.07*)
R^2		0.031	0.229	0.261	0.026	0.092	0.147	0.039	0.045	0.059
Adjusted R^2		0.018	0.213	0.242	0.012	0.073	0.126	0.025	0.025	0.036
F		2.33	14.24***	14.39***	1.89	4.84***	6.99***	2.91*	2.25	2.56*
ΔR^2		-	0.198	0.032	-	0.066	0.055	-	0.006	0.014
F for ΔR^2		-	38.01***	12.77***	-	10.47***	19.02***	-	0.89	4.19***

Notes:
N=296-303 due to missing values
* p≤0.05 ** p≤0.01 *** p≤0.001

Table 2.4   Summary findings for the mediating effect of job attitudes on the relationship between organizational politics (OP) and work outcomes for study 2

Variable	Zero-order correlations		Standardized regression coefficients controlling for OP		Differences	
	Exit	Neglect	Exit	Neglect	Exit	Neglect
Job attitudes						
Job satisfaction	−0.40***	−0.25**	−0.19**	−0.14*	0.21***	0.11*
Organizational commitment	−0.41***	−0.19***	−0.27***	−0.07	0.14*	0.12*
Organizational politics (OP)						
Perceptions of organizational politics (POPS)	–	–	0.19***	0.25***	–	–

Notes:
N = 296–303 due to missing values
* p ≤ 0.05   ** p ≤ 0.01   *** p ≤ 0.001

DISCUSSION AND SUMMARY

In this chapter I have tried to answer several important questions such as:
(1) What is the effect of perceived politics on organizations and employees?
(2) Is politics a factor that improves our understanding of employees' job attitudes, behavioral intentions, and actual behavior at work? (3) What is the nature of this relationship and what implications does this relationship have for the public sector?

The empirical analysis yielded interesting answers. I found that organizational politics had a strong impact on two variables that have received little, if any, attention in previous studies. These variables were negligent behavior and job performance. I further found that job attitudes mediated the relationship between organizational politics and work outcomes.

According to study 2 special attention should be paid to the relatively strong relationship between the perception of organizational politics and negligent behavior. Political perception alone accounted for 5.5 percent out of 14.7 percent of the explained variance in the neglect variable. These findings suggest that reactions to politics in traditional public systems may be more passively than actively negative. One way of interpreting this finding is that employees in the public sector are less willing to give up job security and tenure even if they feel that their work environment is extremely political. Normally they choose to respond with more passive behavior (that is, neglect) that is less risky and does not endanger their career development and occupational status. Since most of the public sector does not compensate employees according to their performance at work, neglecting one's duties or job assignments is less dangerous than in the private sector but at the same time it represents dissatisfaction with the intra-organizational atmosphere. As a result of internal politics, the public sector may be comprised of more 'unsatisfied-neglecting types' than 'unsatisfied-leaving types' of employees. If internal politics breeds negligent behavior and obstructive organizational performance in public agencies, one should also consider the wider effect on all service recipients. When a public sector employee neglects his or her job, organizational outcomes are damaged and the general public is the most likely to suffer. Negligent behavior and negative job attitudes may thus yield low quality work outcomes and poor and ineffective public services. Inefficient public systems threaten large populations and can potentially damage the societies they are supposed to be serving. Such inefficiency also reflects the obstacles facing public organizations as they attempt to implement reforms in an effort to become more responsive and businesslike and to improve the vocational skills of public servants (Pollitt, 1988, 1990).

Study 2 thus extends the findings of study 1 and promoted our knowledge of organizational politics by elaborating on the relationship between the perception of organizational politics and employees' performance. Here a supervisory measure of performance was applied, and its results were collected six months after the original survey. As far as I could find, the study done by Hochwarter et al. (1997) was the only one that has used such a measure to examine the relationship between performance and organizational politics. The findings of study 2 support the usefulness of such an approach and demonstrate the potential advantages of using a separate measure of employees' performance together with job attitudes and behavioral intentions in one model. An examination of employees' performance as a possible work outcome that relates to organizational politics also adheres to the basic model of workplace politics suggested by Ferris et al. (1989). A weak negative relationship was found between these variables, which indicates that such a relationship may exist and is worth further examination. The findings also adduce a negative relationship between perceptions of organizational politics and both job satisfaction and organizational commitment, as mentioned in previous studies (Cropanzano et al., 1997; Drory, 1993; Ferris et al., 1996a, 1996b).

The relationship between the perception of organizational politics and other work outcomes is also in line with the theory on organizational politics suggested by Ferris et al. (1989) and reinforced in subsequent studies. Nonetheless, study 2 deserves special consideration mainly in light of other works that have examined the side effects of organizational politics on work outcomes (Bozeman et al., 1996; Ferris et al, 1989, 1996b; Parker et al., 1995). These studies could not point to any direct relationship between organizational politics, intentions of turnover, job satisfaction, and loyalty. Instead they suggested that control or self-efficacy mediates the organizational politics–work outcomes relationship. The findings of study 2, however, portray a more complex connection, suggesting that different types of politics–outcomes relationships (direct and indirect) may emerge in different sectors and cultures. The empirical support provided by Ferris et al. (1996b) for an indirect relationship may hold for non-public or semi-public organizations (for example, universities) but is true to a lesser degree for more traditional public structures such as the government agencies and municipalities tested here. This discrepancy may be due to the extra-organizational pressures from parties, interest groups, and governmental institutions that play a larger role in the internal politics of public agencies than they do in the life of non-public groups. Employees' degree of control over the political game in public organizations may be small and less significant because of external political influences, which are usually powerful. Mediators such as control or self-efficacy that were proposed earlier may not have any effect in such organizations while job attitudes may. In study 2 organizational commitment and job satisfaction showed a mediating effect on the relationship between organizational politics and work outcomes. This effect was additional to the independent main effect of organizational politics on work outcomes and also additional to the causal relationships that were found in study 1 (described in the previous chapter). They all imply that job satisfaction, organizational commitment and perceptions of organizational politics are related in a bi-directional way which is more complex than the one proposed by the original work of Ferris et al. (1989). Hence I recommend future examinations of the direct and indirect relations, as well as the relational and causal relations, among these variables as dependent in the specific organization and sector.

The personal variables that were used in study 2 showed some interesting relationships with the outcome variables. These relationships should also be examined in light of the relevant findings of study 1. First, women, highly educated employees, and those with higher incomes showed fewer intentions of neglect than other employees. A possible explanation is that such employees are more vulnerable and sensitive to their achievements in the organization; they are more careful and less willing to engage in negligent behavior that may risk their position and job security. Another explanation may be the level of acceptance of organizational politics among these employees. When organizational politics is accepted as an integral part of daily life in the workplace employees feel less worried and less capable of doing something about it. They thus treat organizational politics as something they have to put up with if they wish to stay with the organization. This idea is supported by the theory of control and self-efficacy mentioned early in this chapter. Highly educated employees were more willing to leave the organization, perhaps because they felt that other job options were available to them. Naturally, low-income employees also expressed higher intentions of exit; however, they were also those who received better performance evaluations from supervisors. Working better but receiving fewer rewards, perhaps due to high levels of organizational politics, may lead to negligent behavior and even eventual resignation from the organization. Nonetheless, the contribution of organizational politics to the explanation of all the work outcomes was significant and was beyond the contribution of the personal variables. This finding implies that organizational politics is an important variable that makes an independent contribution to the explanation of job performance, intentions of exit, and especially negligent behavior of public personnel, over and above other variables.

Future research on the relationship between workplace politics and work outcomes would benefit from the use of more objective measures of performance. It would be especially interesting to look for the effect of workplace politics on other work outcomes such as absenteeism, lateness, and turnover (Ferris and Kacmar, 1992) as well as performance and organizational citizenship behavior (Cropanzano et al., 1997; Williams and Anderson, 1991). I will try to respond to some of these challenges in the next chapters. Second, I note again that in contrast to most research on organizational politics the data for study 2 were not collected in a North American setting. I consider this to be an advantage but am also aware that the results might be affected by cultural and structural factors unique to Israel. While I will elaborate more on this point in Chapter 5, I feel it necessary to highlight certain aspects of these possible differences here.

The Israeli public sector is markedly different from the American in both size and responsibilities. It is also more conservative and centralized. Israel has adopted the Western European model of the welfare state in which social services are broad and extensive. Services are controlled by the central government and affected by powerful social elites (Nachmias, 1991). In contrast with the North American public sector Israeli public agencies face the continuous problem of political involvement in administrative processes. This makes the public sector more sensitive to political pressures, political appointments and the involvement of interest groups in the professional decisions of public officials. Scholars agree that, due to its singular cultural and structural characteristics, Israeli public administration suffers chronically from a bloated bureaucracy and a relatively high politization of many of its units (Deri, 1993; Nachmias, 1991). In this environment perceived politics is presumably higher than in smaller organizations that are more businesslike and detached from the external pressures of the political system. Moreover, since political behavior inside organizations as well as outside is subject to cultural influences (Pfeffer, 1992), this research should be replicated in other settings to enable a better understanding of cultural implications.

Hence this chapter has accomplished several goals that are milestones in the arena of organizational politics. The study has (1) explored the relationship between perceptions of organizational politics, job attitudes, exit, neglect, and job performance; (2) further illuminated the special role of organizational politics in traditional public systems and its implications for employees as well as for citizens/customers; and (3) utilized a non-American setting to allow a cross-cultural examination of organizational politics. In the next chapter I will try to develop further some of the ideas that have been mentioned so far with a special emphasis on the possible impact of political perceptions on employees' formal and informal performance in the workplace.

NOTE

1. Some parts in this chapter are based on Vigoda (2000) 'Organizational politics, job attitudes, and work outcomes: Exploration and implications for the public sector' *Journal of Vocational Behavior*, *57*, 326-47. Copyright with permission from Elsevier Science.

3.   Organizational politics, in-role performance, and organizational citizenship behavior[1]

The previous chapters and the two studies presented so far have explored some new directions in the study of organizational politics, especially (1) the relationship between political perceptions and actual politics and (2) the more extensive examination of the impact of workplace politics on work outcomes and employee performance in public domains. To date, studies on organizational politics have relied partly on the expectation of finding new answers to some old questions, such as what (dis)motivates individuals at work and how we can better explain variations in employees' behavior and productivity. The previous chapters have also shown how studies became particularly interested in the potential relationship between workplace politics and individuals' performance. The primary goal of these attempts was to examine whether internal politics plays a significant role in setting organizational outcomes and, if so, the nature and characteristics of this relationship.

Politics and political behavior in organizations seemed a promising field for theoretical inquiry not only because of their practical implications but also for some other reasons. First, modern societies have sought better efficiency and effectiveness in organizations in order to successfully respond to the increasing demands of their citizens. Scholars were urged to provide new explanations of and remedies for the decline in organizational outcomes in both the business and the public sector. Internal politics and power relations between organizational members appeared to account at least for some of these problems. Second, politics represented a creative approach to the understanding of organizational dynamics, which for many years had been particularly overlooked. Many scholars agreed that politics was a common phenomenon in every organization (for example, Bozeman et al., 1996; Cropanzano et al., 1997; Ferris and Kacmar, 1992; Ferris and King, 1991; Mayes and Allen, 1977; Mintzberg, 1983; Pfeffer, 1992; Zhou and Ferris, 1995) yet only a handful of comprehensive attempts were made to fully understand it. Studies were preoccupied with other, mainly formal, aspects of workplace activities and characterized the political arena as a less significant dimension of the organizational nature. Consequently the field was much under-studied until the 1970s and 1980s. Third, this approach was interdisciplinary and employed classic terminology rooted in conventional political science and sociological theory. The common perception was that politics in the workplace was a necessary evil that no individual or society could avoid but no different from many other unpleasant realities of the work world. Therefore management literature consistently considered politics, power, and influence relations among stakeholders as illegitimate, informal, and dysfunctional, as opposed to authority and formal organizational design that were described as apolitical and functional (Hardy, 1995). Scholars like Block (1988:5) stated bluntly that 'politics (in organizations) is basically a negative process. If I told you you were a very political person, you would take it either as an insult or at best as a mixed blessing'. Organizational politics was presumed to describe a dark and exceptional aspect of workplace activity (Ferris and King, 1991).

With the growing interest in workplace politics, some studies have suggested promoting a more empirical approach to the examination of its outcomes. However, only recently have a small number of scholars responded positively to this challenge (Bozeman et al., 1996; Ferris et al., 1996a, 1996b, 1998) and, as presented in Chapters 1 and 2, most of them have focused on employees' attitudes as the prime outcomes of organizational politics. As a result, scant empirical evidence exists today that can support the (negative?) effect of internal workplace politics on employees' outcomes and especially on objective performance evaluations.

The main goal of this chapter is to contribute to the development of theoretical and empirical thinking about organizational politics and more specifically to demonstrate the relationship between job congruence, perception of organizational politics, and two constructs of employees' reactions: formal/in-role performance and informal performance currently known under the name 'organizational citizenship behavior' (OCB) (Organ, 1988). The thesis developed here is that employees respond to the political climate of their work environment both formally and informally. As the general model has suggested, job congruence (that is, met expectations and person-organization fit) is expected to affect individuals' perception of politics, and both politics and congruence with the work sphere are presumed to have an influence on employees' performance.

JOB CONGRUENCE AND ORGANIZATIONAL POLITICS

In the present chapter we will examine the direct and indirect effect of job congruence (met expectations and person–organization fit) on employees' performance through their perception of organizational politics. Studies have mentioned job congruence as an important determinant of employees' productivity and performance. For example, Elchanan et al. (1994) found job congruence to be related to job stability/persistence and to performance evaluations in 774 employees in Israel. Other studies also mentioned the importance of job congruence, organizational climate and general culture as crucial factors that may facilitate employees' coping abilities in a new work environment and during the initial integration stages in organizations (Ferris et al., 1998). Schein (1968, 1978) suggested that newcomers are aware of the ongoing politics within the organization but must go through a learning process of gaining the acceptance of others. Job congruence can help them successfully cope during this period and adapt to the political environment. Therefore it is only natural to try to relate job congruence to organizational politics, which represents a meaningful part of the workplace atmosphere.

Job congruence generally refers to the basic compatibility of an employee with his or her workplace and specific job. It also reflects a level of fulfilled aspirations and expectations of the work environment in its broad sense. This book treats job congruence as comprising two constructs: employees' level of met expectations (ME) and person–organization fit (POF). ME and POF are two well established factors reflecting the adaptability of an individual to his or her work surroundings. Wanous et al. (1992) defined ME as the discrepancy between what a person encounters on the job in the way of positive and negative experiences and what he or she expected to encounter. Bretz and Judge (1994) defined POF as the degree to which individuals (skills, needs, values and personality) match job requirements. The higher the ME and POF are, the better the congruence of the individual's characteristics and expectations with the organizational environment and demands.

The congruence between an individual and the workplace is expected to have a negative effect on employees' perception of organizational politics. The rationale for this relationship is based on Cropanzano et al. (1997:163) and Hulin (1991) who argued that individuals are more likely to have a positive evaluation of an organization when their goals are met than when their aspirations are threatened. The basic model of Ferris et al. (1989) and Ferris and Kacmar (1992) also mentioned the job/work environment influences as potential predictors of political perceptions. Variables such as job autonomy, job variety, feedback, advancement opportunity, and interaction with others represent one's level of fit and compatibility with the workplace. This fit may reduce employees' perception of organizational politics. Those who better fit the organization and have more realistic expectations are presumed to view the environment as less aggressive, less power hungry, more just and equitable, and thus apolitical.

The importance of fit and expectations in social life and their implications for the study of politics was further advanced by Molm (1997:4), according to whom actors in every social political system are motivated by the cost and benefits of their activities and the mutual political exchange relations with the environment. Those who better fit the organization and succeed in fulfilling self-aspirations will tend to develop positive perceptions toward their social and work environment. When such congruence exists employees will perceive the organization as less political and more responsive to their needs and aspirations. They will probably attribute their success to factors other than politics, such as their own qualifications and level of performance at work. However, individuals who do not fit well with a specific job or work unit are expected to perceive the organization more negatively. When job congruence is low it is more likely that employees will feel disappointed and frustrated and will become alienated from the organization and their surroundings. Such feelings may broaden the emotional as well as the functional gap between a person and his or her job. Consequently employees will tend to attribute their failure to achieve their goals to the political system of the organization rather than to themselves.

The relationship between job congruence and performance at work is even more established in management theory. Vroom (1964) developed the expectancy theory, which argued that expectations significantly affect employees' motivation, perceptions, and performance in the workplace. The expectancy theory suggests that a better fit between individuals and their work environment enhances employees' met expectations. When one's personal characteristics and attitudes are close to those of the workplace a better fit can be expected between the individual and his or her job or work. Those organizations that employ individuals who fit better with them have significant advantages over other organizations. They enjoy high levels of productivity and quality performance and they encounter only minor problems with absenteeism and turnover.

Empirical evidence exists today to support these claims. An extensive meta-analysis of 31 studies and 17 241 people was conducted by Wanous et al. (1992), who found a correlation of -0.29 between met expectations (ME) and intentions to leave the organization. A correlation of 0.19 was reported between ME and job survival and of 0.11 between ME and job performance. Bretz and Judge (1994) examined person–organization fit (POF) as a construct of work adjustment. They affirmed a positive effect of POF on tenure, satisfaction, and other constructs of career success. These arguments led to the first hypothesis in this chapter:

Hc1. *Job congruence is negatively related with perception of organizational politics and positively related with employees' performance.*

EMPLOYEES' PERFORMANCE AS CONSEQUENCE OF ORGANIZATIONAL POLITICS

Most studies of organizational politics naturally expected to find it related with poor employee performance (Cropanzano et al., 1997; Eisenhardt and Bourgeois, 1988) or a potential source of work stress (Ferris et al., 1996b). However, this relationship seems far more complex. As mentioned in the previous chapters, Bozeman et al. (1996) elaborated on the effect of the perception of politics on four outcome variables: organizational commitment, job satisfaction, intention to turnover, and job stress. No direct relationships were found in this two-study investigation yet some interactive relationships were found between perception of organizational politics, feelings of self-efficacy, and the outcome variables. Specifically, individuals with high job self-efficacy perceived organizational politics as a threat and thus exhibited lower levels of organizational outcomes (organizational commitment and job satisfaction) than persons with low job self-efficacy. Ferris and King (1991) found that influence tactics of employees contributed to being liked by the supervisor, which led the supervisor to rate the employees' job performance more favorably. Tziner et al. (1996) further developed and supported this idea and thus promoted the Janus-face image of organizational politics proposed by Mintzberg (1985) and Rollinson et al. (1998).

A more balanced approach to organizational politics was adopted in other studies. In a survey conducted by Gandz and Murray (1980) more than half of the respondents thought that politics in an organization was synonymous with unfair, negative, irrational, and unhealthy behavior. Nonetheless, many believed that political behavior is necessary if one wants to be a good employee or a successful manager and get ahead in the organization. An early work of Hirschman (1970) suggested that political behavior is a legitimate fight response to conflict or to a decline in organizations. It was also argued that organizational politics is a legitimate way for people to take effective action in the organizational context by having control over information, flexibility, and statecraft (Hirschman, 1970; Ryan, 1989). As also suggested in the previous chapters the above studies imply that organizational politics is not necessarily related to negative work outcomes. Ferris et al. (1989a) and Kumar and Ghadially (1989) stated that organizational politics is a natural social influence process. Workplace politics may have functional as well as dysfunctional consequences and can be helpful or harmful for members of the organization. Organizational politics may have several positive outcomes (for example, career advancement, recognition and status, enhanced power and position, accomplishment of personal goals, control, and success). It may also result in harmful outcomes (for example, loss of strategic power, position credibility, negative feeling toward others, internal feelings of guilt). More importantly for our case a majority of these works argued that organizations with extremely high levels of internal politics will eventually have to face hampered job performance by their members.

EMPLOYEES' PERFORMANCE: IN-ROLE BEHAVIOR AND ORGANIZATIONAL CITIZENSHIP BEHAVIOR IN RELATION WITH ORGANIZATIONAL POLITICS

So far this chapter has discussed employees' performance as one construct. However, there are at least two aspects of such activities, namely formal (in-role) and informal (extra-role) performances of individuals. In-role performance usually refers to duties and responsibilities one executes as an integral part of one's job assignments. Extra-role behavior describes some activities beyond formal job requirements that one chooses to do without expecting any direct reward. These formal and informal activities contribute to the general health and prosperity of the work unit. Among them organizational citizenship behavior (OCB) is the one that has received considerable attention in management literature during the past decade.

OCB had its roots in the work of Katz and Kahn (1966) who argued that an important behavior required of employees for the effective functioning of an organization is the undertaking of innovative and spontaneous activities beyond the prescribed role requirement. OCB consists of informal contributions that participants can choose to make or withhold without regard to sanctions or formal incentives. Examples of such behavior may be exceptional willingness to assist others with their work duties, helping new employees, or using the organizational resources only when necessary. Many of these contributions aggregated over time and people were believed to enhance organizational effectiveness (Organ and Konovsky, 1989). OCB was described by Organ (1988) as the 'good soldier syndrome' that every organization must foster.

Subsequent researchers suggested that a better measurement of OCB should also include items representing in-role behaviors because such an analysis would clarify whether the respondents differentiated intra-role and extra-role behaviors (Williams and Anderson, 1991). This recommendation was strongly supported by Morrison (1994) who found that the boundary between intra-role and extra-role behavior was poorly defined and varied from one employee to the next and between employees and supervisors. While OCB refers to informal behaviors aimed at enhancing organizational outcomes, in-role performance refers to a set of required behaviors one is expected to display in one's job and for which one is directly rewarded. These activities include duties, routine tasks, and ad-hoc requests of the immediate supervisor. Sometimes they are part of the organization's formal procedures and regulations but they are always perceived as an essential part of the production process. For this reason the present chapter has taken an integrative approach to the measurement of OCB, using both in-role and extra-role behaviors in one scale.

Perception of organizational politics is predicted to be negatively related to OCB and in-role performance. High levels of organizational politics usually reflect an unfair organizational environment in which those who hold more political power determine the criteria for resource allocation and distribution. This is generally done with only minor concern for objective standards, fair priorities, and the actual needs of the rest of the organization members. Ferris et al. (1996a, 1996b) suggested a relationship between constructs of procedural justice (for example, time since last promotion or time since last appraisal) and perception of politics. Arguments that support the relationship between justice and performance in the workplace can also be found in numerous other studies (Farh et al., 1990; Konovsky and Pugh, 1994; Moorman, 1991; Niehoff and Moorman, 1993; Schnake, 1991; Tansky, 1993; Wayne and Green, 1993). For example Schnake (1991) argued that a leader's fair or supportive behavior might create a need in subordinates to reciprocate. One way to 'pay back' a leader for his or her supportive and fair behavior is by performing better or engaging in positive citizenship behavior. Employees consider their leader the key representative of the organizational justice process because of his or her frequent contact with them. An employee's sense of the organization's fairness would depend very much on the leader's behavior and fairness values.

Moorman (1991) found that supervisors who increase the fairness of their interactions with their subordinates have a direct influence on the latter's behavior. This idea can be extended to include other organizational members as well. Managers and co-workers are responsible for the formation of the political climate in the workplace. Organizations rife with political manœuvring and power struggles are usually less concerned about fairness and equity values. They enable the powerful employees to gain more advantages and benefits than others. Therefore in-role performance and especially OCB may be negatively related with the general political atmosphere in a given work unit. The study of Farh et al. (1990) partially supported this notion. These authors found that higher levels of justice and fairness (lower levels of organizational politics) encourage employees to respond with higher levels of OCB. Building on the exchange approach, employees with high job congruence will perceive their environment as more fair and therefore will reciprocate with better performance. That is, organizations that create a culture and atmosphere of better equity and a fair distribution of social and political resources may increase employees' formal performance as well as willingness to engage in OCB. Thus a second hypothesis in this chapter is proposed:

Hc2. *Perception of organizational politics is negatively related to in-role performance and organizational citizenship behavior.*

Since perception of organizational politics largely reflects attitudes toward fairness and equity in the organizational arena (Ferris and Kacmar, 1992; Kacmar and Ferris, 1991) it is also expected to mediate the relationship between individuals' congruence with the job/work environment and personal performance. Schein (1968, 1978) argued that employees may be expected to develop attitudes to the political climate of the work unit only after they had spent a reasonable period of time in the organization. During the first stages of entering the organization they experience political events only as bystanders. However, with time they are bound to actively enter into situations where their personal power and influence abilities are confronted with other employees' ambitions. The results of such confrontations can be translated to positive or negative work outcomes.

The proposition that perception of organizational politics is a mediator between job congruence and employees' performances is based on previous studies (Bozeman et al., 1996; Cropanzano et al., 1997; Ferris et al., 1996a, 1996b; Ferris and Kacmar, 1992; Parker et al., 1995). These studies argued that perception of politics mediates the relationship between some job/work influences and individuals' outcomes such as job anxiety, job stress and burnout, organizational withdrawal, turnover, absenteeism, job satisfaction, effectiveness, loyalty, and commitment. However, there is little direct evidence about how politics affects formal and informal performance evaluations of employees' by their supervisors. Relying on these findings and on the mediating role of perception of politics recently found by Ferris et al. (1996b), it is expected that:

Hc3. *Perception of organizational politics mediates the relationship between job congruence and employees' performance.*

STUDY 3   POLITICAL PERCEPTIONS, PERFORMANCE AND CITIZENSHIP BEHAVIOR IN LOCAL GOVERNANCE

The sample for study 3 relied on 303 participants for whom we received supervisory evaluations of formal and informal performance. Like study 2 here too I have distinguished two time phases. The first time phase represents information about employees' met expectations, person–organization fit and perceptions of organizational politics. The second time phase represents information collected from the employees' direct supervisors on in-role and extra-role performance such as organizational citizenship behavior (OCB). As mentioned before, 22 supervisors participated in the second stage, each providing between 12 and 17 performance evaluations.

Two models were suggested to test the contribution of organizational politics to the understanding of variations in employees' performance. These models have the advantage of examining the entire theoretical conception of the study from one integrative view. They extend the implications of the hypotheses that elaborate on some meaningful, yet specific and relatively limited relationships between organizational politics, job congruence, and performance.

The Indirect/Research Model

This model relies on the literature about the perception of organizational politics. It assumes that organizational politics does make a difference and can affect employees' performance. The general conception is that internal politics mediates the relationship between job congruence and employees' performance. High job congruence results in a reduced perception of organizational politics and a perception of fair resource distribution. In this environment employees feel that they are treated equally and have a reasonable chance of achieving their goals and ambitions. Also expected is an increase in job performance, which is the reaction to such positive attitudes toward the organization, managers and co-workers. Thus it is anticipated that a reduced perception of organizational politics will lead to an increase in formal outcomes (in-role performance) as well as informal outcomes (OCB).

The Direct/Alternative Model

This model excludes organizational politics from the analysis of individuals' performance in the workplace and expects to find that job congruence is directly related to employees' performance. Thus organizational politics, fairness, and justice in the workplace have only a minor effect or no effect at all on employees' performance. The alternative model must be examined in comparison with the research model in order to more strongly support the latter (Joreskog and Sorbom, 1994). It also represents the null hypothesis in study 3, and if supported it implies that analysing the perception of organizational politics makes no meaningful contribution to the understanding of employees' performance.

The two models were assessed using path analysis with LISREL VIII. A covariance matrix among the research variables, using listwise deletion of missing values, formed the input for the path analysis. The common approach is to estimate structural relationships among variables that are free of measurement errors. However, I implemented another technique. Here the multi-item scales were treated as single indicators of each construct because of the large number of parameters (54 observed variables) relative to the size of the sample and to the structural theoretical parameters (9–10). As mentioned by Bollen (1989) the ratio of the number of observed variables to the sample size should be at least 1:5 in order to allow the common estimation approach. Otherwise the alternative method should be implemented as was done here. To correct for random measurement errors the random error variance associated with each construct was equated to the value of its variance multiplied by the quantity one minus its estimated reliability (Bollen, 1989). Other studies have also used this approach (Farkas and Tetrick, 1989; Frone et al., 1992). Moreover, the utility of the approach was supported in another study (Netemeyer et al., 1990) that showed that latent variable analysis yielded virtually identical parameter estimates, direction, magnitude, and significance. Results of this procedure however diverged substantially from the uncorrected single-indicator analysis.

Fit Indices

Ten indices were used to assess the fit of the models. The first one was the chi-square test, which is the most basic and essential for the nested model comparison. A low and insignificant value of chi-square represents good fit to the data. The chi-square test is sensitive to sample size, so the ratio of the model chi-square to degrees of freedom was used as another fit index. A ratio up to 2 was considered in this study as a satisfactory value. Moreover, the use of chi-square is based on the assumption that the model holds exactly in the population. As noted by Joreskog and Sorbom (1994) this may be an unreasonable assumption in most empirical research because it means that models that hold approximately in the population will be rejected in large samples. Therefore Browne and Cudeck (1993) suggested using Steiger's (1990) Root Mean Square Error of Approximation (RMSEA). A value of 0.05 indicates a close fit, and values up to 0.08 represent reasonable errors of approximation in the population. Some other fit indices are also reported as less sensitive to sample size differences and to the number of indicators per latent variable increase (Medsker et al., 1994). Six of these indices were used in this study: the Relative Fit Index (RFI), the Comparative Fit Index (CFI), the Normed Fit Index (NFI), the Non-Normed Fit Index (NNFI), the Goodness of Fit Index (GFI), and the Adjusted Goodness of Fit Index (AGFI).

The RFI (Bollen, 1989) and the CFI (Bentler, 1990) were developed to facilitate the choice of the best fit among competing models that may differ in degree of parameterization and specification of relations among latent variables. They are recommended as being the best approximation of the population value for a single model. The closer their value to 1, the better the fit. NFI was proposed by Bentler and Bonett (1980) and is additive for the nested-model comparison. Its value should be close to 1 to indicate a good fit. However, it has the disadvantage of being affected by sample size, and on some occasions it may not reach 1.0 even when the model is correct (especially in small samples). This difficulty was resolved with the modified index called NNFI, which has the major advantage of reflecting model fit very well at all sample sizes. As with NFI a value closer to 1 reflects better fit. The last two indices do not depend on sample size explicitly and measure how much *better* the model fits than no model at all. Both these measures should be between zero and 1, and a value higher than 0.90 is considered very good. Another recommended index for the selection of one of several a priori specified models is the Expected (single sample) Cross-Validation Index (ECVI) suggested by Browne and Cudeck (1989). This index is a measure of the discrepancy between the fitted covariance matrix in the analysed sample and the expected covariance matrix that would be obtained in another sample of the same size (Joreskog and Sorbom, 1994).

Path Coefficients

Testing the quality of two or more a priori alternative models should mainly rely on a variety of fit indices as described above. However it does not necessarily imply that one model is the best or the correct causal model. Another important criterion for the quality of the model is the plausibility criterion (Joreskog and Sorbom, 1994). This criterion means that the path coefficients in the possibly better fitting model adhere well to the general theoretical conception and to the hypotheses. This adherence should hold in terms of magnitude as well as in the expected directions. Accordingly a model that fits the data well but many of whose theoretical paths do not support the theoretical arguments cannot be defined as correct. There has to be some balance between the fit indices and the theoretical predictions or hypotheses regarding the relationships among research variables. The accuracy of the theoretical predictions can be tested by the path coefficients in each of the models as was done in study 3.

The descriptive statistics and intercorrelations of the variables used in study 3 are presented in Table 3.1. Reasonable psychometric properties were found for all the measures. The correlations between the OCB constructs and in-role performance were relatively high ($r = 0.36$ to $r = 0.58$; $p < 0.001$) yet still typical for such variables. More importantly they did not exceed the critical point of 0.60. These findings reduce the possibility of multicollinearity among the independent variables. Other correlations among the variables indicate that perceptions of organizational politics was negatively related to ME and POF ($r = -0.46$; $p < 0.001$ and $r = -0.53$; $p < 0.001$ respectively). POPS was also found to be negatively related to OCB altruistic and to OCB compliance ($r = -0.16$; $p < 0.01$ and $r = -0.14$; $p < 0.01$ respectively). As mentioned in the previous chapter these conditions are suggested by Baron and Kenny (1986) and James and Brett (1984) as necessary for the support of a mediating effect and therefore imply that perceptions of organizational politics may indeed play a mediating role in the research model.

A confirmatory factor analysis (CFA) using LISREL VII was performed to estimate the internal dimensionality of the dependent variables. This was done to support more strongly the use of formal and informal measures of performance in one model. It also confirmed the assumption that the two OCB constructs (altruistic and compliance) substantially differ from each other and deserve separate representation in the models. The three-factor model placed the 20 indicators of OCB altruistic, OCB compliance, and in-role performance on separate latent factors. This model was compared with three two-factor models that forced the indicators of two subscales into a single factor and forced the remaining indicators of the remaining subscale into a single factor. The three-factor model was also compared with a single-factor model where all 20 indicators were forced into a single latent factor. The findings, presented in Table 3.2, reveal that the three-factor model fits the data better than any of the two-factor models or the single-factor model. A chi-square difference test (Bollen, 1989) shows that the restrictions added to all the alternative models significantly reduced the fit of these models in comparison with the three-factor one. Another analysis was performed to test the dimensionality of the two OCB subscales. In this analysis only the indicators of the two OCB subscales were tested. The two-factor model placed the 13 indicators of OCB altruistic and OCB compliance on separate latent factors. It was compared with a single-factor model that placed all 13 indicators on a single latent factor. The findings presented in the lower portion of Table 3.2 reveal a better fit with the data of the two-factor model than the single-factor model. The chi-square difference test also shows that the single-factor model reduced the fit with the data. The above analyses reconfirm the examination of both formal and informal performances as well as the separate use of OCB altruistic and OCB compliance in one model.

Models Assessment

Figure 3.1 describes the two models evaluated here. Table 3.3 estimates the goodness of fit statistics for these models. As Table 3.3 shows the indirect model (Model 1) clearly provides the best fit. The fit indices for this model show a small, non-significant chi-square (6.89); the ratio of chi-square to the degrees of freedom is lower than 2 (1.15); RFI is 0.96, NNFI is 0.99, CFI is 1.00, AGFI is 0.97, ECVI is 0.12, and RMSEA is 0.02. The alternative direct model (Model 2) provides a relatively inferior fit with the data. The chi-square is significant (42.07; $p < 0.001$), indicating a poorer fit of this model than the mediating model. Other fit indices of the direct model also show a poor fit with the data: RFI is 0.63, NNFI is 0.65, CFI is 0.91, AGFI is 0.77, ECVI is 0.25, and RMSEA is 0.18. These findings provide some support for hypothesis Hc3, which expected to find that perception of organizational politics mediates the relationship between job congruence and performances.

Figure 3.1 also provides the structural coefficients for the models. As mentioned, the path coefficients, their significance and their magnitude furnish the important plausibility criteria for model evaluation. Thus an additional indication that the mediated model is better than the alternative/direct model can be found in the path coefficients. All of the paths in the mediated model (6 out of 6) were significant, as compared with only 3 out of 7 in the direct model.[2] Needless to say, the mediated model also contained a smaller total number of paths and therefore was more parsimonious than the direct model. All of these measurements further support hypothesis Hc3.

In line with my theory ME and POF showed a negative relationship with perception of organizational politics (-0.40; $p < 0.05$ and -0.31; $p < 0.05$ respectively). These findings support hypothesis Hc1, which suggests that employees with high job congruence perceive their work environment as less political and more just. In addition, perception of organizational politics was negatively related to job performance. It was negatively related to the two OCB constructs (-0.24; $p < 0.05$ with OCB altruistic and -0.23; $p < 0.05$ with OCB compliance, and also to in-role performance (-0.16; $p < 0.05$). These findings support hypothesis Hc2, which expected to find a negative relationship between perception of organizational politics and employees' performance. In addition these relationships support the positive relationship between job congruence and job performance as suggested in hypothesis Hc1. Further support for this hypothesis can be found in the positive relationship between ME and OCB altruistic and ME and in-role performance (0.20; $p < 0.05$ and 0.17; $p < 0.05$ respectively) as described in the second mode. Note that these paths, together with the path between POF and ME (0.59; $p < 0.05$), were the only significant relationship found in the direct model. In sum, the path coefficients of the mediated model strongly demonstrate its superiority over the alternative/direct.

Model 1: Perceptions of organizational politics and performance: an indirect model

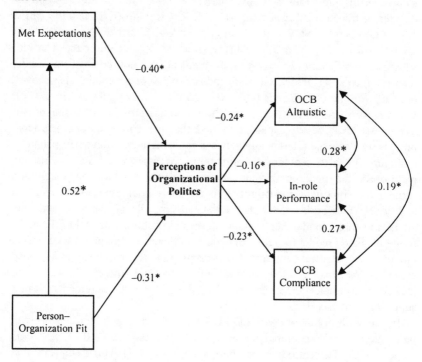

Model 2: Perceptions of organizational politics and performance: a direct model

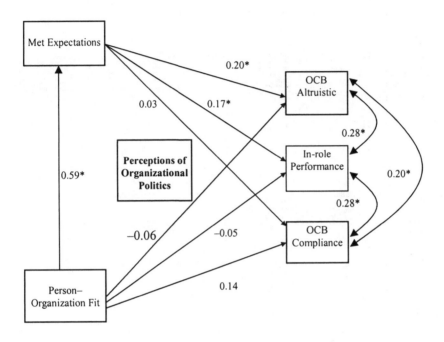

Figure 3.1   Path analysis for two alternative models

Table 3.1 Descriptive statistics and intercorrelations among the variables (reliabilities in parentheses) for study 3

Variable	Means	S.D.	1	2	3	4	5	6
1. Person–Organization Fit (POF)	3.36	0.67	(0.78)					
2. Met Expectations (ME)	3.05	0.67	0.45***	(0.83)				
3. Perceptions of Organizational Politics Scale (POPS)	3.06	0.60	−0.46***	−0.53***	(0.77)			
4. OCB Altruistic	3.40	0.80	0.01	0.12*	−0.16**	(0.93)		
5. OCB Compliance	3.77	0.68	0.11	0.09	−0.14**	0.36***	(0.80)	
6. In-role Performance	4.19	0.66	0.12*	0.03	−0.14*	0.55***	0.58***	(0.92)

Notes:
N = 298–303 due to missing values
* p ≤ 0.05   ** p ≤ 0.01   *** p ≤ 0.001

Table 3.2   Confirmatory factor analysis for employees performance (20 items of OCB and in-role behavior) for study 3

Model/ Description	df	X^2	Model comparison	X^2	df	X^2/df	RFI	NFI	NNFI	CFI	GFI	AGFI	ECVI	RMSEA
All variables **Three-factors** 1. OCBA vs. OCBC vs. INR#	149	411.25*	-	-	-	2.76	0.88	0.90	0.92	0.93	0.87	0.84	1.63	0.076
Two-factors 2. OCBA and OCBC vs. INR	151	846.77*	1 vs. 2	435.52*	2	5.61	0.76	0.79	0.79	0.82	0.71	0.63	3.06	0.120
3. OCBA and INR vs. OCBC	151	1267.51*	1 vs. 3	856.26*	2	8.39	0.64	0.68	0.67	0.71	0.56	0.45	4.46	0.160
4. OCBC and INR vs. OCBA	151	612.94*	1 vs. 4	201.69*	2	4.06	0.83	0.85	0.86	0.88	0.79	0.73	2.29	0.100
One-factor 5. OCBA and OCBC and INR	152	1470.94*	1 vs. 5	1059.69*	3	9.68	0.59	0.63	0.61	0.65	0.53	0.42	5.12	0.170
OCB constructs **Two-factors** 6. OCBA vs. OCBC	64	219.27*	-	-	-	3.42	0.88	0.91	0.92	0.93	0.90	0.85	0.90	0.090
One-factor 7. OCBA and OCBC	65	567.55*	6 vs. 7	348.28*	1	8.73	0.71	0.76	0.73	0.78	0.71	0.60	2.05	0.160

Notes:
OCBA:OCB altruistic, OCBC:OCB compliance, INR:in-role performance
* P≤0.001

Table 3.3   *Goodness of fit summary for the research models in study 3*

Model/Description	df	X^2	X^2/df	RFI	NFI	NNFI	CFI	GFI	AGFI	ECVI	RMSEA
1. Perceptions of organizational politics and performance: an indirect model	6	6.89	1.15	0.96	0.98	0.99	1.00	0.99	0.97	0.12	0.02
2. Perceptions of organizational politics and performance: a direct model	4	42.07*	10.52	0.63	0.90	0.65	0.91	0.96	0.77	0.25	0.18

Note:
* p≤0.001

DISCUSSION AND SUMMARY

Study 3 tried to support the idea that internal politics should be considered an important behavior with significant consequences for employees' performance in public administration systems. Building on the previous chapters and on other studies that have found a relationship between politics and performance, the current chapter supported the notion that perception of organizational politics is a good mediator between constructs of job congruence and employees' performance. These findings affirm the complex relationship between politics and performance that was mentioned by Drory (1993).

Recent findings of Maslyn and Fedor (1998) and Witt (1998) are also in line with this idea. For example the study of Maslyn and Fedor (1998) found varying levels of organizational politics (work-group and organizational) and indicated that they are related to different outcomes in the workplace. Witt (1998) tested the assertion that the efforts of first-line supervisors to enhance agreement on organizational goal priorities among their employees would decrease the impact of organizational politics on outcomes for those employees. Having examined five organizations, Witt supported the notion that individual-level performance may be an outcome of organizational politics. Study 3 also demonstrated that perceptions of politics and actual employee–supervisor goal congruence have interactive effects on organizational commitment and job performance. As one may observe, the concept of congruence is mentioned as a critical element that relates organizational politics to performance. For individuals with priorities different from those of their supervisors, politics may have had some impact on commitment and job performance. For those with priorities similar to those of their supervisors, politics had comparatively little impact. Drawing on the above, future studies that examine attitudes and behaviors in the workplace must not neglect the effect of job congruence and political perceptions on employees' performance.

Moreover studies have overlooked the relationships between these constructs in the public sector, and only scarce empirical evidence exists today about the nature of internal politics in public administration systems. What accounts for the lack of data in this area? As mentioned earlier, studies about organizational politics began to flourish only in the late 1970s and were conducted mostly in private organizations. Since the public sector represents classic bureaucracy with a large number of formal structures, many scholars assumed that internal politics played only a secondary role in these organizations and hence paid little attention to the examination of this sector. Another reasonable cause for the lack of studies about organizational politics in public organizations may be rooted in the environment of modern societies. Ferris et al. (1998) argued that the magnitude and rapidity of technological change occurring within industry has created an environment rife with ambiguity, hence rife with political behavior. Thus many studies have examined organizational politics in the private-industrial sector but have somehow neglected its investigation in public organizations, which have also undergone fundamental changes in recent years. Many scholars also presumed that internal politics in public administration systems is an extremely sensitive issue and very difficult to measure by the conventional methods of the social sciences. This speculative assumption discouraged many from obtaining original field data on this behavior. Limitations of time, cumbersome bureaucracy, and the small likelihood of finding a willingness to cooperate in such studies also impeded the advancement of knowledge in this field.

This chapter thus provides useful information regarding internal politics in two public organizations. Since these data were collected in two phases (T1, T2) and from two different sources (employees and supervisors) they have stronger validity and reliability than those presented in other studies, which generally used self-reported data. Job congruence, especially ME and POF, were found to be good predictors of perceptions of politics. These findings contribute to the basic model of Ferris and his colleagues by adding two new constructs to the study of organizational politics. These variables are based on the expectancy theory of Vroom (1964), and they reconfirmed its usefulness for the understanding of power relations, politics, and influence in organizations. Thus ME, POF and other factors that may better reflect job congruence deserve further inquiry in future studies. Furthermore the perception of politics was successfully related to the objective information on the formal and informal performance of public personnel. The CFA, which was conducted for the OCB and in-role behaviors, certified the use of separate measures for every one of the performance constructs in study 3. The findings also provided support for the idea of mediation that has been recently promoted by Ferris et al. (1996b, 1998).

The findings of study 3 thus reveal that politics contributes to our understanding of organizational dynamics and outcomes. The most profound finding of study 3 is that internal politics are pervasive and do make a difference in public administration systems. The significant paths of the indirect/research model showed that politics had a modest negative effect on formal performances (in-role behavior). It also maintained a stronger negative influence on informal performances as represented by the two OCB dimensions. These findings contradict a recent study of Cropanzano et al. (1997) who found an insignificant relationship between perception of politics and OCB among manufacturing employees and students who were working part-time. The findings here imply that politics may function as the *silent enemy* within organizations and can be even more destructive for public administration systems than for private organizations. According to Hirschman (1970) the option of exit is more realistic for employees in the private sector. Public sector employees do not tend to give up job security and tenure even if they feel that politics is pervasive and sometimes personally harms them. Normally they choose to respond with more passive behaviors, such as neglect or apathy, which are less risky. Today most of the public sector still does not reward employees according to their performance at work. The absence of a direct link between performance and compensation may lead public employees to be more neglectful of job assignments and duties than employees of private organizations. In many cases labor unions provide some informal legitimacy for such behaviors and protect even poorly performing employees. As a result of internal politics the public sector may comprise more 'unsatisfied-neglecting types' than 'unsatisfied-leaving types' of employees. Another aspect of neglect in the workplace is reflected informally in the decreased motivation to engage in volunteer and spontaneous behaviors such as OCB. This lack of motivation functions as a silent enemy because it is usually not measured by existing performance evaluations that generally apply to formal outcomes. However, organizations with lower levels of OCB lose some elementary parts of their internal health and thus are considerably harmed (Katz and Kahn, 1966).

As also mentioned in the summary of Chapter 2 the silent effect of internal politics can spill over beyond the formal boundaries of public organizations. Attitudes and behaviors of public servants toward citizens/clients partially reflect the effectiveness and efficiency of public administration. Higher levels of internal politics may lead employees to perform in a mediocre manner. When public organizations offer mediocre formal or informal service, citizens are negatively affected. They obtain inferior services from discouraged public servants and as a result may develop negative attitudes toward the entire public system. Thus internal politics works against modern approaches to the management of public agencies (for example, the quality movement of the 1980s and 1990s, and the new public management approach [NPM]). Together with the discouragement of service orientations of public personnel, internal politics may have a negative effect on entrepreneurial activities and spontaneous and creative ideas that are vital for the prosperity of modern society and a healthy public administration. Practitioners and managers in the public sector must not ignore internal politics and should be aware of its hazardous consequences for both public personnel and citizens. Of course these implications deserve further examination in future studies that will be able to compare the current results with findings from the private arena.

The main limitation of study 3 is however that it focused on the perception of organizational politics but did not examine the entire political environment of public organizations. As suggested in Chapter 1 perception of organizational politics is an important construct of organizational politics but it does not fully describe other political rituals inside and outside organizations (for example, influence tactics between internal and external stakeholders). To do this other measures should be used and examined more thoroughly. In particular we should evaluate actual political behaviors, influence tactics, and power strategies and relate them to perceptions of organizational politics. As suggested in the introductory chapter this line of research will be able to provide insights into the relationship between the perception of politics and actual political behavior and the way they relate to organizational outcomes. While some literature exists on this topic (Ferris et al., 1998) it is still largely uncharted territory waiting to be explored.

Another limitation of study 3 lies in its relatively narrow examination of other variables that are thought to affect politics and performance in the workplace. The basic theory of Ferris and his colleagues (1989, 1992), as well as studies that followed it, mentioned many constructs that should be considered in this regard. However, as in other studies in the field of organizational behavior, it is impossible to test all of them in a single effort. Nevertheless the theoretical model suggested in this chapter emphasized the functionality of job congruence in explaining perception of politics and employees' performance. The findings demonstrated the usefulness of this idea, so further studies should follow up on it and examine the job congruence–politics–performance relationships more extensively.

NOTES

1. Some parts of this chapter are based on Vigoda, (2000) 'Internal politics in public administration systems: An empirical examination of its relationship with job congruence, organizational citizenship behavior and in-role performances', *Public Personnel Management, 29,* 185-210. Copyrights by permission from IPMA – International Personnel Management Association.
2. This excludes the paths among the depended variables that were set to describe their interrelationships according to Morrison (1994) and others

4. Organizational politics and job distress[1]

To date most studies about the consequences of organizational politics have been concerned with work attitudes (for example, job satisfaction and organizational commitment) or behavior intentions (for example, turnover intentions and negligent behavior). However, some other potential reactions to organizational politics were invariably overlooked. For example little attention has been paid to the possibility that politics in organizations may cause job distress on a level beyond conventional work-related results (Bozeman et al., 1996; Valle and Perrewe, 2000). Moreover studies have not been able to attest to additional consequences related to job stress such as burnout or somatic tension. Except for the work of Cropanzano et al. (1997), the only study to investigate a larger number of stress-related outcomes, theory and empirical evidence on this topic remain vague. The present chapter offers a deeper discussion of this topic and an empirical assessment of stress-related reactions to organizational politics. The importance of these reactions lies in their potential relationship with productivity, effectiveness, and performance at work, as well as with individuals' health and behaviors in non-work domains such as family life or social affairs in general.

The goals of this chapter are fourfold: (1) to conduct a theory-guided examination of the relationship between organizational politics and stress-related factors; (2) to examine empirically the effect of organizational politics on employees' job stress and burnout; (3) to link these possible stress-related outcomes of organizational politics to more specific reactions such as aggressive behavior of individuals; and (4) to derive implications for future developments and examinations in this field.

As demonstrated in the previous chapters research to date has assembled a large body of knowledge about the consequences of organizational politics. However, most of these studies have concentrated on a relatively limited set of outcome variables. Among these, job satisfaction, organizational commitment, and turnover intentions were the most frequently studied variables, while less studied ones were variants of job performance, job involvement, and organizational citizenship behavior (OCB). These outcome variables can be classified into groups such as work attitudes, behavioral intentions, or actual behaviors. Furthermore most if not all of the studied consequences of organizational politics were related directly to the workplace. Very few studies have mentioned the possibility that organizational politics may cause other, more general reactions. Such reactions, as presented in Table 4.1, constitute a separate group of variables, which may be called *stress-related aftermaths* of organizational politics. These stress-related constructs may have affective, cognitive-psychological, or behavioral outcomes, as will be shown in the following sections.

Table 4.1 A summary of studies on stress-related aftermaths to organizational politics

Study	Reactions to OP
1. Ferris et al. (1994)	Job anxiety (+)
2. Ferris et al. (1996b)	Job anxiety (+)
3. Bozeman et al. (1996)	Job stress (+)
4. Cropanzano et al. (1997)	Job tension (+) Somatic tension (+) General fatigue (+) Burnout (+)
5. Kacmar et al. (1999)	Job anxiety (+)
6. Valle and Perrewe (2000)	Job stress (+)

Note: all relationships are positive (+)

In fact it was Ferris et al. (1989) who originally mentioned the possibility that workplace politics may affect employees emotionally or psychologically and have a potential impact on the individual's behavior outside the workplace (that is, in family life or other social contacts). Such reactions may include anxiety (Ferris et al., 1996a, 1996b; Kacmar et al., 1999), stress (Bozeman et al., 1996; Valle and Perrewe, 2000), general fatigue, job and somatic tension, and burnout (Cropanzano et al., 1997). The above studies, as well as the work by Jex and Beehr (1991), define anxiety as a psychological strain that involves feelings of tension, nervousness, worry, and apprehension. It may thus also include somatic tension and general fatigue. Stress is defined in these studies either as an environmental event requiring some type of adaptive response or as an individual's response to environmental stressors. Burnout is viewed as a unique consequence of long-lasting stress culminating in emotional exhaustion, depersonalisation or dehumanization, and a belittling of personal accomplishment (Maslach and Jackson, 1981, 1986). Finally, Selye (1975) suggested that stress-related outcomes may result in exceptional behaviors such as verbal and physical aggression. However, most of the studies on reactions to organizational politics have not devoted adequate attention to stress-related outcomes of organizational politics that are psychological, physical, or behavioral.

THE RELATIONSHIP BETWEEN POLITICAL BEHAVIOR AND JOB DISTRESS

Several studies to date have mentioned the possibility that employees' political behavior may lead to various stress-related outcomes in the workplace (for example, Ferris et al. 1996b; Gilmore et al., 1996; Jex and Beehr, 1991; Matteson and Ivancevich, 1987). These studies have treated stress in numerous ways, but all are basically rooted in Selye's classic work (1975). Selye treated stress as the psychological, physiological, or behavioral reaction of the organism to stressful events. According to Beehr (1990) stress can be defined as any feature of the workplace that causes an employee to experience discomfort. Following Folkman and Lazarus (1991) and Edwards (1992), Cropanzano et al. (1997) adopted another definition, arguing that stress is the subjective feeling that work demands exceed the individual's belief in his or her capacity to cope. Jex et al. (1992) suggested that stress is associated with what was earlier called strain. In line with this definition, stress is an individual's response to work-related environmental stressors, one of which would be politics.

Only recently have studies begun to show an interest in the role of organizational politics as a possible work stressor. The relationship between organizational politics and various aspects of job stress was mentioned and empirically tested in several studies from the mid 1990s, for example, Ferris et al. (1994), Gilmore et al. (1996), Ferris et al. (1996b), Bozeman et al. (1996), and Cropanzano et al. (1997). Gilmore et al. (1996) proposed organizational politics as one source of stress and conflict in the work environment with the potential for dysfunctional outcomes at both the individual and the organizational level. Ferris et al. (1994) found that understanding moderated the relationship between perceptions of organizational politics and job perceptions and served as an antidote for the dysfunctional consequences of perceptions of politics as a stressor. Ferris et al. (1996b) surveyed 822 employees at a large university in the southwestern part of the United States. They empirically supported the relationship between organizational politics and job anxiety ($\beta = 0.56$; $p < 0.01$) and argued that there was a strong connection between patterns of politics and the possibility of stress.

First, politics and stress are both perceptual in nature. As originally noted by Lewin (1936) they do not refer to reality per se but to individuals' perceptions of reality. Second, politics and stress share the characteristics of ambiguity and uncertainty. Political behavior is usually a covert activity accompanied by a high degree of uncertainty. Likewise stress, strain, and tension are frequently related to uncertainty in an individual's environment and are exacerbated by an individual's inability to forecast future situations (Ferris et al., 1989). Third, both politics and stress 'create situations where people may gain or lose depending on how they respond to a situation' (Gilmore et al., 1996:483). One's ability to successfully handle political and stress-related situations determines one's gains or losses in the work environment. As further argued by Ferris et al. (1996b) stress in organizations, like politics, seems to provide options and opportunities for individuals and 'thus can be construed in a comparable manner' (p. 236).

In their study Cropanzano et al. (1997) extended this examination of the relationship between organizational politics and individual-based stress factors. While in their early works Ferris, Gilmore and colleagues chose to focus on job anxiety, which is only one aspect of job stress, Cropanzano et al. (1997) assessed various other aspects of job stress such as job tension, somatic tension and general fatigue. Their findings revealed a positive relationship between organizational politics and the outcome variables.

ORGANIZATIONAL POLITICS AND JOB BURNOUT

The study of Cropanzano et al. (1997) was also important because the researchers found that organizational politics was positively correlated with burnout, which may be viewed as a late outcome of job stress and work stressors. Still, despite the importance of these findings, to the best of my knowledge they have never been examined in additional studies. Thus a question arises: if organizational politics leads to job anxiety and job stress, can we assume even more extensive impacts such as a positive effect on work burnout or even other behavioral consequences, as suggested by Selye (1975)?

For a deeper discussion of this question it may be useful to explain the meaning of job burnout. Nowadays its most commonly accepted definition is that suggested by Maslach and Jackson (1981, 1986). According to them burnout is a unique type of stress made up of three components: (1) emotional exhaustion characterized by a lack of energy and a feeling that one's emotional resources are used up; (2) depersonalization or dehumanization, evidenced by a detached and emotional callousness and a cynical approach to others (co-workers, clients, organization); (3) belittling of personal accomplishment characterized by a tendency to evaluate oneself negatively.

Today, theory speaks almost univocally of the positive relationship among work stress, tension, anxiety, and burnout. In an extensive review of research on job burnout Cordes and Dougherty (1993) described the evolution of the concept and compiled a long list of studies that had examined it theoretically and empirically (for example, Golembiewski and Mounzenrider, 1981, 1984; Maslach, 1978, 1982; Maslach and Jackson, 1981, 1986, 1984; Pines and Maslach, 1980 and many others). Most if not all of these studies suggest that burnout is more likely to develop among service-oriented employees (for example, nurses, teachers, policemen, social workers) where the work environment is stressful and pressing. Ganster and Schaubroeck (1991) supported the notion that burnout is a chronic affective response pattern to stressful work conditions that feature high levels of interpersonal contact. A more recent global process model for the understanding of burnout was suggested by Golembiewski et al. (1996). According to this study, advanced burnout implies that an individual experiences a collection of stressors. These job stressors cause so much strain that normal coping skills and attitudes do not suffice (p. 83) and in such an environment burnout is an inevitable result.

As shown in previous studies, organizational politics may function as a potential work stressor so it too may lead to burnout. Since workplace politics is usually not a passing event but a continuous activity that encompasses the organizational sphere, its impact on individuals accumulates over time. Cropanzano et al. (1997) suggested that stress and tension are manifested as nervousness and apprehension about work, so they may result in burnout, poor health, and other physical symptoms. One possible reason may be that workplace politics encourages and preserves a situation of inequity, unfairness, and disharmony among members of the organization (Ferris and Kacmar 1992:93; Kacmar and Ferris, 1991:193–4). This rationale was partially supported by an experiment-based study by Dierendonck et al. (1998). Their longitudinal effort compared one experimental group with two control groups. Findings showed that reduced perceptions of inequity in the relationship with the organization and with other individuals caused burnout, absenteeism, and deprived feelings to diminish among the experimental group with significant differences from the control groups. These findings support the central role of equity and fairness as highly reflected by organizational politics in affecting job burnout as well as other work outcomes.

According to other studies (for example, Ferris et al., 1996b; Folger et al., 1992) those who feel that they cannot cope with a political and hence unfair and unjust environment (and at the same time have other employment alternatives) usually adopt a 'flight' response and quit their job. Others who choose to stay must decide whether to 'fight' the system or adjust and comply with its norms (Selye, 1975). Note that these reactions are very similar to the 'exit' and 'voice' patterns of Hirschman (1970) that were described in Chapters 1 and 2. Either way, many of those who stay in the organization are exposed to a higher risk of burnout due to their inability or unwillingness to play the political game. Most employees find it hard to adjust to or comply with such a reality. Their perception of the organization as an unfair or unresponsive environment where people do not receive rewards or recognition for their personal efforts is translated into an emotional state of stress and strain that eventually turn into breeding grounds for job burnout.

ORGANIZATIONAL POLITICS AND AGGRESSIVE BEHAVIOR

Taking our discussion one step forward it is also interesting to ask what may be the possible behavioral outcomes of organizational politics. The idea that will be developed here is that workplace politics is also related to an individual's aggressive behavior. Both direct and indirect relationships are expected in this case where organizational politics may lead to job stress and job burnout, and in turn that job burnout will be positively and directly related to aggressive behavior. Cordes and Dougherty (1993) suggested four major groups of consequences of job burnout: physical and emotional, interpersonal, attitudinal, and behavioral. In Selye's (1975) typology these groups may be narrowed down to two major constructs: (1) physiological results and (2) behavioral results. First, burnout may cause severe physical disorders. Maslach and Jackson (1981:99–101) mentioned several physical symptoms such as high rates of headaches, lingering colds, backaches, gastro-intestinal disturbances, etc. However, in addition, and more importantly for our case, job burnout may also influence individuals' actual behaviors. People who face a great deal of pressure on the job may become highly stressed and behave nervously and impulsively or evince far less tolerant behavior toward others. In fact such symptoms may also be typical of aggressive behavior of various kinds.

Aggressive behavior was described by Baron (1977:7) as 'any form of behavior directed toward the goal of harming or injuring another living being who is motivated to avoid such treatment'. Similarly, Berkowitz

(1993:3) refers to aggressive behavior as 'any form of behavior that is intended to injure someone physically or psychologically'. In a more recent study Andersson and Pearson (1999) define aggression as deviant behavior with intent to harm (p. 456). They thus distinguish it from other similar terms such as violence, deviant behavior, antisocial behavior, and incivility. Andersson and Pearson (1999) also provide further evidence that most of the aggression occurring in work settings is of a less intense form, namely verbal rather than physical, passive rather than active, indirect rather than direct and subtle rather than overt (Baron and Neuman, 1996).

A closer look at the organizational politics literature provides some hints as to the possible emergence of aggressive behavior in highly political atmospheres. Gilmore et al. (1996) suggested that organizational politics has many negative consequences, including conflict and disharmony, which emerge when individuals and/or groups are pitted against each other or against the organization. In their analysis Gilmore et al. (1996:482) use the term 'hostile environment' to refer to the possible atmosphere that organizational politics may create. Hence if politics enhances conflicts among individuals and groups as well as creating a hostile work environment, it is likely that employees' behavior will be affected in some way at least, perhaps even reaching extreme levels such as aggressive behavior toward co-workers either verbally or physically.

In light of the above discussion Figure 4.1 presents a detailed framework for the examination of direct and indirect relationships between organizational politics and stress-related aftermaths. Job stress is one of the immediate responses to a high level of organizational politics. Individuals who perceive their work environment as more political, hence less fair and equal in terms of resource sharing, opportunities for influence on decision-making processes and accessibility to organizational power centers, will show more symptoms of stress, tension, tiredness, and a general feeling of exhaustion that are also typical of job burnout. Consequently the model predicts the emergence of interpersonal hostility and aggressive behavior by the employee himself or herself or around him or her.

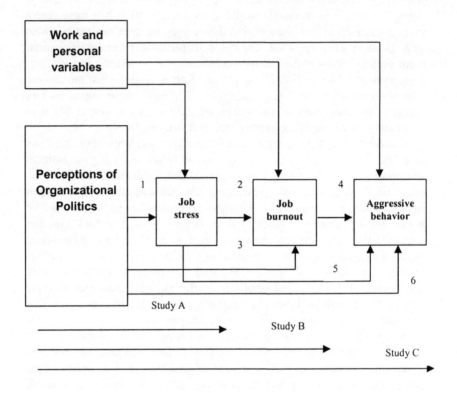

Note:
 Main paths are numbered (1-6)

Figure 4.1 Perceptions of organizational politics, job stress, burnout, and aggressive behavior

Along with the core constructs of the research model I decided to control for two additional work attitudes that were mentioned in the previous chapters and may prove relevant in this context as well. These are job satisfaction and organizational commitment. I chose these two variables because they figure prominently in the study of organizational politics and should be controlled wherever organizational politics is studied. Moreover job satisfaction and organizational commitment have also been examined in other works that investigated job stress and job burnout (for example, Cropanzano et al., 1997; Tan and Akhtar, 1998; Wolpin et al., 1991). According to these studies employees reporting high levels of job satisfaction are expected to feel less stressed at work. These studies further suggest equivocal relationships between organizational commitment and job burnout. For example, Cropanzano et al. (1997) reported a moderately negative relationship that is in line with the findings on the relationship between job satisfaction and job burnout. However Tan and Akhtar (1998) found a contradictory positive relationship. This finding may be explained by the more intensive care, attachment, and personal resource investment by highly committed employees who consequently deplete their energies more quickly and run the risk of job burnout. Thus I concluded that both of these variables merited inclusion in the model. Despite disagreement as to their exact function in relation with the other stress-related variables I chose to integrate them as additional predictors of job stress, burnout, and aggressive behavior together with organizational politics, but I also decided not to provide specific hypotheses for these variables. Nonetheless future studies are encouraged to do so in order to examine competitive relationships. Finally I also controlled for several other personal variables including age, education, and job status, but here again no specific hypothesis was formulated for these variables in order to maintain the compactness of the model.

Hence in this chapter I propose four hypotheses, the first of which predicts that organizational politics is expected to increase job stress. Moreover as job stress is positively related to job burnout, organizational politics is likewise expected to be positively related to job burnout. Thus, Hd1 is formulated as follows:

Hd1. *Organizational politics is positively related to employees' job stress and job burnout.*

In an attempt to examine the relationship between organizational politics, job stress, and burnout in greater detail I further hypothesized that job stress functions as a mediator between a political workplace environment and burnout. This hypothesis treats organizational politics as one predictor of job stress, which in turn positively relates with burnout. Therefore Hd2 included an important extension of Hd1 by noting that organizational politics may relate with burnout indirectly, via job stress (Kenny et al., 1998; http://nw3.nai.net/~dakenny/mediate.htm).

> **Hd2.** *Job stress mediates the relationship between organizational politics and job burnout.*

The third hypothesis of the model concerns the possible relationship between organizational politics and aggressive behavior. While the previous hypotheses treat workplace politics as a possible predictor of job stress and burnout, this hypothesis proposes a more broad-based relationship based on the assumption that Hd1 and Hd2 will prove valid. Based on the logic that politics leads to job stress and/or job burnout, I expect that aggressive behaviors are a natural consequence of such a stressful and uncomfortable working environment. Thus Hd3 proposes that:

> **Hd3.** *Organizational politics is positively related to aggressive behavior in the workplace.*

The final hypothesis again focuses on a more specific relationship based on the model. It suggests that burnout functions as a mediator between the independent variables (including job stress) and the only behavioral outcome in the model, which is aggressive behavior. The reasoning behind this hypothesis is quite similar to what has been described so far: politics may lead to higher levels of job burnout due to its competitive and combative nature, and higher levels of job burnout may exacerbate aggressive workplace behaviors. Hd4 thus implies an indirect, mediating relationship between organizational politics and aggressive behavior via job burnout.

> **Hd4.** *Job burnout mediates the relationship between organizational politics and both job stress and aggressive behavior in the workplace.*

STUDY 4   POLITICAL PERCEPTIONS AND JOB DISTRESS AMONG EMPLOYEES FROM THE PUBLIC, PRIVATE, AND THIRD SECTOR

Three separate studies were devised to examine the model and hypotheses. All three studies were based on a survey. Participation was voluntary, and employees were assured full confidentiality during the entire process. Data of all samples were collected between 1998 and 1999 and together constituted one set of data. Note also that the samples were representative of the internal populations of the organizations. The various demographic characteristics of each sample (that is, gender, age, job status, education, and marital status) were compared with the general population statistics as provided by the human resource departments in the organizations. The results confirmed that the three samples were very representative of the target populations.

The first sample in study 4 (sample 1, study A) was designed to examine the basic relationship between organizational politics and job stress as originally proposed in the literature. Participants in this study were 155 third-sector employees who provided child-care services in a northern Israeli city. Using a direct return method we achieved a response rate of 77.5 percent in this study. All participants were women with an average age of 46 years (s.d. = 9.8) and an average tenure of 9.4 years in the organization (s.d. = 6.7). Of the employees 76 percent had a high school education and 24 percent held an academic degree; 79.7 percent were married, 82.1 percent worked part-time and 83 percent had tenure.

The second sample in study 4 (sample 2, study B) extended the theoretical boundaries of the first by testing the levels of burnout among employees. This study was based on the reports of 185 private-sector employees who worked for the Israeli branch of a large international company. This high-tech company, which developed and manufactured sophisticated electronic chips for the computer and telecommunication industry, was also located in the northern part of Israel. Here again we used a direct return method, which resulted in a response rate of 88.3 percent. In this study 83.2 percent of the respondents were men and 16.8 percent women, the average age was 27.8 years (s.d = 5.3), and the average tenure in the organization was 2.9 years (s.d. = 2.4). Of the employees 31.4 percent had a high school education, 52.4 percent had a partial academic education, and 16.2 percent held an academic degree; 50.3 percent were married, and 89.7 percent worked part-time.

The third sample in study 4 (sample 3, study C) was designed to be the most inclusive and detailed. It gathered information from public-sector employees who worked for two major organizations; one was a governmental authority supplying energy and the other a local municipality. As in the previous studies, here too we employed a direct return method to maximize the return rate. This resulted in 201 usable questionnaires and a response rate of 57.4 percent, somewhat lower than the other two samples. In this study 58.2 percent of the respondents were men and 41.8 percent women, the average age was 39.9 years (s.d = 10.4), and the average tenure in the organization was 15 years (s.d. = 10.9). Of the employees 49.8 percent had a high school education, 28.8 percent had a partial academic education and 21.4 percent held an academic degree. All of the employees worked full-time; 74.1 percent were married and 23.9 percent worked on a temporary basis.

To support the hypotheses in this chapter I employed three strategies. First, I performed a correlation analysis for all three samples to examine internal relationships that may prove useful for further evaluation. Second, I used standard multiple regression analysis to test for direct relationships. Third, I used hierarchical regressions to analyze the mediating relationships. To support the hypotheses regarding indirect-mediating relationships I again followed Baron and Kenny (1986), Kenny et al. (1998), and also Kenny's web page on mediation (http://nw3.nai.net/~dakenny/mediate.htm). In line with the strategy used in Chapters 1 and 2 to test for mediation one should estimate the following three regression equations. First, the dependent variable is regressed on the independent variable, whereby the independent variable must affect the dependent variable to establish that there is an effect that may be mediated. Second, the mediator is regressed on the independent variable, whereby the independent variable must affect the mediator. Third, the dependent variable is regressed on both the independent variable and on the mediator, whereby the mediator must affect the dependent variable while controlling for the independent variable. If these conditions all hold in the predicted direction, a certain level of mediation exists. An additional fourth condition concerns a case of full mediation. Here the effect of the independent variable on the outcome variable controlling for the mediator should be zero. If this effect is anything other than zero (that is, only the first three equations hold), a partial mediation is indicated.

Table 4.2 presents descriptive statistics of the three samples included in study 4. All psychometric properties of the variables appear reasonable. Cronbach alpha ranged around the high 0.70s with a minimum of 0.68 and maximum of 0.90. Absolute level of job stress was lowest among participants of sample 1 (M = 1.88; s.d. = 0.94) and highest among participants of sample 2 (M = 3.03; s.d. = 0.90). Following this, burnout among participants of sample 2 (M = 2.87; s.d. = 0.77) was higher than burnout among participants of sample 3 (M = 2.46; s.d. = 0.98). As expected, level of aggressive behavior (measured only in sample 3) was not very high but still high enough to justify further investigation (M = 1.94; s.d. = 0.79).

Table 4.3 provides a correlation matrix for each of the studies. According to this table organizational politics was positively related to job stress in all of the three studies (r = 0.33; p < 0.001, r = 0.44; p < 0.001, and r = 0.33; p < 0.001 respectively). It was also negatively related to job satisfaction (r = − 0.49; p < 0.001, r = −0.36; p< 0.001, and r = −0.43; p < 0.001 respectively) and to organizational commitment ($r = -0.45$; $p < 0.001$, $r = -0.31$; $p < 0.001$, $r = -0.38$; $p < 0.001$ respectively). Job stress was negatively related to job satisfaction in all of the three samples ($r = -0.31$; $p < 0.001$, $r = -0.41$; $p < 0.001$, and $r = -0.38$; $p < 0.001$ respectively) and to organizational commitment in studies A and B ($r = -0.19$; $p < 0.05$, $r = -0.23$; $p < 0.01$, and $r = -0.43$; $p < 0.001$ respectively). Job stress was also positively related to burnout in study B ($r = 0.57$; $p < 0.001$). It is noteworthy that this value was high but not high enough to be interpreted as multicollinearity. Therefore I concluded that job stress and burnout as measured here were correlated but still represented distinct and separate constructs that can be analysed individually. These relationships also confirmed the construct validity of the measures as used in study 4. In study C all stress-related constructs appeared to intercorrelate: job stress was correlated with burnout and aggressive behavior ($r = 0.64$; $p < 0.001$ and $r = 0.40$; $p < 0.001$ respectively) and burnout was correlated with aggressive behavior ($r = 0.53$; $p < 0.001$). All in all, the zero-order correlations were consistent with the research hypotheses, and specifically with hypothesis Hd1, which expected a positive relationship between organizational politics and job stress.

Table 4.4 summarizes the results of six regression equations. The first three equations (1–3) were conducted to examine the direct effect of the independent variables on job stress in each of the three studies. The next two equations (4–5) regressed burnout on the independent variables and on job stress in studies B and C. Each of these equations was run twice: first with the exclusion of the suspected mediator (job stress) and then controlling it. Finally, in the last equation we regressed aggressive behavior on the independent variables as well as on job stress and burnout. This equation refers only to study C. Here also two separate models were run: with and without the suspected mediator (burnout).

Analysis of the first three equations revealed that job stress was positively related to organizational politics in all of the three studies ($\beta = 0.27$; $p < 0.05$, $\beta = 0.32$; $p < 0.001$, and $\beta = 0.20$; $p < 0.05$ respectively). These findings were thus consistent with the first part of Hd1. Moreover, they were also consistent with the second condition for mediation, which requires that the independent variable (organizational politics) in a model be correlated with the plausible mediator, which, in the case of Hd2, was job stress. Finally, according to the first three equations job stress was also negatively related to job satisfaction in all three studies ($\beta = -0.23$; $p < 0.05$, $\beta = -0.29$; $p < 0.001$, and $\beta = -0.47$; $p < 0.001$ respectively) as well as to organizational commitment in study C ($\beta = -0.30$; $p < 0.01$).

Analysis of the fourth and fifth equations provided additional support for the research hypotheses. These equations referred only to studies B and C. When these equations were run without the suspected mediator, organizational politics was positively related to burnout in both studies (β = 0.25; $p < 0.001$ and $\beta = 0.21$; $p < 0.05$ respectively). This finding was consistent with the second part of Hd1, which expected to find a positive relationship between organizational politics and burnout. It was also consistent with the first condition for mediation as set forth by Kenny et al. (1998). This condition requires that the independent variable (organizational politics) correlate with the dependent variable (which in this case was burnout). In addition, when job stress was added to the equations it was strongly and positively related to burnout in study B as well as in study C (β = 0.42; $p < 0.001$ and $\beta = 0.52$; $p < 0.001$ respectively). These findings were consistent with Kenny et al.'s third condition for mediation, which requires that the mediator (job stress) affect the dependent variable (burnout). Finally the fourth condition for mediation requires that for complete mediation, the effect of the independent variables on the dependent variables, controlling for the mediator, should be zero. As seen in the fourth and fifth equations this condition was not met. The effect of organizational politics on burnout was down from 0.25 to 0.12 in study B and down from 0.21 to 0.11 in study C. Nonetheless, in both studies it was far from zero. Hence, we must conclude that studies B and C were consistent with partial rather than complete mediation. In other words, job satisfaction partially mediated the relationship between organizational politics and burnout while similarly a direct effect existed among the independent variables and burnout. Hence the findings generally supported Hd2, which expected that job stress would mediate the relationship between organizational politics and job burnout. However, this mediation was not of a complete type but of a partial one.

To test hypotheses Hd3 and Hd4, equation 6 was needed. Hd3 suggested that organizational politics would be positively related to aggressive behavior. When equation 6 was run without the suspected mediator (burnout), organizational politics was positively related to aggressive behavior ($\beta = 0.24$; $p < 0.05$), which was consistent with Hd3. This finding was also in line with the first condition for mediation, which was tested in Hd4. According to this condition a correlation should exist between the independent variables (organizational politics and job stress) and the dependent variable (in this case, aggressive behavior). Since job stress was also positively correlated with aggressive behavior ($\beta = 0.29$; $p < 0.01$) I concluded that this condition was met. In addition, recall that the correlation between the independent variables and the mediator (in this case, burnout) was supported in equation 5. This led to the examination of the third condition for mediation, which requires that the mediator (burnout) affect the dependent variable (aggressive behavior). When burnout was controlled in equation 6, this condition was met by a strong positive relationship between these two variables ($\beta = 0.41$; $p < 0.001$). Last is the fourth condition for mediation, which requires that the effect of the independent variables on the dependent variables, controlling for the mediator, should be zero. While this condition was not met I found a significant decrease in the effect of the independent variables on the dependent variable. The effect of job stress on aggressive behavior was down from 0.29 to 0.08 while the effect of organizational politics on aggressive behavior was down from 0.24 to 0.19. As Kenny et al. (1998) argue, this does not indicate complete mediation, yet it may definitely be considered partial mediation. Thus we may conclude that the findings of study C were consistent with Hd4 but in the form of partial rather than complete mediation.

Finally, I summarized the main direct and indirect effects of the model in Table 4.5. According to this table the indirect effect of organizational politics on burnout was lower than the direct effect in both study B and study C (0.134 versus 0.250, and 0.104 versus 0.210). Similarly, the total indirect effect of organizational politics on aggressive behavior in study C was lower than the direct effect (0.187 versus 0.240). Note however that while the direct effects were dominant the indirect effects were also prominent and deserve consideration. The meaning and interpretations of these results are discussed more extensively below.

Table 4.2 Descriptive statistics and reliabilities among the research variables for study 4

		Study A (Third sector, $n = 155$)			Study B (Private sector, $n = 185$)			Study C (Public sector, $n = 201$)		
		Mean	S.D.	α	Mean	S.D.	α	Mean	S.D.	α
1.	Organizational politics	2.69	0.78	0.77	2.90	0.65	0.78	3.29	0.64	0.68
2.	Job stress	1.88	0.94	0.75	3.03	0.90	0.75	2.80	1.10	0.83
3.	Burnout	–	–	–	2.87	0.77	0.81	2.46	0.98	0.87
4.	Aggressive behavior	–	–	–	–	–	–	1.94	0.79	0.76
5.	Job satisfaction	3.74	0.66	0.70	3.70	0.56	0.70	3.65	0.70	0.78
6.	Organizational commitment	4.05	0.87	0.90	4.03	0.60	0.78	4.06	0.70	0.79
7.	Age	46.05	9.81	–	27.85	5.28	–	39.88	10.41	–
8.	Education	1.65	1.12	–	2.61	0.83	–	2.56	1.22	–

Table 4.3   Correlation matrix (Pearson's r) for studies A, B, and C in study 4

Study A	1	2	3	4	5	6		
1. Organizational politics	–							
2. Job stress	0.33	–						
3. Job satisfaction	−0.49	−0.31	–					
4. Organizational commitment	−0.45	−0.19	0.58	–				
5. Age	0.03	0.14	0.09	0.24	–			
6. Education	0.04	0.07	−0.07	−0.20	−0.29	–		
7. Job status (temporary)	0.11	−0.07	−0.04	−0.10	−0.34	0.27		

Study B	1	2	3	4	5	6	7	
1. Organizational politics	–							
2. Job stress	0.44	–						
3. Burnout	0.40	0.57	–					
4. Job satisfaction	−0.36	−0.41	−0.42	–				
5. Organizational commitment	−0.31	−0.23	−0.30	0.48	–			
6. Age	0.01	0.12	0.09	−0.03	0.16	–		
7. Education	0.08	0.10	0.15	−0.13	−0.04	0.34	–	
8. Job status (temporary)	−0.03	−0.28	−0.15	−0.03	−0.16	−.031	−.07	

Study C	1	2	3	4	5	6	7	8
1. Organizational politics	–							
2. Job stress	0.33	–						
3. Burnout	0.32	0.64	–					
4. Aggressive behavior	0.37	0.40	0.53	–				
5. Job satisfaction	−0.43	−0.38	−0.34	−0.20	–			
6. Organizational commitment	−0.38	−0.07	−0.02	−0.11	0.61	–		
7. Age	0.17	0.15	0.20	0.17	−0.08	0.07	–	
8. Education	−0.01	−0.06	−0.11	−0.15	−0.16	−0.10	0.11	–
9. Job status (temporary)	−0.24	−0.25	−0.28	−0.28	0.09	0.06	−0.51	0.14

Notes:
Correlations equal to or greater than 0.16, 0.23, and 0.28 are significant at the 0.05, 0.01, and 0.001 alpha levels, respectively.

Table 4.4 Regression analysis (study 4) for studies A, B, and C (standardized coefficients). The effect of organizational politics on job stress (studies A–C), the effect of organizational politics and job stress on burnout (studies B–C), and the effect of organizational politics, job stress and burnout on aggressive behavior (study C), (t test in parentheses)

Equation No.	1	2	3
Independent variables	Job stress (Study A)	Job stress (Study B)	Job stress (Study C)
1. Burnout	–	–	–
2. Job stress	–	–	–
3. Organizational politics	0.27 (2.30*)	0.32 (4.72***)	0.20 (2.20*)
4. Job satisfaction	–0.23 (–2.18*)	–0.29 (–3.85***)	–0.47 (–4.45***)
5. Organizational commitment	0.03 (0.29)	–0.04 (–0.50)	–0.30 (2.87**)
6. Age	0.16 (1.74)	0.03 (0.36)	–0.02 (–0.25)
7. Education	0.12 (1.35)	0.01 (0.17)	–0.07 (–0.85)
8. Job status (temporary)	–0.07 (–0.81)	–0.28 (–4.24***)	–0.17 (–1.79)
R^2	0.18	0.35	0.27
Adjusted R^2	0.14	0.33	0.23
F	4.43***	15.04***	7.00***

Note:
* $p \leq 0.05$ ** $p \leq 0.01$ *** $p \leq 0.001$

(Continued)

Table 4.4 (Continued)

	4		5		6	
	Burnout (Study B)		Burnout (Study C)		Aggressive Behavior (Study C)	
	Mediator not controlled	Mediator controlled	Mediator not controlled	Mediator controlled	Mediator not controlled	Mediator controlled
	–	–	–	–	–	0.41 (3.96***)
	–	0.42 (5.54***)	–	0.52 (6.48***)	0.29 (3.06**)	0.08 (0.72)
	0.25 (3.52***)	0.12 (1.68)	0.21 (2.28*)	0.11 (1.31)	0.24 (2.48*)	0.19 (2.13*)
	−0.27 (−3.45***)	−0.15 (−2.00*)	−0.45 (−4.26***)	−0.21 (−2.10*)	0.02 (0.15)	0.10 (0.92)
	−0.11 (−1.44)	−0.10 (−1.35)	0.33 (3.18**)	0.17 (1.90)	−0.02 (−0.22)	−0.10 (−0.92)
	0.02 (0.28)	0.01 (0.15)	0.03 (0.32)	0.04 (0.53)	0.05 (0.51)	0.03 (0.34)
	0.07 (1.00)	0.07 (1.01)	−0.13 (−1.50)	−0.09 (−1.24)	−0.12 (−1.43)	−0.09 (−1.06)
	−0.16 (−2.27*)	−0.04 (−0.61)	−0.17 (−1.77)	−0.08 (−0.96)	−0.11 (−1.07)	−0.07 (−0.78)
R^2	0.28	0.40	0.28	0.47	0.26	0.35
A.R^2	0.26	0.37	0.24	0.44	0.21	0.30
F	10.85***	15.36***	7.42***	14.62***	5.66***	7.55***

Note:

* $p \leq 0.05$ ** $p \leq 0.01$ *** $p \leq 0.001$

Table 4.5   *Summary of the main direct and indirect effects of the model (standardized coefficients) in study 4*

Path	Study A	Study B	Study C
Direct effects:			
1. OP →JS	0.27*	0.32***	0.20*
2. JS → JB	–	0.42***	0.52***
3. OP →JB	–	0.25***	0.21*
4. JB →AG	–	–	0.41***
5. JS → AG	–	–	0.29**
6. OP → AG	–	–	0.24*
Indirect effects:	–		
7. OP → JS → JB		0.32 X 0.42 = 0.134	0.20 X 0.52 = 0.104
8. OP →JB → AG	–	–	0.21 X 0.41 = 0.086
9. OP →JS → AG	–	–	0.20 X 0.29 = 0.058
10. OP → JS→ JB → AG	–	–	0.20 X 0.52 x 0.41 = 0.043
Total indirect effect of OP on AG	–	–	Path 8 + Path 9 + Path 10 = 0.086 + 0.058 + 0.043 = 0.187*

Notes:
* p ≤ 0.05   ** p ≤ 0.01   *** p ≤ 0.001
OP = Organizational politics; JS = Job stress; JB = Job burnout; AG = Aggressive behavior

DISCUSSION AND SUMMARY

With the growing scholarly interest in organizational politics, studies have suggested assessing the possible relationship of influential behavior, perceptions of workplace politics and job stress (Ferris et al., 1994, 1996b). While some evidence does exist today about the nature of this relationship, no explicit model has been advanced so far for a comprehensive examination of longer-range stress-related aftermaths of organizational politics. I believe that this gap in the literature deserves closer scholarly attention and exploration.

As suggested by Cropanzano et al. (1997) work stress has an obvious negative impact on the individual and equally deleterious effects on the organization and the economy. Studies have demonstrated that the costs of stress and burnout can be enormous due to lost time, reduced effectiveness and production, loss of interpersonal co-ordination, higher rate and severity of accidents, as well as an increase in absenteeism and turnover, and other human considerations (Ganster and Schaubroeck, 1991; Golembiewski et al., 1996; Jackson and Maslach, 1982; Leiter and Maslach, 1988; Shirom, 1989). The purposes of the present chapter were first to offer a relationship between stress and politics and to integrate some empirical results in a useful manner. Second, the chapter focused on two stress-related consequences of workplace politics that have been overlooked in the literature. Relying on previous knowledge and accumulated evidence from closely related yet separate sub-fields, I developed and empirically examined a general model that related politics to job distress, burnout, and aggressive behavior at work.

The findings of study 4 (based on the three samples included) supported four hypotheses. First, previous knowledge was reconstructed and reconfirmed about the fundamental relationship between perceived organizational politics and job stress. This relationship was consistent across three samples, three sectors and more than 540 subjects. Next, the interrelationships were evaluated among organizational politics, job stress, and job burnout. The findings supported both direct and indirect relationships, which generally cohere with the study of Cropanzano et al. (1997). As far as I could ascertain, to date theirs is the only study to relate workplace politics to job burnout, as was done here. In addition the findings provide some initial evidence of another possible consequence of organizational politics, namely its effect on aggressive behavior. Literature on the consequences of job burnout has dealt with possible behavioral reactions to stressful personal conditions, yet knowledge is scarce about the effect of burnout on aggressive behaviors at work.

This chapter thus suggests that stress and burnout play an important mediating role, interfacing the relationship between organizational politics and aggressive behavior by employees. However, the power of the indirect/mediating effects is still less than the power of the similar direct effects. One implication of the findings is that employees who work in political environments develop an emotional alienation from work as a result of the inequitable and unjust organizational climate (Ferris and Kacmar, 1992; Kacmar and Ferris, 1991). Such a psychological state may lead employees to suffer high levels of stress, strain, tension, and job burnout which may eventually translate into harmful behaviors. One such behavioral reaction is aggression toward others (co-workers, clients, supervisors). As demonstrated here, aggression can take the form of verbal assault or, at its most dangerous, actual violent physical attack. As mentioned, one should keep in mind that these relationships cohere with other significant direct effects that are even stronger than the indirect relationships.

These findings of study 4 should be interpreted both theoretically and practically. First, I believe that they contribute to knowledge about the possible reactions to organizational politics. These reactions are affected directly by politics in the workplace but also indirectly through job stress and burnout. Second, until recently studies were generally interested in the direct implications of organizational politics such as changes in employees' work attitudes, performance, and intentions to stay with or leave the organization (for example, Gilmore et al., 1996; Parker et al., 1995; Randall et al., 1999; Witt et al., 2000; Zhou and Ferris, 1995). The possible effect of organizational politics on stress-related constructs demonstrates another impact that may prove significant beyond the boundaries of the workplace. Stressed employees are those who are more likely to face higher levels of burnout, somatic symptoms of strain and tension and, as suggested here, also aggressive behaviors. These reactions can be easily transferred from the workplace into day-to-day life. This notion is supported by extensive literature on work and non-work domains (Cordes and Dougherty, 1993; Jackson and Maslach, 1982). Future studies are thus encouraged to re-examine organizational politics in its wider social context and to apply it as a possible explanation for human conduct outside the workplace as well as inside it. The theory underlying such relationships undoubtedly needs to be extended too, and this is a serious challenge for future work.

The practical implications of study 4 are several. Most importantly I suggest that managers consider the possibility that organizational politics breeds stress and burnout among employees. Our knowledge from the field of work stress and job burnout suggests that such psychological indicators strongly correlate with general organizational efficiency and performance (Golembiewski et al., 1996). A phase model of politics–stress aftermaths may suggest a continuous deterioration in organizational stability and productivity where politics exceeds a certain level and magnitude.

Employees who are detached from the political process in the workplace and perceive it as deleterious to their goals and interests will react emotionally with higher levels of stress and burnout. Since stress is costly in organizational terms even those who perceive politics as personally beneficial will eventually lose out because of the negative reactions of others and the need to handle stress and burnout on an organizational level. Managers should also be aware that at least some work stressors may be translated into aggressive behavior at work. According to Andersson and Pearson (1999) data have confirmed that aggression and violence of various kinds occur in the American workplace. Romano (1994) reported that more than 20 percent of the human resource managers participating in a study stated that their organization had experienced workplace violence in the previous three years, and an additional 33 percent reported that there had been threats of violence. According to the Northwestern National Life Insurance Company report (1993), in 1992 alone almost 25 million American workers were exposed to some kind of aggressive behavior at work. Such behavior might be actual aggression (physical attacks), threats of attack, or sexual harassment (O'Leary-Kelly et al., 2000). In light of this evidence managers need to develop mechanisms to cope with such dangerous activities that may harm both the internal social structure of the organization and its reputation and image in the eyes of clients and customers. Employees who experience large-scale political activities in the workplace may react aggressively, and it is the managers' duty to identify such potential situations and eliminate them.

While the above sections discussed the main findings of study 4, secondary findings exist that also deserve attention. Originally I did not hypothesize on the relationship between job satisfaction and organizational commitment, and the dependent variables. Nonetheless findings revealed that both constructs showed a significant statistical relationship in numerous ways. Job satisfaction significantly correlated with job stress across the three samples, and organizational commitment also showed a relationship with job stress but in a less consistent and weaker manner. While the literature on job stress and burnout frequently treats these variables as potential consequences I made them control variables, together with personal variables, to monitor the effect of organizational politics on the dependent variables. This is a somewhat unconventional approach but I found that it served the purpose. One should not assume however that job satisfaction and organizational commitment are necessarily antecedents of stress and burnout. On the contrary, as one may notice in Figure 4.1 a bi-directional arrow more accurately describes the role of these constructs in the model, implying that job stress and job burnout may also lead to variations in job satisfaction and organizational commitment as at least some of the literature suggests (Wolpin et al., 1991).

Among the personal variables only job status was found to have a significant impact on some of the job–distress dependent variables. For example, temporary employees reported a lower level of job stress and burnout in study B. In addition, study C provided some indication that temporary employees participate less in organizational politics, have lower levels of job stress and burnout, and display fewer aggressive behaviors. Yet these findings represented zero-order correlations, which proved inconsistent in a subsequent multivariate analysis, so they should be treated with caution. The possible explanation for job status playing some role in this model may be the feeling in temporary employees of lesser attachment to the organization, so they are less influenced by its internal processes. Nonetheless these findings, like others, should be replicated in future works to test their validity.

Another notable contribution of study 4 is its cross-sectoral orientation. As mentioned earlier, the present findings have the advantage of providing limited but important information about the organizational politics–stress aftermaths based on data from three different sectors. At least one variable (job stress) was examined across all three sectors while another variable (burnout) was examined across two sectors, namely the third-sector and the private-sector organizations. The cross-sectoral nature of the data is an important contribution of this study that will hopefully lay the groundwork for more extensive research in this field. The findings suggest that job stress may be treated as a reaction to organizational politics that transcends sectoral differences. The fact that I used the same research tools in all studies (A, B, C) and conducted all of them in the same cultural arena and time frame further supports this argument. Thus the organizational politics–job stress relationship, and to a lesser extent the organizational politics–job burnout relationship, acquired a more global meaning with stronger external validity than had been demonstrated in previous works.

Like the previous studies this one also has its limitations. First, although this section applied three samples that were also cross-sectoral, only study C fully examined the suggested model as presented in Figure 4.1. The other two studies (A and B) could examine only part of the model so some of the hypotheses suggested here received support from only one or two sources. Second, although the data collection was spread over time our design was definitely not longitudinal. This is a limitation of the study because the theoretical basis of this research could benefit from a longitudinal design to test these hypotheses. Future studies would do well to adopt such an approach to re-examine this model. Third, the findings used in study 4 were all based on cross-sectional and self-report data, incurring the possibility of source bias (for example, social desirability effect) or common method error. However, other studies that have tested similar concepts were also based on self-report data (for example, Cropanzano et al., 1997; Ferris et al., 1996a, 1996b). Nevertheless, other psychometric properties of the variables firmly support the validity of the data and the findings. Finally, with the exception of one item, the measurement of aggression in the present study does not refer entirely to aggressive behavior performed by the respondent (see Appendix 1). The other items may or may not indicate such behavior, so future studies may benefit from the use of other measures that are more direct and inclusive. Note also that the scale of aggressive behavior combined two types of aggression (verbal and physical) into one construct. It is recommended that future projects retest this model or a similar one using the two types of aggressive behavior that are suggested here separately. However, it is noteworthy that the scale used here provides important information about aggression that occurs around the respondent and by which he or she may be affected even if only indirectly.

Despite its limitations I believe that study 4 has discussed a missing link in the organizational politics literature and provided interesting empirical findings that will stimulate future efforts. The sparse research on the relationship between organizational politics and job burnout, as well as the scant knowledge that we possess today about other possible behavioral reactions such as aggressive behavior, should encourage both theoretical development and empirical examination. Since neither organizational politics nor job stressors are expected to diminish in modern worksites it is essential that we understand them better in order to provide managers with practical tools for improvement. While this chapter has demonstrated the soundness of examining workplace politics in relation to stress factors, more work is needed to provide these relationships with satisfactory external validation and predicting power.

NOTE

1. Some parts of this chapter are based on Vigoda (2002), 'Stress-related aftermaths to workplace politics: the relationship among politics, job distress, and aggressive behavior in organizations' *Journal of Organizational Behavior*, 23, 571-91. Copyright with permission from John Wiley & Sons, Ltd.

5. Cross-cultural perspectives of organizational politics[1]

I have so far tried to convince readers that organizational politics is an indispensable construct of workplace dynamics. However I must admit that it is also an elusive phenomenon that, as suggested in various studies, represents some unique aspects of organizational culture and climate (Frank, 1993; Shaker, 1987). I have mentioned that the foremost characteristics of organizational politics are the readiness of organization members to use power in their efforts to influence others and advance their own interests or alternatively to avoid negative outcomes within the organization (Bozeman et al., 1996). I have also suggested that studies have taken two alternative approaches to the field. The first treats organizational politics as a simple aggregated measure of influence tactics by employees in organizations (for example, Kipnis et al., 1980). The second is a more cognitive analysis proposed by Lewin (1936) and is measured by the perceptual measure of organizational politics (POPS). Moreover all of the relevant studies have also shown that organizational politics, and especially perceptions of politics, reflect fairness and justice levels inside the work arena. Therefore they have a significant effect on organizational climate and on a variety of work outcomes (Ferris and Kacmar 1992; Ferris et al., 1996b; Folger et al., 1992; Kacmar and Ferris, 1991; Vigoda, 2000, 2000a). Accordingly politics in organizations has received increasing scholarly attention during the past decade. Theory on the topic has expanded rapidly and, as I have shown in the first four chapters of this book, has contributed to a better understanding of various organizational dynamics as well as employee performance.

However, most studies have so far evinced limited interest in the cultural applications of political behavior in the workplace. With the exception of Romm and Drory (1988) and Ralston et al. (1994) data have usually been collected in one cultural sphere (often the North American) while cross-cultural aspects, which might prove important for the development of a comprehensive theory in the field, have been overlooked. The scant attention accorded to the possibility that workplace politics are culturally dependent is especially surprising considering that broader theories of political science and political psychology have accumulated a great deal of evidence indicating that politics and political behavior vary across cultures (for example, Almond and Verba, 1965; Hofstede, 1980, 1991; Pateman, 1970; Verba et al., 1995). Since political behavior inside and outside organizations has psychological and sociological roots (for example, Bacharach and Lawler; 1980; Mintzberg, 1983; Peterson, 1990; Sobel, 1993) I assumed that a culture-based investigation into workplace politics might make both theoretical and practical contributions to the field. All of these considerations motivated us to compare the consequences of political perceptions in two non-American cultures. In the following sections I report on my attempt to develop a culture-oriented theory and a set of specific hypotheses about workplace politics. To this end I integrated existing organizational politics theory and findings from the cross-cultural organizational and sociopolitical literature into a meaningful explanatory model.

Using the most conservative approach to workplace politics, as well as identical measures in both settings, I investigated employees' reactions to perceptions of organizational politics in two very similar samples from substantially different cultures, Israel and Britain. While some studies have examined the political behavior of Israeli employees (for example, Drory, 1993; Drory and Romm, 1988) no such data could be found about British or other EU subjects. The exploration of the perceptions of organizational politics among British employees is thus another contribution of this chapter. At the heart of the theory are the influential activities that generate a political atmosphere in organizations affecting a range of employees' behaviors, attitudes, and outcomes. Most importantly it is argued that employees' reactions to organizational politics may be culturally dependent and that further generalization of any theory about organizational politics should take into consideration social norms, values, and cultural forces relevant to the specific organization, its members, and its unique external environment (Hofstede, 1980). This strategy is in keeping with recent attempts to point out mediators and moderators in the study of organizational politics (for example, Cropanzano et al., 1997; Ferris et al., 1996b; Valle and Perrewe, 2000; Witt et al., 2000). The extra-organizational culture is proposed as a possible moderator in the study of the reactions to perceptions of organizational politics.

CULTURAL ANALYSIS OF ORGANIZATIONAL POLITICS: EXPLORING ANOTHER MISSING LINK

Scholarly journals listed in several academic databases[2] have to date published about 32 empirical articles concerned with perceptions of organizational politics from various psychological viewpoints.[3] Of these, 26 studies (about 81 percent) reported findings based on North American samples, four (12.5 percent) used Israeli samples, and one incorporated data collected from Hong Kong managers; the exact cultural context of the remaining samples was not reported. These figures reveal that most of our knowledge about workplace politics comes from one cultural arena, the North American. As far as I could find hardly any study examined the nature of political perceptions, their antecedents or their outcomes in other cultures such as the European or the Asian, both of which have emerged as increasingly important in modern world economics.

The study by Romm and Drory (1988) was the first and the only one to date to examine workplace politics in more than one culture. An Israeli and a Canadian sample were tested to evaluate differences in the perceptions of politics. Findings of that study indicated that (1) Canadians perceived situations in their work environment as more political than did Israelis; (2) Israeli subjects were less likely to view organizational politics as immoral than Canadian subjects; and (3) Canadians perceived organizational politics as less prevalent in their organization than the Israelis. It was thus concluded that 'the greater familiarity of Israelis with political processes within and outside the workplace and the greater tolerance of informal and non-routine behaviors is expected to make them perceive organizational politics as a more acceptable normative and therefore more morally legitimate behavior' (p. 101). This is a very important implication to which we shall refer later. A more recent study by Ralston et al. (1994) compared ethical perceptions of organizational politics between American and Hong Kong managers. Differences were found in a variety of areas. Focusing on ethical differences and actual influence tactics instead of perceptions of organizational politics, the authors were not interested in work outcomes. However, their findings indicate that ethical perceptions of organizational politics varied according to the employees' social background and specific culture. This finding is meaningful, providing solid ground for the assumption that *reactions* to organizational politics may also differ across cultures.

A cognitively oriented interpretation (Lewin, 1936) suggested that politics is in the eye of the (organizational) beholder. When individuals share a set of ethical values, norms, and behaviors, their views of reality may be substantially alike. Potentially their reactions to such reality may also have much in common and differ significantly from the views of other cultural groups. A slightly different perspective was adopted by Rao et al. (1997) who compared actual political behavior as represented by influence tactics used by Japanese managers with those reported by Kipnis et al. (1980) in a sample of North American managers. The researchers found that Japanese managers used some unique influence tactics and strategies that were less common among American managers (for example, socializing or personal development). Like Ralston et al.'s (1994) study this research did not examine perceptions of politics directly. Nonetheless it provided additional support for the idea that culture plays an important role in creating an atmosphere of organizational politics.

In light of the above studies I found the cross-cultural approach to workplace politics a promising and challenging research endeavor with the potential of filling a gap in organizational politics literature. However, these studies also had several shortcomings that limited their relevance to the current research: (1) Some of the studies referred to influence tactics in the workplace and not to perceptions of politics, as this chapter intended; (2) studies that did refer to perceptions of politics were not concerned with reactions to politics across cultures; (3) none of the above studies compared two non-American samples, as I try to do here.

REACTIONS TO ORGANIZATIONAL POLITICS ACROSS CULTURES

As shown in the first chapters of this book previous studies provide a fairly reasonable starting-point for an investigation of reactions to organizational politics. A wide range of outcome variables were found to correlate with workplace politics in the American culture, thereby furnishing necessary elements for my thesis. As we have noted in the several other chapters, the original model of Ferris et al. (1989) suggested that organizational politics could result in several work outcomes, such as job anxiety, job involvement, job satisfaction, turnover, and absenteeism. Other studies elaborated on additional reactions such as organizational commitment, loyalty, innovation, tension-related and stress-related factors, job performance, and even organizational citizenship behaviors (OCB) (Bozeman et al., 1996; Cropanzano et al., 1997; Drory, 1993; Kacmar et al., 1999; Parker et al., 1995; Randall et al., 1999; Vigoda, 2000, 2000a). In the current chapter I focused on seven possible reactions to organizational politics. As observed from Table 5.1, four of them have received much attention in the literature outlined above (job satisfaction, exit/intentions of turnover, voice or job involvement, and loyalty/commitment) while the other three (met expectations, neglect, and absenteeism) have enjoyed little or no empirical examination. These reactions, as well as perceptions of organizational politics and other variables, were examined here by means of similar research tools, scales, and methods in two cultural groups.

My decision to focus on intentions of Exit, Voice, Loyalty, and Neglect (EVLN) was rooted in Hirschman's (1970) theory on employees' responses to organizational decline that was mentioned in the introductory chapters. Since high levels of organizational politics may indicate negative organizational processes, with a damaging effect on productivity, effectiveness, and efficiency, I found the EVLN variables useful and relevant for the purposes of this chapter. I also relied on the study of Ferris and Kacmar (1992), who proposed several responses to organizational politics that 'appear similar in nature to Hirschman's (1970) exit, loyalty and voice' (p. 97). Two additional reactions are job satisfaction and met expectations (ME). As seen from Table 5.1, job satisfaction is perhaps the most studied variable related to organizational politics and was originally suggested in the basic model of organizational politics by Ferris et al. (1989). ME, however, has received much less attention. As presented in the previous chapters Victor Vroom's theory of expectations provided the rationale for the inclusion of this variable in the model. According to Vroom (1964), a match of expectations between individuals and organizations is a key element for higher performance at all levels. A meta analysis of 31 studies and 17241 people by Wanous et al. (1992) extensively supported this argument. It found a correlation of –0.29 between ME and intentions to leave the organization, of 0.19 between ME and job survival and of 0.11 between ME and job performance. I consequently found ME an interesting dimension of work outcomes, meriting examination in an organizational politics study. The last variable tested here was absenteeism. Kacmar et al. (1999) suggested this construct as an important part of organizational withdrawal that may be affected by workplace politics and therefore deserving further inquiry and empirical examination. The analysis also incorporated several structural variables, in conformity with the basic model of organizational politics as suggested by Ferris et al. (1989). I examined formalization, centralization as reflected by participation in decision making, job autonomy, and hierarchical level, as well as personal variables of age, gender, education, and full-time/part-time job. All of these variables are part of the general model presented in Figure I.3.

Finally, as Table 5.1 shows, only two studies (Ralston et al., 1994; Romm and Drory, 1988) have conducted an empirical comparison of organizational politics across cultures. Of the other 15 empirical studies on reactions to organizational politics, at least twelve used American samples and three applied Israeli samples. The main conclusion stemming from these data is that implications regarding employees' reactions to organizational politics are at present limited to the American culture and perhaps to the Israeli one. Further generalizations to other cultures are, at this point, questionable and inconclusive.

Table 5.1 Cross-cultural studies on organizational politics and reactions to organizational politics across cultures: a summary of empirical findings

Study	Sample characteristics	Culture	Possible reactions to organizational politics[a]
1. Romm and Drory (1988)	86 Israeli university faculty and 86 Canadian university faculty	Israel and Canada	Canadians perceive situations as more political, less moral, and less prevalent in their organization than Israelis
2. Kumar and Ghadially (1989)	278 male managers in one public and one private organization	Not specified	Interpersonal trust (–) Alienation (+) Feelings about job performance (–)
3. Ferris and Kacmar (1992)	Study 1: 264 employees from a factory, a hospital, and a nursing care facility Study 2: 95 hospital nurses	USA USA	Job involvement (+) Job satisfaction (–)
4. Drory (1993)	200 employees in 3 public and 2 private organizations	Israel	Organizational commitment (–) Satisfaction with supervision and co-workers (–)
5. Ralston et al. (1994)	161 US managers and 144 Hong Kong managers	USA and Hong Kong	Ethical differences in managers' perceptions of organizational politics were found across the two cultures
6. Parker et al. (1995)	1641 employees at a governmental R&D organization	USA	Perceived innovation (–) Positive organizational values (–) Loyalty (–) Overall satisfaction (–) Senior management effectiveness (–)
7. Zhou and Ferris (1995)	822 non-academic employees at a southwestern university	USA	Satisfaction with pay, promotion, supervision and co-workers (–)
8. Ferris et al. (1996a, 1996b)	514 (1996a) and 822 (1996b) non-academic employees at a southwestern university	USA	Job anxiety (+) Job satisfaction (–)
9. Bozeman et al. (1996)	Study 1: 146 managers in the hotel industry Study 2: 189 managers in the hotel industry	USA USA	Organizational commitment (–) Intention to turnover (+) Job stress (+) Job satisfaction (–)

(Continued)

Table 5.1 (Continued)

10 Cropanzano et al. (1997)	Study 1: 69 employees in a manufacturing firm	USA	
	Study 2: 185 part-time working students	USA	Job involvement (–) Job satisfaction (–) Organizational commitment (–) Psychological withdrawal (+) Turnover intentions (+) Antagonistic work behavior (+) Job tension (+) Somatic tension (+) General fatigue (+) Burnout (+) Organizational Citizenship Behavior–OCB (–)
11. Randall et al. (1999)	128 employees	USA	Job satisfaction (–) Organizational commitment (–) Turnover intentions (+) OCB (–) Job performance (–)
12. Kacmar et al. (1999)	1255 participants of whom 786 were employees of a large division of a state government agency and 469 were employees of a private electrical cooperative	USA	Job satisfaction (–) Job anxiety (+) Turnover intentions (+) Organizational satisfaction (–) Supervisor effectiveness (–) Self-reported performance (–)
13. Vigoda (2000, 2000a)	303 local municipalities employees	Israel	OCB (–) In-role performances (–)
14. Valle and Perrewe (2000)	260 employees from two aerospace service firms, three manufacturing firms and one university.	USA	Job satisfaction (–) Organizational commitment (–) Intentions of leaving (+) Negligent behavior (+) Job satisfaction (–) Job stress (+) Intention to turnover (+)
15. Witt et al. (2000)	1251 public sector employees	Not-reported (USA assumed)	Job satisfaction (–)

Notes:
a: direction of relationship in parentheses
+ = positive relationship;   – = negative relationship;   ~ = very weak or no relationship

137

REACTIONS TO ORGANIZATIONAL POLITICS: ISRAEL AND BRITAIN IN A COMPARATIVE VIEW

Politics goes hand in hand with the art of people exercising power over others in their surroundings. Referring to the meaning of power across cultures, Wildavsky (1989) suggested that 'power is a social phenomenon and power, therefore, is constituted by culture' (p. 65). Other classic cross-cultural studies of political behavior (for example, Almond and Verba, 1965, 1980; Verba et al., 1995) demonstrated how individuals from one culture perceive politics and political behavior differently from individuals from another culture. People interpret power, politics, and conflict-filled relationships according to their set of beliefs, norms, and culturally based experience. As a vast literature has confirmed in recent years, such interpretations frequently result in unique patterns of dealing with conflicts and with politics (for example, Gabrielidis et al., 1997; Gire and Carment, 1992; Leung and Wu, 1990).

Proceeding logically from these facts, a proper discussion of power should rely heavily on its nature and implications in a given culture. Therefore, and in light of the study by Romm and Drory (1988) specifically on the intra-organizational and cross-cultural aspects of power and politics, I argue that reactions to power and politics in the workplace may depend on the way political activities are viewed, translated, and understood by organization members according to their cultural orientations, socialization, and environmental determinants.

Two theory-based explanations underpin this argument. The first was promulgated by Mintzberg (1983:26), who suggested that the internal political game in a workplace is strongly influenced by external forces relevant to the cultural, political, and economic systems surrounding the organization. This argument was also supported by Peterson (1990) in an extensive interdisciplinary study of political behavior. According to Peterson's idea, later substantiated by Sobel (1993), a spillover effect exists in social life that allows a transmission of political norms, values, and codes of behavior from one arena (the general social one) to another (the organizational one). Since organizations in Israel and Britain are set in substantially different environments (human, social, political, economic, etc.) the political game within organizations is likewise expected to be different. People may respond to organizational politics in various ways and degrees, depending on their values, norms, and understanding of reality. This idea is also supported by studies that examined the relationship between non-work and work domains. According to this approach, attitudes, perceptions, and behaviors in one social arena (for example, non-work) are transferred into other areas of social life (for example, the workplace). Thus a national political environment/culture may be reflected in the organizational environment/culture (Cohen and Vigoda, 1999; 2000). One's attitudes and behaviors regarding non-work realms of life such as family, leisure activities, and membership in social clubs can affect one's attitudes and behaviors in the work setting (Near et al., 1987).

This is one way in which national culture manifests itself in a more narrow organizational culture represented by work attitudes and behaviors. However, the second hypothetical explanation may be even more cogent. It arises from the theory of conflict management within different cultures (Hofstede, 1980, 1991; Triandis, 1994, 1995). According to this line of thought, cultural differences in values may determine how individuals deal with conflicts (Leung and Wu, 1990). These studies distinguished between individualistic and collectivist cultures, relating the differences between them to a variety of organizational dynamics. Ohbuchi et al. (1999) suggest that people in highly individualistic cultures view interactions in a given sphere as occurring between independent individuals, so disagreements and conflicts are accepted as a natural and inevitable aspect of social life. In other cultures (collectivist or with a strong appreciation of tradition and social norms), on the other hand, people dislike social disagreements and therefore are expected to show less tolerance for individual influence tactics and internal organizational politics that go beyond certain acceptable boundaries. Similarly cultures in which aggressive political activities and offensive influence tactics are considered violations of desirable norms and acceptable codes of behavior will differ from other cultures in which political behavior by individuals is treated as a necessity stemming from environmental constraints or as acceptable human activity.

I found these arguments useful in the present cross-cultural examination of organizational politics because of the significant social differences between Israel and Britain. Moreover I related these arguments to the relative social stability in each of the examined cultures. For example Israel is defined as a relatively unstable society where power relationships are intense and are the predominant human contacts (Hofstede, 1980; Sagy et al., 1999). Confronting a diverse ethnic structure and unique security problems that continuously threaten its existence, Israel is perceived as a democracy 'at war', 'under stress', or at least in transition, which makes for intensive power relationships among parties (Barzelay, 1987; Sprinzak and Diamond, 1993). Exposure to multiple types of conflicts (national, religious, ethnic, and social) makes Israeli citizens more familiar with and accepting of power struggles and teaches individuals how to cope with them effectively in daily life. Moreover in recent decades Israeli culture has undergone fundamental changes. It has become far more individualistic than ever before (Herzog and Shapira, 1986; Sagy et al., 1999) and has been strongly influenced by American values and norms, especially regarding work values (Bar-Haim and Berman, 1991). In addition, over the years rifts in Israeli society have become wider and deeper. In consequence the last two decades have witnessed a rapid transformation of Israel into a more individualistic and polarized political and social arena. The country has departed sharply from the socialist, collectivist heritage of its founding fathers and has adopted many American-oriented values that place great emphasis on the prosperity of the individual and his or her quality of life instead of the general welfare and cohesiveness of the nation (Triandis, 1995). In many respects Israel in the late 1990s was far more individualistic than in the 1960s and 1970s, and people developed a profound understanding of the potential value of political pressures that might assist them in achieving their personal goals. All of these phenomena cohere with the typology of the State of Israel as reflecting a culture in transition and an unstable social democracy. In fact the same argument was used by Romm and Drory (1988) in their study on organizational politics in Israel and Canada. Romm and Drory suggested that Israelis have a greater familiarity with political processes within and outside the workplace that allows them to recognize and respond to this behavior differently from individuals from other, perhaps more stable, cultures who are less accustomed to such intensity in political dynamics. Therefore I expected that in general Israeli employees would be relatively tolerant of intense political processes in the workplace because of their greater familiarity with its nature, construct, and necessity in their unstable social environment.

British culture presents a different case. First, Britain is classified as a very stable society (Kavanagh, 1980), far more stable than that of Israel. Second, like the United States and perhaps also like Canada, Britain is generally categorized as an individualistic culture (Hofstede, 1980, 1991; Triandis, 1995). Still, its cultural attitudes are far different from the American individualism presently reflected in Israeli culture. Unlike the United States, Britain preserves some important traditional and collectivist characteristics that significantly impact its society. Despite (or some say because of) recent fundamental changes in the free-market economy, Britain is still a model of a relatively successful welfare state where governmental responsibilities to citizens are extensive and deeply rooted in society (Ryan, 1977; Valocchi, 1989). Kavanagh (1980) has further suggested that for many years Britain enjoyed 'widespread consensus about political procedures and the deference to rulers' (p. 124), which implies more acceptance of traditional authority and greater respect for the holders of formal power in society. In addition social justice and concern for the community at large remain valued and appreciated ideals that are supported by public opinion. I argued that these traditional and collectivistic domains are central to the British legacy, softening its modern individualist nature and markedly distinguishing it from American individualism, which Israel is assimilating. I posited that British individuals are less accepting of informal conflicts and the power seeking behaviors of others in daily life. This argument draws substance from both socio-political theory (for example, Almond and Verba, 1965; Kavanagh, 1980; Verba et al., 1995) and conflict resolution theory (Gire and Carment, 1992; Leung and Wu, 1990). I further believed that, due to its longstanding political stability and traditions, British culture in general appreciates the good manners of individuals and socially rejects aggressive behaviors that upset widely accepted norms. It thus substantially differs from Israeli culture, which has enjoyed a far shorter period of political stability, suffers from a high degree of social fragmentation, and is accustomed to aggressive behaviors in daily life because of its stressful environment and intense political climate. Drawing additional support from the spillover effect suggested earlier, I expected that British employees would also react differently to workplace politics. In general I expected British employees to be less welcoming of political behavior in others. When, despite all social constraints, conflicts and politics did emerge in the workplace, the reaction of British employees as reflected in job performance would be more extreme than that of Israelis.

Note too that a literature review did not yield any specific up-to-date theory on the differences between Israeli and British cultures in terms of individualistic versus collectivist attitudes or responses to politics in and around the workplace. Presuming that such a theory does not exist, I was left with a more general theoretical perspective, as suggested by Hofstede (1980, 1991) and Triandis (1994, 1995), namely that cultures differ in terms of interpreting power, understanding relations involving conflict, and struggling over resources (Triandis, 1989; Reykowski, 1994). Beyond the possibility of personal bias and the effect of stereotypes, which are of great significance, I predicted that reactions to conflicts, influential behaviors, and general politics in the workplace would not evince the same intensity and form in the two cultures. More specifically I anticipated that reactions to political perceptions by British employees would be more negative than those by Israeli employees because of group norms and attitudes to conflict. British employees would be more willing to leave the organization or to be absent. As an active response they would be less likely to voice their objections and as a passive response more likely to neglect their job duties. They would also be less loyal and less satisfied with their job and would show lower levels of met expectations. In light of the above I formulated the following hypotheses:

He1. *Organizational politics will cause a greater willingness in British employees to exit the organization or alternatively to neglect their job duties than in Israeli employees.*

He2. *Organizational politics will cause British employees to be less loyal to the organization and to show lower voice activities than Israeli employees.*

He3. *Organizational politics will make British employees less satisfied with their job and have lower levels of met expectations than Israeli employees.*

He4. *The relationship between organizational politics and absenteeism will be stronger and more positive among British employees than among Israeli employees.*

STUDY 5   POLITICAL PERCEPTIONS AND WORK PERFORMANCE OF ISRAELI AND BRITISH EMPLOYEES

Study 5 was based on a survey of Israeli and British public sector personnel from two medium-size cities of about 300 000 inhabitants. Employees in both samples held a variety of administrative positions in local government and in the high-school educational system (for example, real estate departments, human resource units, financing, citizens' services, computing and technical departments, archives and documentation, planning). The Israeli sample relied more heavily on public personnel in the city administration while the British sample comprised public personnel in the municipal high-school educational system. However, the two samples were similar in demographic variables and professional characteristics. The target population comprised 411 Israelis and 208 Britons. Of these 303 Israeli employees ($n1$; 73.7 percent response rate) and 149 British employees ($n2$; 71.6 percent response rate) agreed to take part in the study. They returned usable confidential questionnaires directly to the researchers. Subsequent analyses confirmed no significant demographic differences between respondents and non-respondents in each culture. All together the sample comprised 452 Israeli and British employees with very similar characteristics in most regards. For example, 56 percent of the Israeli sample were women (61 percent in the British sample), 33 percent of the Israeli sample were managers (37 percent in the British sample) and 11 percent of the Israeli sample were part-time employees (14 percent in the British sample). The British employees, however, were slightly older than the Israelis (M = 44.2; s.d. = 10.31 and M = 37.2; s.d. = 10.66 respectively) and also reported a higher level of education (M = 1.93; s.d. = 0.98 and M = 1.56; s.d.= 1.21 respectively). These differences are not unusual in intergroup comparisons (for example, deLeon and Ewan, 1997:27–8). Moreover I controlled for all of these variables in the multivariate analyses. To increase the similarity between the two studied groups I further controlled for professional and departmental characteristics. Individuals were employed in very similar professions and departments with the same ratio in the total sample: 15 percent of the sample were in the real estate department in the British sample and 18 percent in the Israel sample; 14 percent were in the human resource department in the Israel sample and 16 percent in the British sample; 12 percent were in financing departments in the Israel sample and 13 percent in the British sample; 17 percent were in citizens'/clients' services in the Israel sample and 19 percent in the British sample; 9 percent were in planning departments in the British sample and 14 percent in the Israeli sample; about 22 percent were in computing and technical departments in both samples; about 9 percent were in archives and documentation departments in both samples. A comparison by profession (Israel and Britain respectively) showed that 16 percent and 18 percent were blue-collar employees, 43 percent and 40 percent held a clerical job, 16 percent and 17 percent were engineers or architects, and about 25 percent in both samples had another technical position. All in all I believe that these findings furnished solid grounds for a cross-cultural comparison of the samples.

Participation in either survey was voluntary, and employees were assured full confidentiality regarding all information provided. Data were collected between 1997 and 1998 by means of identical questionnaires in Hebrew and English. A pre-test among 110 graduate students at a large Israeli university and a cross-examination of the two versions of the questionnaires by 10 professional Israeli and British ratters were performed to ensure appropriate content validity and internal reliability of the scales. These methods yielded a reliable research tool, which had the same meaning in the two languages.

Three methods were applied to support the hypotheses. First I used a conservative independent sample *t*-test (equal and non-equal variance assumed) to examine mean differences across cultures. This method revealed significant, basic differences in the perceptions of politics across the two samples as well as differences in work outcomes. It is widely accepted in cross-cultural studies of unrelated groups to ensure that core-variables show differences or similarities as predicted in the hypotheses (for example, Sato and Cameron, 1999; van den Berg et al., 1998). Here I expected to find similar levels of perceptions of organizational politics in the two cultures that would allow for further examination of work outcomes. I also expected to find initial indications of dissimilarities in various reactions to organizational politics. In the second phase I produced two separate correlation matrices (for the Israeli and British samples) to examine zero-order relationships among all variables. The third phase was developed according to this matrix and employed seven moderated hierarchical regressions to test the effect of independent variables on employees' reactions. In addition to the independent variables this procedure used a dummy variable of culture and an interaction effect of POPS x culture as predictors of the dependent variables. The procedure was recommended by Aiken and West (1991) and Cohen and Cohen (1983) and enables us to examine the major and incidental effects of perceptions of organizational politics and culture, as well as their relative contribution to the tested models.

Table 5.2 presents means (M), standard deviations (s.d.), and an independent sample *t*-test for all of study 5's variables in both the Israeli and British samples. The basic finding was that Israeli and British employees showed similar levels of perceptions of organizational politics. In light of this finding it was interesting to discover that many other outcome variables differed across the two cultures (assuming a conservative non-equal variance). Intentions of exit among British employees were higher than among Israeli employees (M = 2.51; s.d. = 1.31 and M = 2.07; s.d. = 0.85 respectively with $t = 3.74$; $p < 0.001$). The level of voice was lower among British employees than among Israeli employees (M = 2.76; s.d. = 0.91 and M = 3.22; s.d = 0.74 respectively with $t = -5.38$; $p < 0.001$). Loyalty was lower among British employees than among Israeli employees (M = 2.93; s.d. = 0.74 and M = 3.43; s.d. = 0.60 respectively with $t = -7.21$; $p < 0.001$). Job satisfaction of British employees was lower than that of Israeli employees (M = 3.23; s.d. = 0.91 and 3.54; s.d. = 0.67 respectively with $t = -3.73$; $p = 0.001$). Met expectations of British employees was slightly lower than that of Israelis (M = 2.93; s.d. = 0.59 and M = 3.07; s.d. = 0.67 respectively with $t = -1.96$; $p < 0.05$). No significant differences in negligent behavior and absenteeism were found between the samples. These basic findings indicated that differences between the two cultures were possible, so I was encouraged to proceed with further statistical examinations. Table 5.3 shows intercorrelations and reliabilities for the research variables separately for both samples. As is evident, the perception of organizational politics was significantly correlated with all of the outcome variables in the British sample and with all of the outcome variables in the Israeli sample except voice, loyalty, and absenteeism. Directions of the relationships were as expected.

To support the hypotheses on differences in reactions to organizational politics across cultures I employed a moderated hierarchical regression analysis with interactions. As shown in Table 5.4, seven statistical models were tested, and each regressed an outcome variable on all other variables. The independent structural and control variables were entered into the equations in the first step while perception of organizational politics was added in the second step. In this way it was possible to evaluate the relative contribution of perceptions of organizational politics to the explanation of the outcome variables. The third step added a dummy variable of culture (1 =

British; 0 = Israelis), while the fourth step included an interaction effect of POPS X culture. Here I followed the procedure recommended by Aiken and West (1991) and by Namboodiri et al. (1975).

Table 5.4 shows the effects of perceptions of organizational politics and culture on the dependent variables. Perceptions of organizational politics had a positive and consistent main effect on exit (β = 0.24; p < 0.001) and neglect (β = 0.29; p < 0.001) and a negative main effect on job satisfaction (β = – 0.17; p < 0.01) and met expectations (β = –0.49; p < 0.001). Less consistent indications were also found for a negative effect of perceptions of organizational politics on loyalty (β = –0.20; p < 0.001) as well as on absenteeism (β = 0.14; p < 0.01) in the third step of the regression. Perceptions of organizational politics contributed 16 percent of the total variance in exit, 4 percent of the variance in loyalty, 11 percent of the variance in neglect, 13 percent of the variance in job satisfaction, 14 percent of the variance in met expectations, and a low 1 percent of the variance in absenteeism. Culture had a main effect on exit (β = 0.10; p < 0.05), voice (β = –0.31; p < 0.001), loyalty (β = –0.22; p < 0.001), and neglect (β = 0.12; p < 0.05). It showed no main effect on any of the other dependent variables. The contribution of culture to the explained variance in the dependent variables was 1 percent in exit and neglect, 7 percent in voice, and 4 percent in loyalty. However, an interaction of culture X POPS had a strong effect on the dependent variables. According to these findings British employees tended to have more exit intentions than Israelis (β = 0.28; p < 0.001), lower levels of loyalty (β = –0.23; p < 0.001), higher levels of negligent behavior (β = 0.12; p < 0.05), lower levels of job satisfaction (β = –0.31; p < 0.001), and lower levels of met expectations (β = 0.13; p < 0.05). These findings indicate that British and Israeli employees react differently to organizational politics in the workplace.

Table 5.2.   Means, standard deviations and independent samples t-test for the research variables in Israel and Britain (study 5)

Variable	Israel ($n = 303$) Mean (S.D.)	Britain ($n = 149$) Mean (S.D.)	df (equal variance) df (non-equal variance)	t-value (equal variance.) t-value (non-equal variance)
1. Perceptions of organizational politics scale (POPS)	2.94 (0.77)	3.03 (1.12)	446.00 220.64	N.S. N.S.
2. Participation in decision making	1.93 (0.96)	2.49 (1.08)	482.00 257.95	5.73*** 5.49***
3. Formalization	2.39 (0.57)	2.19 (0.73)	486.00 233.42	−3.24*** −2.96**
4. Job autonomy	3.63 (0.93)	3.36 (0.95)	486.00 279.23	−2.90** −2.88**
5. Exit	2.07 (0.85)	2.51 (1.31)	446.00 211.88	4.29*** 3.74***
6. Voice	3.22 (0.74)	2.76 (0.91)	445.00 250.48	−5.74*** −5.38***
7. Loyalty	3.43 (0.60)	2.93 (0.74)	447.00 246.16	−7.74*** −7.21***
8. Neglect	1.88 (0.63)	1.82 (0.74)	445.00 260.49	N.S. N.S.
9. Job satisfaction	3.54 (0.67)	3.23 (0.91)	489.00 220.19	−4.20*** −3.73***
10. Met expectations	3.07 (0.67)	2.93 (0.59)	442.00 316.33	−1.76 −1.96*
11. Absenteeism	4.70 (6.15)	5.47 (9.97)	465.00 189.49	N.S. N.S.
12. Job hierarchy (1 = manager)	0.33 (0.47)	0.37 (0.49)	483.00 257.16	N.S. N.S.
13. Full-time/part-time job (1 = part-time job)	0.11 (0.31)	0.14 (0.35)	487.00 252.45	N.S. N.S.
14. Age	37.2 (10.66)	44.2 (10.31)	465.00 263.82	−6.68*** −6.60***
15. Education	1.56 (1.21)	1.93 (0.98)	474.00 311.17	3.23*** 3.53***
16. Gender (1 = female)	0.56 (0.50)	0.61 (0.49)	488.00 280.55	N.S. N.S.

Notes:
Values printed bold represent t-test when equal variance not assumed
* $p \leq 0.05$ ** $p \leq 0.01$ *** $p \leq 0.001$

Table 5.3   Intercorrelations for the research variables in the Israeli and British samples *(reliabilities in parentheses)*

Variable	1	2	3	4	5	6	7	8	9	10	11	12	13	14	15	16
1. Perceptions of organizational politics scale (POPS)	(0.79) (0.94)	-0.06	-0.15	-0.09	0.27	0.01	-0.11	0.27	-0.25	-0.46	0.11	-0.04	-0.13	-0.12	0.05	0.21
2. Participation in decision making	-0.38	(0.85) (0.89)	-0.01	0.35	-0.04	0.39	0.09	-0.02	0.25	0.11	0.02	0.47	-0.06	0.18	-0.12	-0.17
3. Formalization	0.19	-0.28	(0.65) (0.70)	0.14	-0.19	0.07	0.20	-0.08	0.31	0.20	-0.13	-0.11	0.03	0.01	0.11	-0.20
4. Job autonomy	-0.47	0.47	-0.60	(0.87) (0.86)	-0.19	0.34	0.22	-0.18	0.42	0.25	-0.03	0.25	0.02	0.16	-0.01	-0.10
5. Exit	0.60	-0.27	0.31	-0.51	(0.84) (0.94)	-0.01	-0.32	0.51	-0.40	-0.43	0.08	-0.02	-0.03	-0.16	-0.10	0.08
6. Voice	-0.19	0.61	-0.22	0.40	-0.04	(0.77) (0.84)	0.35	-0.16	0.20	0.12	-0.04	0.37	-0.09	0.04	-0.06	-0.09
7. Loyalty	-0.38	0.23	0.04	0.17	-0.36	0.20	(0.68) (0.74)	-0.39	0.28	0.23	-0.09	0.12	-0.13	0.13	-0.01	-0.13
8. Neglect	0.50	-0.27	-0.08	-0.31	0.53	-0.14	-0.49	(0.67) (0.67)	-0.25	-0.31	-0.01	-0.08	-0.06	-0.07	-0.06	-0.07
9. Job satisfaction	-0.71	0.23	-0.20	0.47	-0.71	-0.01	0.40	-0.54	(0.77) (0.85)	0.50	-0.15	0.13	0.11	0.07	-0.04	-0.15
10. Met expectations	-0.49	0.16	-0.19	0.34	-0.51	-0.02	0.23	-0.32	0.62	(0.80) (0.81)	-0.18	0.06	0.11	0.09	-0.01	-0.18
11. Absenteeism	0.21	-0.10	0.12	-0.13	0.21	0.04	-0.08	0.08	-0.22	-0.15	– –	0.01	-0.01	-0.05	0.04	0.18

(Continued)

147

Table 5.3 (Continued)

	1	2	3	4	5	6	7	8	9	10	11	12	13	14	15	16
12. Job hierarchy (1=manager)	-0.07	**0.55**	-0.14	**0.19**	-0.07	**0.40**	0.15	-0.05	0.02	-0.01	-0.03	-	-0.13	**0.25**	-0.12	-0.12
13. Full/Part time job (1=part-time)	**-0.17**	**-0.18**	0.10	-0.09	-0.06	**-0.18**	**0.17**	**-0.19**	0.14	0.10	0.04	-0.15	-	-0.07	0.01	**0.25**
14. Age	0.10	-0.03	**-0.19**	0.16	-0.16	0.07	0.14	-0.12	0.02	-0.04	-0.01	0.04	-0.13	-	-0.02	**-0.25**
15. Education	**-0.21**	**0.31**	-0.04	0.12	0.07	**0.29**	-0.04	0.03	-0.02	0.05	-0.03	0.06	-0.02	**-0.31**	-	-0.06
16. Gender (1=female)	**-0.30**	0.06	**0.29**	**-0.17**	-0.10	-0.08	**0.20**	**-0.25**	**0.21**	0.13	0.03	-0.08	**0.33**	**-0.23**	0.05	-

Note:
Values above diagonal-Israeli sample, values below diagonal-British sample; significant values are in bold. For the British sample: correlations equal to or greater than 0.17, 0.22, and 0.25 are significant at the 0.05, 0.01, and 0.001 alpha levels, respectively. For the Israeli sample: correlations equal to or greater than 0.11, 0.15, and 0.19 are significant at the 0.05, 0.01, and 0.001 alpha levels, respectively.

Table 5.4 Moderated hierarchical regression results (standardized coefficients) of reactions to organizational politics across cultures (t-test in parentheses) for study 5

Variable	Exit β(t) Step 1	2	3	4	Voice β(t) Step 1	2	3	4	Loyalty β(t) Step 1	2	3	4	Neglect β(t) Step 1	2	3	4
1. Participation in decision making	-0.05 (-0.79)	0.04 (0.78)	0.01 (0.08)	0.03 (0.56)	0.17** (3.12)	0.17** (3.06)	0.28*** (5.06)	0.28*** (4.92)	-0.05 (-.84)	-0.09 (-1.60)	-0.01 (-0.15)	-0.03 (-0.52)	-0.10 (-1.73)	-0.03 (-0.56)	0.01 (.12)	0.02 (.27)
2. Formalization	-0.02 (-.40)	0.01 (.12)	0.02 (0.35)	-0.01 (-0.30)	0.06 (1.25)	0.06 (1.24)	0.03 (0.56)	0.03 (0.71)	0.17*** (3.57)	0.16*** (3.39)	0.14** (2.95)	0.16*** (3.43)	-0.07 (-1.48)	-0.05 (-1.15)	-0.07 (-1.38)	-0.08 (-1.58)
3. Job autonomy	-0.32*** (-4.37)	-0.22*** (-4.63)	-0.20*** (-4.11)	-0.17*** (-3.72)	0.25*** (5.17)	0.25*** (5.01)	0.18*** (3.79)	0.18*** (3.65)	0.22*** (4.33)	0.17 (3.28)	0.12* (2.36)	0.10* (2.02)	-0.20*** (-3.74)	-0.11* (-2.20)	-0.14** (-2.59)	-0.13* (-2.41*)
4. Job hierarchy (1=manager)	0.08 (1.51)	0.04 (.87)	0.06 (1.14)	0.04 (0.88)	0.24*** (4.52)	0.24*** (4.51)	0.20*** (3.86)	0.20*** (3.92)	0.11* (1.98)	0.12* (2.27)	0.09 (1.73)	0.11* (1.97)	0.02 (0.33)	-0.01 (-0.24)	-0.03 (-0.50)	-0.03 (-0.59)
5. Full-time/part-time job (1=part time)	-0.08 (-1.57)	-0.01 (-0.25)	0.01 (0.23)	-0.00 (-0.02)	0.06 (1.21)	0.06 (1.20)	-0.01 (-0.24)	-0.01 (-0.19)	0.14** (2.76)	0.11* (2.12)	0.06 (1.12)	0.06 (1.33)	-0.03 (-0.58)	0.02 (0.42)	-0.01 (-0.05)	-0.01 (-0.16)
6. Age	-0.21*** (-4.12)	-0.17*** (-3.79)	-0.14** (-2.97)	-0.16*** (-3.35)	0.06 (1.33)	0.06 (1.32)	-0.03 (-0.64)	-0.03 (-0.57)	0.23*** (4.45)	0.21*** (4.19)	0.14** (2.71)	0.15*** (2.98)	-0.08 (-1.59)	-0.06 (-1.16)	-0.09 (-1.74)	-0.10* (-1.96)
7. Education	0.10* (2.05)	0.12** (2.76)	0.11** (2.55)	0.12** (2.66)	0.03 (0.70)	0.03 (0.70)	0.06 (1.36)	0.06 (1.34)	-0.06 (-1.23)	-0.07 (-1.48)	-0.05 (-1.06)	-0.05 (-1.11)	0.07 (1.38)	0.09 (1.80)	0.10* (2.00)	0.10* (2.03)
8. Gender (1=female)	-0.08 (-1.62)	-0.06 (-1.44)	-0.06 (-1.29)	-0.02 (-.32)	0.01 (0.06)	0.01 (0.06)	0.01 (0.29)	0.06 (0.95)	0.10* (1.96)	0.09 (1.81)	0.07 (1.53)	0.04 (.76)	-0.18*** (-3.48)	-0.17*** (-3.46)	-0.17*** (-3.62)	-0.16*** (-3.20)
9. Perceptions of organizational politics scale (POPS)		0.43*** (9.63)	0.42*** (9.55)	0.24*** (3.87)		0.01 (0.06)	0.01 (0.29)	0.06 (0.95)		-0.22*** (-4.41)	-0.20*** (-4.27)	-0.05 (-0.68)		0.35*** (7.24)	0.36*** (7.37)	0.29*** (4.20)
10. Culture (1=Britain)			0.10* (2.07)	0.10* (1.96)			-0.32*** (-6.29)	-0.31*** (-6.17)			-0.23*** (-4.37)	-0.22*** (-4.11)			0.11* (2.01)	0.12* (2.13)
11. POPS x culture				0.28*** (4.44)				-0.07 (-1.06)				-0.23*** (-3.44)				0.12* (1.97)
R²	0.17	0.33	0.34	0.37	0.24	0.24	0.31	0.31	0.15	0.19	0.23	0.25	0.08	0.19	0.20	0.21
Adjusted R²	0.15	0.31	0.32	0.35	0.23	0.23	0.29	0.29	0.13	0.17	0.21	0.23	0.06	0.17	0.18	0.18
ΔR²	-	0.16	0.01	0.03	-	0.00	0.07	0.00	-	0.04	0.04	0.02	-	0.11	0.01	0.01
F for ΔR²	-	106.66***	6.70**	21.43***	-	N.S.	44.87***	N.S.	-	22.22***	22.86***	11.76***	-	61.11***	5.55*	5.60*
F	9.71***	20.95***	19.44***	20.31***	15.54***	13.78***	17.58***	16.09***	8.53***	22.22***	11.42***	1.74***	4.33***	10.19***	9.65***	8.99***

Note:

N=410-452 (sum of Israeli and British samples) due to missing values

N.S.-Not significant

* p≤0.05   ** p≤0.01   ***p≤0.001

(Continued)

Table 5.4 (Continued)

Variable	Job Satisfaction β(t) Step 1	2	3	4	Met Expectations β(t) Step 1	2	3	4	Absenteeism β(t) Step 1	2	3	4
1. Participation in decision making	0.09 (1.72)	0.02 (0.36)	0.04 (0.81)	0.01 (0.28)	0.03 (0.50)	-0.05 (-0.84)	-006 (-1.02)	-05 (-.79)	0.02 (0.26)	0.04 (0.68)	0.04 (0.62)	0.05 (0.79)
2. Formalization	0.17*** (3.68)	0.15*** 3.50	0.14*** (3.32)	0.17*** (4.15)	0.09 (1.78)	0.07 (1.44)	007 (1.51)	06 (1.22)	0.03 (0.49)	0.03 (0.66)	0.04 (0.67)	0.02 (0.41)
3. Job autonomy	0.43*** (9.00)	0.34*** (7.51)	0.33*** (7.05)	0.30*** (6.69)	0.28*** (5.31)	0.17*** (3.52)	0.18*** (3.58)	19*** (3.75)	-0.04 (-0.76)	-0.01 (-1.13)	-0.01 (-0.11)	0.01 (0.06)
4. Job hierarchy (1=manager)	-0.03 (-0.51)	0.09 (0.17)	-0.01 (-.10)	0.01 (.30)	-0.04 (-.60)	-0.00 (-.02)	0.01 (.07)	-00 (-.06)	-0.02 (-0.29)	-0.03 (-0.48)	-0.03 (-0.46)	-0.03 (-0.55)
5. Full-time/part-time job (1=part time)	0.20 (4.22)	0.14** (3.22)	0.13** (2.81)	0.14** (3.18)	0.17*** (3.24)	0.11* (2.27)	0.12* (2.36)	11* (2.23)	-0.13* (-2.40)	-0.11* (-1.99)	-0.11* (-1.96)	-0.11 (-2.00)
6. Age	0.09* (1.96)	0.06 (1.45)	0.04 (.92)	0.06 (1.32)	0.05 (.98)	0.01 (028)	0.02 (.48)	02 (.35)	-0.03 (-0.55)	-0.02 (-.34)	-0.02 (-0.29)	-0.02 (-0.41)
7. Education	-0.04 (-0.87)	-0.06 (-1.40)	-0.05 (-1.24)	-0.06 (-1.33)	-0.01 (-.18)	-0.03 (-.65)	-0.03 (-.71)	-03 (-.69)	-0.01 (-0.21)	-0.00 (-.08)	-0.01 (-.09)	-0.00 (-.08)
8. Gender (1=female)	0.07 (1.49)	0.06 (1.30)	0.05 (1.19)	0.01 (0.08)	-0.04 (-.77)	-0.06 (-1.23)	-0.06 (-1.18)	-04 (-.76)	0.12* (2.32)	0.13* (2.45)	0.13* (2.45)	0.15** (2.75)
9. Perceptions of organizational politics scale (POPS)		-0.38*** (-8.76)	-0.37*** (-8.68)	-0.17** (-2.82)		-0.41*** (-8.64)	-0.41*** (-8.66)	-0.49*** (-7.53)		0.14** (2.60)	0.14** (2.59)	0.05 (0.72)
10. Culture (1=Britain)			-0.07 (-1.45)	-0.05 (-1.04)			-0.04 (0.68)	-0.03 (0.48)			0.06 (0.10)	-0.01 (-0.05)
11. POPS x Culture				-0.31*** (-5.11)				-0.13* (-1.99)				0.12 (1.60)
R²	0.24	0.37	0.37	0.41	0.11	0.25	0.25	0.27	0.04	0.05	0.05	0.06
Adjusted R²	0.23	0.35	0.35	0.39	0.09	0.24	0.24	0.25	0.02	0.03	0.03	0.03
ΔR2	-	0.13	0.00	0.04		0.14	0.00	0.02		0.01	0.00	0.00
F for ΔR2	-	92.85***	N.S.	30.77***		82.35***	N.S.	12.12***		4.76*	N.S.	4.70*
F	15.56***	25.03***	22.80***	24.43***	5.89***	14.52***	13.10***	13.32***	1.71	2.29**	2.06*	2.11*

Note:
N=410-452 (sum of Israeli and British samples) due to missing values
N.S.=Not significant

* p≤0.05   ** p≤0.01   ***p≤0.001

150

Figure 5.1 (a–e) presents the significant two-way interaction plots of the relationship between perceptions of organizational politics and the independent variables, by culture. The findings strongly support hypothesis He1, which predicted higher levels of exit and neglect among British employees than among Israelis as a result of perceptions of organizational politics. The findings also partly support hypothesis He2 for the variable loyalty, but not for voice. Hypothesis He3, which predicted that perceptions of organizational politics would make British employees less satisfied with their jobs and have lower levels of met expectations than Israeli employees, was also supported. However, no relationship was found between perceptions of organizational politics and absenteeism, so I concluded that He4 was not supported.

Figure 5.1a:

Interaction effect: Exit by POPS

$y=0.274x+0.183z+0.448xz+3.28$

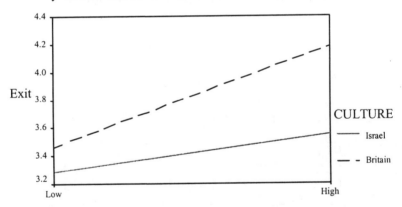

POPS - Perceptions of Organizational Politics Scale

Figure 5.1b:

Interaction effect: Loyalty by POPS

y=-0.034x-0.313z-0.248xz+2.297

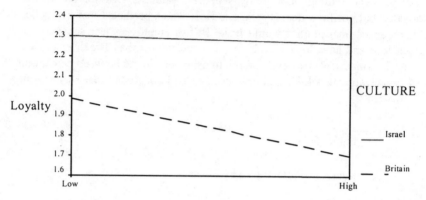

POPS - Perceptions of Organizational Politics Scale

Figure 5.1c:

Interaction effect: Neglect by POPS

y=0.213x-0.161z+0.106xz+2.673

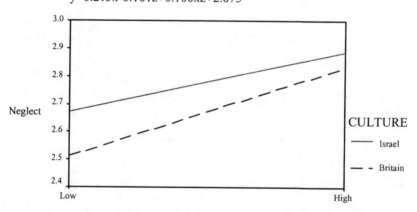

POPS - Perceptions of Organizational Politics Scale

Figure 5.1d:

Interaction effect: Job satisfaction (JS) by POPS

$y=-0.140x-0.078z-0.361xz+1.933$

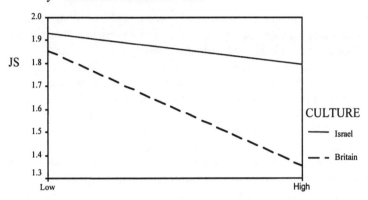

POPS - Perceptions of Organizational Politics Scale

Figure 5.1e:

Interaction effect: Met expectations (ME) by POPS

$y=-0.364x-0.035z-0.130xz+2.456$

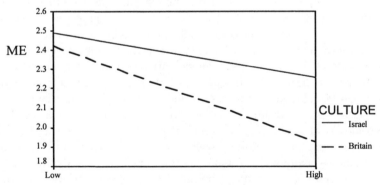

POPS - Perceptions of Organizational Politics Scale

Figure 5.1   Two way interaction plots of the relationship between perceptions of organizational politics, exit, loyalty, neglect, job satisfaction and met expectations

DISCUSSION AND SUMMARY

The lack of empirical findings on organizational politics across cultures has to date hampered our understanding of the field and impeded the development of a comprehensive theoretical framework about political processes in the workplace. This lack of a specific, definitive theory could have led us to conduct a conventional, purely exploratory study. Instead I attempted more than that in this chapter by testing one model of reactions to workplace politics in Israel and Britain.

Indeed the most notable contribution of this chapter is the addition of culture as a possible moderator of various reactions to organizational politics. This idea has been mentioned before (Romm and Drory, 1988) but until now had not undergone any empirical examination. The findings based on study 5 show that British and Israeli employees reported very similar levels of organizational politics in the workplace, but the former responded to organizational politics more negatively than the latter. British employees showed higher intentions of leaving the organization (exit), higher tendencies toward negligent behavior (neglect), lower levels of loyalty, and lower levels of job satisfaction and met expectations. Findings regarding voice tendencies and absenteeism were not robust. All of these results support the prediction of selective reaction to organizational politics as (partly) dependent on cultural characteristics.

It seems that Israelis and Britons have different attitudes to power and politics in their work environment. Such different attitudes must be considered in both intra- and extra-organizational contexts that, according to Peterson (1990) and Sobel (1993) may be related. Hofstede (1980:11) also supported this idea, arguing that 'people carry "mental programs" which are developed in the family in early childhood and reinforced in schools and organizations, and these mental programs contain a component of national culture....most clearly expressed in the different values that predominate among people from different countries.' In keeping with this concept I performed a subsequent analysis of the two samples from study 5 to investigate the idea of different attitudes to politics and power in social life more closely. I found significant differences between Israeli and British employees on three political scales that are relevant to the extra-organizational environment. An independent t-test found that Israelis evinced greater general political participation than Britons (M = 1.97 and M = 1.70 respectively, a scale of 1–3; t = 7.51, p < 0.001), higher levels of community involvement (M = 1.66 and M = 1.33 respectively, a scale of 1–3; t = 9.19, p < 0.001) and higher levels of political efficacy (M = 3.41 and M = 2.85 respectively, a scale of 1–5; t = 8.34, p < 0.001). These findings provide additional support for the argument that Israelis and Britons differ in their general attitudes to politics, influence, and power relations in society, differences that possibly show up in the workplace too. The findings of study 5 may thus expand our knowledge about the relationship between intra- and extra-organizational culture as well as their relationship with work outcomes. Schneider (1990) and Pettigrew (1979, 1990) suggest that a relationship may exist between type of culture and work outcomes, but they note a lack of empirical studies in the field. I believe that state-level politics is a part of general social values and is important for the understanding of organizational culture and organizational politics. Research efforts should accordingly explore these relationships, in particular their possible effect on work outcomes.

Still, what may be the reason for such differences? Two complementary explanations seem possible: (1) perceptual differences as to the meaning of conflict and politics in daily life; and (2) the meaning of individualism and the idea of 'power distance' (Hofstede, 1980) as reflected in Israel and Britain. The first of these differences may stem from distinct perceptions of conflict and power in one's cultural environment. Israeli employees were more likely to accept disagreements and conflicts in the workplace and view them as a natural and inevitable aspect of social life (Romm and Drory, 1988). To judge by the study of Romm and Drory (1988) British employees may be more like Canadian employees who viewed organizational politics as morally objectionable, illegitimate behavior. British employees may dislike social disagreements and therefore would be expected to show less tolerance for individual influence tactics or other aspects of organizational politics that go beyond the traditional bounds of mutual respect and politeness. British culture may be characterized as displaying less intense power struggles than Israel culture. The British view politics as tainted and react more negatively to organizational politics when it appears in their work environment. Moreover the additional findings mentioned above about differences between Britons and Israelis regarding a variety of general political attitudes and behaviors are also in line with this explanation.

The second explanation is more complex. I suggest that the rapidly growing individualistic nature of Israeli society, combined with a highly stressful and divided cultural environment, yields a unique atmosphere which today is substantially different from the British one. Consisting of a heterogeneous population, the State of Israel was born and has grown up as an entity whose existence is in dispute. The fundamental rifts in society are deep and sharp. Some researchers claim that they have not narrowed but indeed have widened over the years. As observed by Landau (1997) Israel has to cope with conflicts on several levels, such as individual, group, and national. Such disputes include the external Israeli–Arab conflict, the Jewish–Arab conflict within the country, the ethnic–economic conflict between Western (Ashkenazi) and Eastern (Sephardi) Jews, as well as between veterans and new immigrants, the normative value-system conflict among orthodox, traditional, and secular Jews, and the political–ideological conflict between left and right. These uniquely Israeli social fissures combine with more traditional ones of economics, geography, and gender to generate special patterns of handling situations involving conflict and political disputes.

Under these conditions individuals have more familiarity with political processes inside and around organizations, a fact attested to in the comparison of the general political attitudes of Israelis and Britons. Political behavior in its numerous human aspects is thus viewed as a legitimate way to get ahead in life and to survive in a more aggressive climate. Such clear individualistic patterns of behavior are also reflected in the workplace. Similarly organizational politics is considered a natural means by which an employee can gain advantages and promote his or her personal goals in the workplace. Unlike in Britain, which is a more stable society, Israelis understand power relations and politics as a necessity that no employee can ignore. As a result all forms of politics are more acceptable in the evolving individualistic culture of Israel. Israelis, more than the British, are accepting of influence tactics and approve of the use of political behavior as a recognized means of succeeding both in life and on the job (Gandz and Murray, 1980). Moreover perhaps Israelis more than Britons are inclined to forgive those who use organizational politics, knowing that they too may one day need to utilize such tactics.

To support this speculation further I turned to yet another idea of Hofstede (1980, 1991). Hofstede uses the concept of 'power distance' as an important gauge of how countries' cultures differ. Power distance is defined as 'a measure of the interpersonal power or influence between B and S as perceived by the less powerful of the two, S' (Hofstede, 1980:98). He then provides empirical data on a Power Distance Indicator (PDI) from 40 countries. According to his findings, power distance among Israelis (PDI = 13) was much lower than power distance among British individuals (PDI = 35) on a scale from 0 to 100. Other studies supported and further developed this idea (Kim et al., 1994; Schwartz, 1990, 1992). For example, Triandis (1995:30) mentions that power distance and individualism are negatively correlated at the level of approximately –0.70. These findings may also imply that Israelis are more individualistic and see smaller power distances in their environment. In general they feel more comfortable with others who are highly powerful and influential and are less accepting of a hierarchical structure. The British, who are ranked higher in the PDI scale, are more accepting of hierarchy (Triandis, 1995) and view power relations and politics in the workplace (which contradict formal hierarchy dynamics) as an unnatural and less acceptable feature. These findings are in keeping with my explanations for the differences between British and Israeli reactions to organizational politics. Even though Hofstede's data and theory refer to the two countries in the 1970s (we could not find any recent study that supports or challenges these findings on the basis of new data) they provide some support for my assumption about cross-cultural differences regarding power, influence, political behavior, and political perceptions in organizations. In Hofstede's terminology the power distance in British work environments is high, at least in comparison with Israeli work sites. In such a culture breaking the unwritten rules and norms of mutual respect and challenging the acceptance of hierarchy by taking steps aimed at achieving individual goals and advancing one's self-interest at the expense of others' needs are socially unacceptable. Interpersonal politics is perceived as a disruption of ordinary life (Hofstede, 1991). Individuals who encounter such behavior in their co-workers respond by reducing their work output. In Israeli culture, however, social relationships in general, and workplace contacts in particular, are less formal and reflect a smaller power distance that grants greater legitimacy to interpersonal influential behaviors.

Beyond these implications study 5 has additional value for a better understanding of reactions to organizational politics. Although not directly postulated in the hypotheses, the findings of this study generally support previous literature on reactions to organizational politics as measured in the North American culture. In line with several studies I found that perceptions of politics were positively related to intention to turnover or exit (Bozeman et al., 1996; Randall et al., 1999; Vigoda, 2000, 2000a), negatively related to loyalty or commitment (Bozeman et al., 1996; Cropanzano et al., 1997; Drory, 1993; Parker et al., 1995; Randall et al., 1999) and negatively related to job satisfaction (Bozeman et al., 1996; Cropanzano et al., 1997; Ferris and Kacmar, 1992; Ferris et al., 1996a, 1996b; Kacmar et al., 1999; Parker et al., 1995; Randall et al., 1999; Vigoda, 2000, 2000a; Zhou and Ferris, 1995). Moreover, the findings on a relatively weak but significant positive relationship between organizational politics and negligent behavior and a negative relationship between organizational politics and met expectations were new and had not been tested, as far as I could find, in previous studies. Some findings also suggest that organizational politics was positively related to employees' absenteeism, but this result was not robust. Most of the findings, though, are in line with previous literature on reactions to organizational politics as presented in Table 5.1.

Along with its unique advantages, study 5, like the previous studies in this book, is not free of limitations. First, in this study I used only a few of the variables mentioned by Ferris et al. (1989). Although this is a very common approach in other studies as well (for example, Bozeman et al., 1996; Ferris and Kacmar, 1992) it is recommended that future studies adhere more closely to the original model to validate the impact of cross-cultural differences, even if such inclusions would result in a more elaborate research model. Second, I am aware that despite the attempts to produce very similar samples that differ only in national–cultural factors, this goal is hard to accomplish. As reported earlier I made sure that the two samples were similar in demographic variables and professional variables and that similar proportions of subjects were taken from each department. Moreover both samples were taken from the public sector. However, dissimilarities may still exist regarding other aspects of the groups sampled (for example, the core-function of the tested organizations or cultural differences in other variables). Future cross-cultural studies on organizational politics would do well to maintain the greatest possible similarity between research units and control also for general cultural variables, which were not included in this study. Third, study 5 was conducted among public sector employees. Other studies should use private sector samples to test whether my proposed ideas can be generalized across sectors. Another limitation of the study is the relatively narrow comparison of only two cultures. Further examination of organizational politics across additional cultures may reveal findings that were not explored here and thus extend our knowledge about reactions to organizational politics. Study 5 also failed to prove clear differences in (self-reported) absenteeism across cultures. Hence at this point the findings can be generalized only to attitudinal and perceptual work outcomes that are self-reported and therefore exposed to common-method error. I suggest that further studies apply more objective measures such as performance evaluations by supervisors, OCBs, data about actual absenteeism, lateness, and turnover rates. This recommendation is also relevant to workplace politics measures that have been defined and utilized in a variety of ways. All of these suggestions may contribute to the development of a more comprehensive theory and method in the field.

Finally, this chapter tried to elaborate on the usefulness of a cross-cultural approach in the study of workplace politics. It has also provided some new research avenues for further examination of power relations in a particular cultural context. The findings, based on study 5, reconfirm the general patterns of reactions to organizational politics by providing evidence from two non-American societies, Britain and Israel. However, the results also question whether we can generalize across cultures about the power of the reaction to organizational politics. It is thus suggested that the study of organizational politics would benefit from the incorporation of cultural factors such as norms, values, and accepted informal rules in other societies as well.

NOTES

1. Some parts of this chapter are based on Vigoda (2001) 'Reactions to organizational politics: A cross-cultural examination in Israel and Britain' *Human Relations*, 54, 1483-518. Copyrights by permission from Sage publications.
2. For example, Social Sciences Citation Index-SSCI, ABI-Inform, Econlit, Psyclit, Sociofile, Business and Industry, Business and Management Practices, Business Dateline.
3. Terms searched were variations of 'organizational politics' or 'perceptions of organizational politics'. Other similar terms (i.e., 'influence tactics' or 'power') were examined separately. This search naturally yielded a much larger group of studies (over 150) but very similar results. Only one relevant cross-cultural study was found in this group.

6.   Organizational politics in virtual work sites and in a global world[1]

As presented in the previous chapters, conventional perspectives on the study of organizational politics have so far analyzed it solely among members of visible, face-to-face groups who operate in close geographic proximity to one another. As far as I could find, studies have ignored the possibility that organizational politics has meaning beyond these visible groups and work sites. Studies so far have not considered that politics is an action without borders and that influence and power relations overflow from one site to another, especially in a global economy where communication channels and modern technologies are dominant in organizational lives.

This chapter argues that workplace politics is relevant for individuals who do not interact with each other face-to-face but communicate using virtual methods that are technology based such as e-mailing, telecommuting, video-conferencing, etc. I generally define political behavior in such technological environments as 'Virtual Organizational Politics' or VOP. I then suggest that both a theory of organizational politics and a theory of virtual teams are incomplete as long as the one does not consider the implications of the other. Politics in virtual work sites and among virtual teams may result in various consequences relevant to these groups' effectiveness and efficiency. On the other hand, the complex, cyber environment of virtual teams is undoubtedly important in helping us understand the implications of multifaceted political maneuvers used as influence tactics in modern organizations.

Hence the goals of this chapter are three, built in sequence. First I try to develop a rationale for the study of political processes in virtual teams, namely VOP. To do so I rely on two separate streams of knowledge as well as on their mutual interaction. Here it is necessary to focus on the possible effect of workplace politics on team effectiveness and outcomes. Second, I suggest a preliminary platform for empirical studies of politics in virtual teams. This platform is based on encouraging past experiences that examined politics in face-to-face work groups quite successfully. My aim is to apply such knowledge and experience to the virtual group arena. Third, I describe the results of a field effort that consisted of ten extensive interviews with members of virtual teams. Finally, I attempt to draw both theoretical and practical conclusions for managers. Nonetheless, the entire research endeavor may be defined as exploratory. It is not intended as a comprehensive empirical study of politics in virtual teams but as an initial exploration of its nature and characteristics. I believe that the main contribution of this effort lies in its discussion of influence and politics outside conventional face-to-face work groups, in the hope that it will pave the way for future, more extensive studies in this direction.

VIRTUAL TEAMS IN A GLOBAL WORLD

Modern organizations have undergone major changes and transformations within the last two decades. Our conventional view of classic organizations as formal entities with direct visible communication channels no longer holds true in work sites of the 'new generation.' During the process of gathering information and data for the present study I found that companies are changing traditional patterns so fast that past assumptions about how and where work should be done and who controls it are becoming irrelevant. For example, one large international company that we visited for the purposes of this study is presently asking employees to work from home at least one day a week. The organization provides employees with a 'computerized package' to be installed at home, and the employees spend flexible time working wherever they want, at whatever time that suits them, surrounded by conditions that are personally determined according to their needs and wishes. Such patterns of working from home using advanced technology create challenges for the old style of work and intensify challenges for virtual teams as well. They are symptoms of a rapid, technology-based change in modern work sites.

Moreover many organizations are going global, transforming their traditional visible platforms into invisible, virtual ones. Their developmental aspirations are frequently cross-national and cross-cultural, and to achieve ambitious goals they must rely more heavily on the power of communication and sophisticated technology as applied to the work of virtual groups. This evolution has resulted from several socioeconomic, technological, and ideological changes in modern life: (1) the tremendous growth in the number of multinational activities and cross-cultural use of various natural resources (Boudreau et al., 1998); (2) the increase in the number of complex undertakings such as international projects and the ambition to design highly sophisticated products that need the mutual effort of separate parties, frequently from separate cultures; (3) the practical processes of globalization and the encouragement of commerce across open markets, also supported by the ideological legitimization of powerful governments; (4) the development of new technologies that allow faster and more efficient transfer of information, knowledge, and cyber-products; (5) the growth of universal interdependency in goods and services that are a result of an increase in the general quality of life in the Western world.

Virtual teams are one way by which organizations adjust to working globally. Definitions of such teams are based on the general perception of virtual organizations. As suggested by DeSanctis and Monge (1999) they represent 'a collection of geographically distributed, functionally and/or culturally diverse entities that are linked by electronic forms of communication and rely on lateral, dynamic relationships for coordination' (p. 693). Using this definition virtual teams may be characterized by their dependence on a federation of alliances and partnerships between individuals, their relative spatial and temporal independence due to distances in geographical space and time, and their increased flexibility for members of the team regarding where, when, and even how to conduct the work. According to Boudreau et al. (1998) these characteristics of virtual teams and transnational organizations potentially contribute to enhanced global competitiveness by yielding a higher responsiveness to customers' needs. However, the greatest challenge of these mechanisms remains co-ordination. Working virtually means moving faster and from numerous directions and locations toward the organizational target, but it simultaneously requires top management to harmonize operations between individuals and units. Creating more efficient and effective patterns of synthesizing the firm's actions is thus a necessity in virtual teams, yet it may also have significant side effects on members of the teams. One important consideration is the psychological and behavioral impact. More specifically the quest for more coordination intensifies (virtual) interactions among group members and at the very least potentially provides fertile ground for the increase in conflicts, influential behavior tactics, contradictory interests, and the creation of an atmosphere rife with organizational politics that is at the heart of our discussion.

POLITICS AND INFLUENCE IN ORGANIZATIONS AND THEIR MEANING FOR VIRTUAL TEAMS

Politics in the workplace is an elusive organizational phenomenon that may be characterized in a number of ways. First, on its intra-organizational level it is an influence process executed by *individuals* or by *groups* in the workplace. Second, it expresses *vertical* or *horizontal* influence process. Vertical politics represents influence relations between supervisors and their employees while horizontal politics expresses influence relations inside a given hierarchical level, for example, among co-workers or managers and themselves. Third, it has some *formal* as well as *informal* aspects. Formal politics denotes the implementation of legal and authorized power to influence others while informal politics refers to the use of different sources of informal power to pressure or influence others (French and Raven, 1959); usually those who do not hold formal power are more likely to use informal power whenever it is necessary. Finally, politics in organizations can be analyzed as an *interorganizational* or *intra-organizational* phenomenon. Politics inside organizations includes only the relationships among formal organizational members while a broader perspective includes the complex variety of groups outside the organization. Therefore an inclusive description of organizational politics refers to the formal and informal power relations and influence processes among individuals or groups in the internal or external organizational environment.

In light of this description various theorists have tried to explain what should and should not be considered political activity in the workplace (Ferris et al., 1998; Mayes and Allen, 1977; Mintzberg, 1983; Pfeffer, 1992; Vigoda and Cohen, 2002).   For example Pfeffer (1992) defined organizational politics as those activities carried out by people to acquire, enhance, and use power and other resources to obtain their preferred outcomes in a situation where there is uncertainty or disagreement. Ferris et al. (1989a) suggest that it is a social influence process in which behavior is strategically designed to maximize short-term or long-term self-interest, which is either consistent with or at the expense of others' interests. Although scholars differ as to the need for and the value of measuring perceptions of politics rather than focusing on actual political behaviors, they all agree that politics in organizations is best reflected by influential activities and tactics engaged in by members to maximize their interests and goals in the workplace. Furthermore, politics in organizations today is generally deemed a necessary evil. It is associated with a variety of negative actions that are harmful and dangerous from the organizational point of view (Ferris and Kacmar, 1992; Ferris and King, 1991; Mintzberg, 1983; Parker et al., 1995). Studies that examined the effect of organizational politics on work outcomes concluded that organizations rife with internal politics usually perform poorly on a variety of measurements.

However, all of this valuable knowledge seems insufficient and incomplete unless it is integrated with the idea of virtual teams. Since virtual teams are generally cross-culturally based it is interesting to look for variations in political behavior and influence tactics among members of multinational virtual groups. In fact several studies on organizational politics have theoretically suggested such differences but few have supported them empirically. The presented in the previous chapter Israelis and Britons react differently to the same levels of organizational politics in their work environment. An earlier study by Romm and Drory (1988) found other significant differences in the perceptions and use of organizational politics between Canadians and Israelis. Individuals from different nations seem likely to perceive organizational politics differently as well as to react to it differently.

Moreover virtual teams comprise a work environment where people do not interact with each other directly, personally, or face-to-face, so patterns of influence tactics may also change in direction, magnitude, and frequency. As demonstrated in the introductory chapter, the seminal study by Kipnis et al. (1980) has proposed the most reliable typology of eight influence tactics used by individuals to engage in what I describe as organizational politics. I further argue that in virtual teams these influence tactics are not used in the same manner, with the same intensity, or in the same situations as in conventional groups. I find some support for this argument in the study of Latane et al. (1995) who suggested that physical space and distance do affect social interactions and social influence. Their study was based on the social impact theory, which states that immediacy (which is generally the inverse of distance) adds to the strength and number of social sources in determining virtually any form of social influence. Relying on three separate populations varying in culture (Americans and Chinese), technology, geography, and age, Latane et al. (1995) found that physical location and intervening distance exerted powerful and predictable effects on social influence as measured by memorable interactions among members of the group. Influence tactics and politics in virtual teams thus seem to merit more extensive comparison with the same activities in conventional groups.

VIRTUAL ORGANIZATIONAL POLITICS (VOP): DEVELOPMENT OF A PRELIMINARY FIELD STUDY

My challenge in the present venture was to explore the meaning and implications of political processes for teams that are cross-culturally and cross-nationally based. To do this I utilized information provided by team members who described their understanding and practices of politics while participating in virtual team dynamics. Practically the study faced two major obstacles. First, the most obvious problem was that empirical studies in the field of organizational politics are very sparse. Previously we have mentioned that several factors have restricted the development of this field: (1) the ambiguity and pervasiveness of concepts and issues relevant to workplace politics; (2) the relatively recent interest in empirical guided research about this phenomena; and (3) the methodological difficulties that arise in studies of this kind (for example, the willingness of organizations to collaborate on such a sensitive topic, individuals' cognitive barriers, and unwillingness to discuss influence tactics for fear of revealing how they jockey for position in workplace interrelations or of losing their advantage over others). Second, researching virtual teams suffers from similar problems. As argued by DeSanctis and Monge (1999) the idea of virtual organizations and other dimensions of virtual work have received considerable attention in the management literature of recent years yet, surprisingly, little empirical research exists about this significant topic. So naturally it was impossible to find a reliable source of empirical data on politics and influence in virtual teams. In consequence I decided on an exploratory effort to design what I define as a first empirical step toward the understanding of VOP.

STUDY 6   A QUALITATIVE ASSESSMENT OF ORGANIZATIONAL POLITICS AMONG EMPLOYEES FROM THE HIGH-TECH INDUSTRY

This exploratory study relied on open interviews with members of virtual teams. Ten interviews were conducted between November 2000 and February 2001; participants were Israeli employees of two international organizations from the high-tech sector. They were middle managers who held a variety of technically oriented positions in the companies. All participants were engaged in virtual team activity and some were members of more than one such group. In these cases we asked the participant to concentrate on the dynamics occurring in the most important and active group of all. Most groups intercommunicated once or twice a week and individuals met each other face-to-face once or twice a year. The total number of members in the groups ranged from three to ten individuals, and most members came from the United States, Canada, Britain, Ireland, Belgium, and countries in the Far East (Hong Kong, Japan), in addition to the Israeli members. Interviews were conducted at the organizations' premises and lasted 90 to 120 minutes. During the interview we followed a ready-made question list, which allowed us both sequential development of ideas as well as flexibility in collecting voluntary information provided by the participants. The interviews were tape-recorded and reconstructed in a written version from which the analysis was made.

Evidence by Experience: is VOP so Different from Conventional Organizational Politics?

The main part of the interviews asked participants to describe and explain various influential behaviors and political processes relevant to their organization, in particular to their working virtual teams. The evidence as provided here portrays an interesting image of power relations, influence, and political behavior in situations where people do not interact face-to-face but use various other alternatives to perform their job tasks (for example, e-mailing, conference calls, video-conferencing, synchronized PC working, etc.). In keeping with the exploratory nature of this work I prefer to use a description of organizational politics as originally provided by one of the participants.

> Organizational politics exists in every organization. There are those who are more aware of it and there are others who are less aware. Whoever gets to do it better survives and succeeds more than others. It is also a legitimate thing. If I am leading a project and I need to convince my staff to do their job in the way I see right – this is organizational politics. When people in virtual teams want to push themselves up and get others to appreciate them more – this is organizational politics. When members of the team want to make a stand or to become more assertive they sometimes speak louder – this is also organizational politics.

Distance, intimacy, and the use of influence tactics

First, most of the participants agreed that regular groups constitute more personal and intimate relationships of all kinds. When immediacy exists people tend to care more about each other, there is a visible and concrete common history, and when conflicts arise they frequently are framed in a clear and overt way. One way to explain such behavior is that people may feel more capable of criticizing each other when they see the other person and have a comprehensive understanding of who is standing in front of them. Most importantly, when facing each other personally people can criticize each other using the checks and balances of face-to-face interactions (for example, interpreting eye contact, gestures, or body language). Virtual teams do not allow such balances. During multiple phone conversations or virtual communication on the PC people miss valuable information about the others' reactions. Physical distance is frequently translated into psychological distance, and individuals must understand and obey different rules of the political game. One participant in the study described these differences.

> One of the most salient characteristics of political behavior inside or outside organizations is that it takes place in inner rooms, in hidden corners, and no one actually knows that it is there. You can't actually see it but you eventually witness

its results. You must be very careful in becoming engaged in such influential behaviors; therefore virtual teams are a bad place to start practicing organizational politics. You can't see the people, you can't evaluate their power and secret weapons, and you have much less control over the entire process compared with face-to-face teams that are just nearby you.

The same participant also mentioned another problem of accurately reading the political map from a distance. In his view it was difficult and sometimes impossible to be practically involved in organizational politics from afar and to become actively engaged in processes when their meaning was vague. Moreover the very strict task orientation of a virtual team left less time for informal political actions to emerge, contrary to what I usually see in conventional teams.

It is much more difficult to read and understand the political map when people are distributed all over the world. You don't know where to start from. You frequently can't see it happening. Also, virtual teams are task oriented. You do not have enough chances to read and understand this politics, if it's there at all. In fact, I don't feel that I actually have enough opportunities to be exposed to such activities in my virtual team: we don't have that much time left for politics; we need to work.

In addition, since distance processes in the end are slower than processes in the same physical environment, people simply do not tend to become engaged in additional influence tactics, which are time consuming or unreliable. They usually accept the idea that work in virtual teams takes more time and that they must become more patient and wait for decisions to emerge naturally rather than stepping up extra political activities that in the future may prove inappropriate or premature. Thus when distance factors and media interface limitations prevent individuals from using other, more direct influence tactics, they need to compensate by other means. One way may be by extending and enhancing rational arguments and logical creative tools. When personal visible gestures such as body language or eye contact are impossible people may turn to available low-cost alternatives. These include higher levels of rationalization, better explanations and logical arguments, or the creation of local coalitions or lobbies for a certain issue.

Anonymity

The anonymity factor also coheres with such explanations. Working in virtual teams creates anonymity, which makes it easier for individuals to use certain manipulations such as hiding information, building coalitions based on cultural similarities, and blocking data or ideas that otherwise (for example, in face-to-face groups) could not be hidden. As one of the managers interviewed for this study framed it:

> I am not sure but it seems like a more personal and face-to-face interaction invites more political maneuvers. When there is a higher level of anonymity people become more careful with each other and try not to escalate situations that otherwise may easily become political. When such situations occur we recommend taking them offline, which means pushing them out of the relevant team dynamic.

Other participants, when referring to e-mailing communication among members of the group, also agreed that it is easier to use ingratiation in writing than orally or face-to-face. The reason is that e-mailing represents an indirect method to do something that is discouraged by the environment but is sometimes simply necessary for getting a certain task done. Furthermore they suggested that in general it is easier to consult, make rational arguments and technical explanations, and create 'across the board' coalitions when communicating face-to-face rather than in virtual teams. The main reason is that such comprehensive activities require a basic direct contact, visibility, and intimacy with people, where one can feel their immediate reactions, body language and unfiltered physical and emotional responses.

The interface factor
First, all technical interfaces used by virtual teams are built and expected to operate on a formal level, so fewer informal transactions are conducted in virtual teams. Issues are discussed in order to find solutions for problems, and neither time nor space is available for informal conversations to occur and develop. Since political behavior relies heavily on informal communication and transactions among individuals, virtual teams simply allow less political behavior.

In the use of e-mail the procedures of forward and reply provide some indication of the intensity and magnitude of political behavior. Who would you like to share information with? Why? At what frequency? Why should he or she be listed on your cc. list? The cc. is a way of influencing people by demonstrating that others are involved. People use the cc. to show others what a wonderful job they have done. This is also another way of giving someone else credit for what he or she has done and compensating them socially for their good work. Do you send senior staff and other powerful individuals every piece of information? Can people receive more prestige by doing so? Can we identify powerful groups by asking who is contacting whom and on what issues? In sum, written words are worth more than oral words. People are more careful about writing things than just saying them orally because of the long-lasting effect of the written word. Thus political behavior takes on a more careful form when it is documented.

Team structure, hierarchy, and authority

Virtual teams are usually built with one person acting as a co-ordinator or leader of the group, but he or she cannot be defined as the formal direct supervisor of all other members in the team. Therefore the distribution of power and resources among team members is more equal, which leads to less diversity and more homogeneity among participants. The structure of virtual teams is flatter; hierarchy plays less of a role in the group dynamics, and authority is acquired on the basis of personal, informal resources (for example, knowledge or experience) rather than formally posited by position or title. Thus again, political behavior aimed at powerful individuals (or alternatively at the least powerful ones) is less frequent. As a result it is more likely that the group as one coherent team will confront other teams in the organization than that individuals in the team will confront each other to engage in high levels of intra-team politics.

Similarly, members of virtual teams generally perceive their own membership as voluntary, and they observe the unwritten rule that their participation and behavior should cohere with the general cultural norms of the organizations. For most of the participants in the study the word 'team' also means 'team work,' or more specifically 'working in teams, not individually.' As one of the participants related it:

> There is a greater need for mutual commitment between members of virtual teams than between members of regular teams to make it work better. People work away from each other, there are considerable differences in work hours, people can't see your face and can't sense your reactions to their remarks, so your answers and promises must be trustworthy so that people will be willing to spend time with you at the next meeting.

Another participant mentioned the fact that in virtual teams there are no direct supervisors who are in charge of writing term evaluations (reviews) for their staff as in traditional teams.

> I think that traditional groups may face more internal politics than virtual groups. Wherever the direct supervisor who provides a term review is also part of the team, politics will increase. In my team, for example, I do not provide the reviews. Instead I am one of many others who give feedback, and the direct manager presents the integrated materials to the employee. On the other hand, people pay more attention to you if you are trying to practice organizational politics in your team.

Therefore a relatively high level of collaboration and spontaneous co-operation must be achieved to secure the group's goals and existence. These values stand opposed to formal hierarchy and authority. Individuals understand that, beyond the objective obstacles to acting politically, in virtual teams such influential behaviors may harm the mutual, integrative, collective dynamics upon which every virtual group is built. Perhaps this is another reason why individuals report reduced and muted levels of political activity in virtual teams.

However, beyond this evidence participants also reported that positions and nominations to attractive managerial jobs are among the most likely topics to be exposed to political and influential behavior. Consequently VOP has much similarity with conventional organizational politics, and influence tactics are employed in both arenas when individuals set their sights on obtaining powerful positions.

> When we have discussions on who is going to lead a sub-project for which the entire team is responsible it is easy to identify those individuals who want to play a formal leading role. They are always concerned about what should they do, what their formal title should be, and they will navigate the conversation to the critical point where all other members will ask them to do the job they so much desire.

The risk effect and the development of perceptions of organizational politics

VOP may also be seen as a risky business mainly because of the distance and anonymity factors that have been explained above. In politics, some individuals gain advantages over others simply by having a better understanding of the competition. Learning about the nature of the person whom you are attempting to influence is a necessary precondition for every strategy of political confrontation. It is definitely not enough to communicate by e-mail, fax, conference phone conversations, video-conferencing, or even meeting other team members on a once- or twice-a-year face-to-face basis. In support of this argument studies have shown that electronic mail is more effective in increasing the range, amount, and speed of factual information (McKenney et al., 1992), whereas face-to-face communication is more effective in circumstances where levels of ambiguity and uncertainty are high and in socially sensitive and intellectually difficult situations (Nohria and Eccles, 1992). Since influence and political behavior are clearly among the most sensitive, ambiguous, and illusive organizational processes they can best be implemented by face-to-face meetings rather than by virtual conferencing. The application of political resources for promoting ideas and obtaining goals in virtual teams carries with it a great deal of uncertainty, which makes the entire process very risky and at times even dangerous. In line with this contention one participant argued that politics in virtual teams is much more risky than in other teams.

> Organizational politics may be contrasted with relevancy. It's a side effect emerging from the basic reliance of organizations on human resources... and it's always interesting to have some politics around you. Usually people do not see it as a positive phenomenon since it can sometimes and somehow harm them, especially in virtual teams. When you work with others in the same place you get to know them faster, you quickly understand what behavior is considered appropriate and what isn't and you let everyone else know the same rules. The risk of working in a multicultural (virtual) team is that they can whisper one to the other while we are not aware of it until suddenly, out of nowhere, we get a phone call from one of them saying, 'By the way, this x guy should not be put in charge of the project since he/she never sticks to timetables'. They know that we can't verify such information since we do not hold their CVs or supervisor's evaluations so we are more easily manipulated.

Without a doubt the risk effect is influential in determining the nature and characteristics of VOP. However, beyond the risk effect lies another important factor, namely perceptions of organizational politics. As argued earlier, politics in organizations may be perceived as an actual influential behavior but also as a cognitive perceptual one. The link between these two constructs is unclear. Yet studies have shown that an effect can be supported both ways, where perceptions of politics may affect actual political behavior and, on the other hand, actual political activity may reshape the cognitive perception of organizational politics (Ferris et al., 1998; Vigoda and Cohen, 2002). In line with the first possibility I suggest that what people think about organizational politics determines to a very large degree the nature of such politics and the way it is executed by all employees. This logic can be easily transferred into the field of virtual teams. Working virtually, people have less available information about other members to support their political activity and tactics. The flat structural characteristics of the team, a more equitable sharing of power resources, as well as greater anonymity supported by a lack of direct interactions combine to make most people feel that the use of influence tactics is a risky proposition. In human lives wherever hard facts and clear information are scarce people will try to compensate by building their personal understanding of reality. Thus perceptions of organizational politics are the politics in the minds of all employees, while perceptions of virtual organizational politics are the politics in the minds of the virtual team members.

Cultural differences

Cultural boundaries restrain people from using extremely aggressive influence strategies. The fact that people engage in activities that involve various cultural norms and multiples codes of behavior, exacerbated by the anonymity of virtual teams, makes the entire political process slower and more careful. In many respects political processes in virtual teams do exist but they are more muted, slower, less intensive, and more covert than in visible teams. In line with this argument some of the participants also mentioned the role of language as a barrier to the effective implementation of political processes. As one participant framed it:

> There is something more mild working in virtual teams (by e-mail, conference calls, or video-conferencing). Since we are talking about multicultural groups there is a diversity in levels of spoken or written English among all members. Although we understand each other pretty well we sometimes do not express ourselves the same way as we do in Hebrew. We also sometimes do not get the bottom line or accurate meaning as expressed by the other unless we have got to know him/her personally and relate the words with his/her face and personality.

Moreover when referring to influence tactics and the political behavior of other members in the virtual team Israelis perceived their foreign colleagues as separate cultural groups who behave differently from themselves. For example, several participants argued that North American members used milder, gentler, and perhaps more sophisticated and covert influence tactics than Israelis, who are more direct and blunt.

> The North American members of our team are frequently indirect in their influential behavior. They will try very gently to convince you, and if you are not convinced they will try once more, and another try, and another one and so on and so forth, but all is done in a very civilized manner. We (Israelis) are different. We are more direct in our approach. We have less time to discuss everything all over again. Explanations are given only once and we expect the other side to understand it fast and either to accept our position or reject it. Our influential approach is more overt and direct, but this does not necessarily mean that we do not practice politics in our own way. Israeli politics (VOP) as distinct from American politics (VOP) is characterized by preparing the background in advance. Prior to the virtual team meeting an Israeli will talk with one or two more members to see how they can support his/her idea or position from another angle or something like this. This does not mean that an American will not engage in the same tactic but he will be much more careful to try and not to exceed accepted social norms ... We on the other hand act differently although we try to adjust ourselves to the team's codes of behavior ... still we remain much more direct than others.

DISCUSSION AND SUMMARY

Boudreau et al. (1998) argued that virtual organizational teams are not a passing fad. They are expected to endure well into the twenty-first century due to the informational, technological, economic, and even ideological revolution that reflects a new perception of the role of modern organizations in responding appropriately to changes in individuals' work style and lifestyle. One important field in the study of virtual teams which to date has not received satisfactory attention is the political and influential dynamics that take place in these groups. Power, influence, and political behavior have always been inherent parts of any human activity that occurs in or around organizations (Mintzberg, 1983), but until today they have not been systematically examined in the virtual team context. Recent developments in modern organizations, particularly the explosion of technology-based virtual activity both in business and in public arenas, call for a closer look into this topic.

This chapter has tried to examine several questions. I was first interested in whether organizational politics diminishes in virtual teams or whether it just assumes different forms. I was also interested in what kind of influence tactics, if any, replace the ones that exist in traditional teams and which are found to be most effective in the eyes of team members. The findings suggest several possible answers, which together construct a fuller picture. First, politics does exist in virtual teams as it exists elsewhere; however, it is much more restrained and muted than politics in face-to-face groups. The reason may be the risks that members need to take into account. These risks are exacerbated by the distance and anonymity factors, which make the virtual political game more dangerous because of a lack of necessary information about other members' actions. Second, the participants in the interviews reported that influential behavior among team members depends on their cultural origins as well as on the interface used for communication. These constructs also play an important role by increasing uncertainty and risk as well as underscoring the boundaries of what is and is not acceptable in one culture as opposed to another. Such findings imply that differences in members' cultures lead to differences regarding political behavior. Thus the political game proves more pervasive and complicated when its participants come from different cultural backgrounds. Third, following Kipnis et al. (1980), the most frequent influence tactics in virtual teams seem to be logic and assertiveness. Most of the participants emphasized the flat structure of the teams and the fact that there are minimal hierarchical differences among the members. I find this the main reason why members use logic and assertiveness more than any other influence tactics mentioned in the literature. Organizations that encourage the development of virtual teams with a flat structure and a more equal division of responsibilities and authority among their members will help reduce the level and intensity of influence tactics and general political behavior. For example, the value of making decisions through *consensus* was mentioned by some of the participants as very efficient and constructive for group dynamics. When one enforces a decision made in such a context on others it is more likely that the team cohesiveness and cooperation will endure. In line with this argument, when we asked the participants to report on the existence of other influence tactics most of them denied any use of sanctions or blocking by team members. They agreed however that ingratiation, exchange, coalition, and even upward-appeal might figure covertly but not overly in team dynamics.

Virtual teams are characterized by the use of advanced technology and telecommunication systems that allow their very existence. According to Wiesenfeld et al. (1999), telecommunication used by virtual teams is highly informal and thus limits the ability to convey social context cues. Yet the same informality may break down perceived hierarchies and promote a feeling of equality that may lead virtual workers to feel that they are central to the organization (Huff et al., 1989). Similarly, team members may feel that they are active participants in the organizational processes and more freely initiate influential and political ventures to affect group outcomes.

Indeed the preliminary findings of this study explore some interesting aspects of politics and influential behavior in virtual teams. However, these findings indicate that VOP may be significantly lower than organizational politics in conventional teams. Generally members of virtual teams report lower levels of political behavior compared with similar activities of conventional face-to-face groups. In addition the influential tactics they use are also different in magnitude and intensity from those of other groups. What may be the reasons for this? Based on the knowledge accumulated so far I propose several alternative explanations, which may be related to each other. These explanations and relationships are presented in a model that can be used for either future academic studies or practical purposes.

Figure 6.1 presents the understanding of VOP as arising from the exploratory findings of this work. Six elements are critical in this regard.

1. *Distance and anonymity.* These factors may also be defined as an objective 'gatekeeper' to politics in virtual teams: the distance effect blocks the practical use of some influence tactics while allowing others to be expressed and practiced more freely. Anonymity is a supplementary dimension to distance and contributes to the creation of a psychological climate and boundary to organizational politics. Distance and anonymity may lead to a higher risk effect that encourages lower levels of VOP.

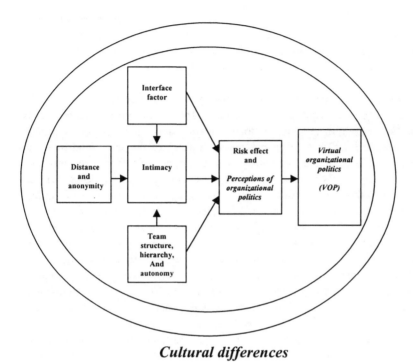

Cultural differences

Figure 6.1   Virtual Organizational Politics (VOP): an exploratory model of the cyber political space

2. *Interface factor.*   This construct is somehow paradoxical in the context of VOP. Basically, advanced interface technology is designed to facilitate transference of information, and in most cases it is very successful in doing so. However, in the context of VOP it has a negative effect. Frequently it limits the flow of necessary information that is required for effective VOP to emerge. The interface factor generally works against VOP or at least changes its meaning compared with conventional organizational politics.

3. *Team structure, hierarchy, and authority.* Virtual teams are characterized by a flat structure, a minimizing of formal hierarchy and the movement of authority from the hands of individuals to those of the entire group. This is a built-in constant factor relevant to most of the virtual teams. It thus has a direct effect on VOP by allowing all members of the team to be

equally involved in decision-making processes and sharing power more equally. It contributes to smaller differences among team members, to more task-oriented activity, and as a result to a lower level of politics and minimal irrelevant (that is, not task-oriented) influential activities.

4. *Intimacy.* Intimacy is central to the model and represents a core social element highly relevant to virtual teams. Most of the virtual teams are by definition less intimate than face-to-face teams simply because people remain at a distance from each other and cannot experience the same kind of social contact that is available in person-to-person connection. Hence the intimacy that arises in virtual groups is a result of several facets, as follows. (a) The interface methods that virtual team members apply to communicate among each other: such methods may run from simple written techniques (that is, e-mailing, chat, or fax), to voice-based techniques (that is, simple telephone calls, conference calls), to video-based techniques (that is, video conferencing). The more sophisticated techniques create a higher degree of intimacy but this can never reach the high level of intimacy people report in face-to-face meetings. (b) The social constructs of distance and anonymity, which add an impersonal factor to human contacts. (c) Team structure, hierarchy and authority, which together with the clear task orientation of most of the virtual teams make the meetings highly focused on the team goals and do not allow intimate social relationships to grow and flourish. The fact that team members hold more or less equal positions in the group causes most of the meetings to be goal oriented. As some of the participants testified, hardly any time is left for small talk or other social gestures among the virtual team members. When two individuals want to talk to each other about a topic that is irrelevant to the task itself, or when the topic is of no interest to the other members, they are kindly requested to take their conversation 'offline', which means out of the general meeting event.

5. *Risk effect and perceptions of organizational politics.* The risk effect is created by the elements of distance, anonymity, the interface factor, and team structure, hierarchy, and authority, as explained above. Moreover intimacy (or lack of intimacy) serves as a facilitator of both the risk effect and perceptions of organizational politics. Higher intimacy provides reliable and trustworthy information that people need to guide their moves, positions, and decisions in the group. Lack of intimacy is thus related to higher risk effect in the general VOP game. Lack of intimacy may also encourage a greater perception of organizational politics. As mentioned in other studies (for example, Ferris and Kacmar, 1992; Kacmar and Ferris, 1991), lower levels of perceptions of organizational politics represent a sense of fairness, equity, and justness among employees. When intimacy is low there are fewer good reasons to

support a sense of such equity and justness. People become more suspicious of each other and may feel that their interests and goals compete with others' ambitions in a zero-sum-game. Such attitudes may then create an organizational climate of unfairness, inequity, and unjustness that is so typical of highly politicized work sites.

In line with the above argument Kurland and Egan (1999) found a general positive relationship between the level and intensity of telecommuting and perceptions of justice. When multiple channels of telecommunication are open and information flows freely from place to place individuals perceive the workplace as fairer and more just, treating its members more equitably. One possible explanation is that transparency and willingness to share information with others is a sign of a healthy work environment where most of the processes are overt and open to questioning and even criticism. Another explanation is that supervisors may perceive individuals who telecommute as more trustworthy, so organizations are encouraged to select only trustworthy employees to telecommute. Trustworthy employees are then not expected to practice politics but to be task oriented and perform only relevant activities. Perhaps this is one reason for their being less involved in VOP. Practically, this view follows Nilles's (1994) recommendation to use telecommuting as a reward for high performing individuals. According to Nilles's idea, the organization might benefit from increasing the involvement of high performing employees in virtual teams; being rewarded with access to broad based telecommunications channels, they can better express themselves and implement their ideas and initiatives more extensively.

6. *Cultural differences*. The cultural impact consists of a discrepancy among members that produces a different social approach to the basic need for and legitimacy of VOP as well as the appropriate way to implement it. Most of the interviewees belonged to multicultural groups, and I found that the majority of them were very much aware of these cultural differences. Such differences were evident mainly in the area of understanding politics or influential behavior but also in practicing it effectively during the team meetings. In sum it is argued that VOP represent one of the most important constructs of group dynamics, and a full understanding of it must take cross-cultural issues into account.

PRACTICAL LESSONS FOR MANAGERS IN THE MASS-COMMUNICATION ERA

The exploratory study and proposed model may contribute to creating better conditions for effective virtual teams in the future. I suggest that the meaning and effect of politics and influence in the emerging field of virtual work sites deserve much more scholarly attention and elaboration. The basic assumption is that virtual teams as distinct and unconventional work units may redefine the boundaries of organizational politics and offer new areas for the study of power relations as yet unexamined. The chapter suggests the idea of VOP as representative of new concepts in the field.

What can managers learn from this experience, and what are the key 'take-aways' for practitioners? I find the answer to this question very complicated, mainly due to the relatively narrow empirical base used in the present venture. The fact that we conducted only ten interviews must limit the implications of this study. However, there are still several important lessons that deserve a closer look. First, this work proves that organizational politics exists in virtual teams although in a different manner and intensity compared with traditional work teams. Thus:

A. *Managers cannot ignore the possibility that influential activities do occur in virtual teams even if in a milder or less intense manner.*

Second, the team structure is crucial in determining the level and type of politics. Insofar as team structure is flatter, employees will rely more heavily on logic, reasoning, and perhaps assertiveness, but definitely not on other overt and more vigorous activities such as sanctions, blocking, coalitions, or upward appeals, which are more frequent in traditional teams. Therefore:

B. *Managers should develop and safeguard team structures that are as flat as possible, dividing responsibilities and authority equally among team members and allowing the teams to decide on their inner dynamics and procedures.*

Still, this should not interfere with managers' duty to define goals clearly for virtual teams as well as to set deadlines to meet these goals and remain in line with the organization's needs and vision.

Third, anonymity is an important construct that affects VOP. While managers cannot manipulate the distance factor they can reduce anonymity in several ways. Hence:

C. *Managers should pay more attention to improving the interface channels that reduce the levels of anonymity in virtual teams (for example, relying more heavily on effective video conferencing).*

Moreover to increase intimacy managers should seek more face-to-face meetings of team members. These have the potential of eliminating or at least decreasing suspicions and culturally-based misunderstandings that may lead to deeper mistrust and intensive 'back-stage' political activities that endanger a group's effectiveness and performance.

A better understanding of VOP may also lead to improved performance by such teams. The literature on group dynamics has long suggested that cultural diversity and heterogeneous work teams combine global and local knowledge bases that may promote the effectiveness and the performance of individuals, teams, and the organization in general (Eisenhardt and Bourgeois, 1988; Elron, 1997). The findings show that cultural diversity is also relevant for the understanding of people's political behavior and influence activity in organizations so VOP may also be related to team performance. Moreover such a proposition receives further support from studies about traditional organizational politics. These studies found that organizational politics is clearly related to various performance indicators on the individual, group, and organizational levels (Cropanzano et al., 1997; Ferris and Kacmar, 1992; Kacmar and Ferris, 1991; Parker et al., 1995; Vigoda, 2000, 2000a). Therefore:

D.   *Managers should be aware of the risk effect in virtual team dynamics and should also pay more attention to the measurement of and follow-up on members' perceptions of organizational politics.*

Such attitudes well attest to the general level of political activity in work groups that embody perceptions of fairness, justice, and equity that are so essential for effective team activity.

Finally, virtual teams will definitely attract more attention in the years to come and more empirical studies will try to determine their meaning for and their effect on the group's general effectiveness and performance. In order to do so it is essential to better understand the virtual political game, defined here as VOP. I believe that the present work is pioneering in its effort to sketch alternative ideas and delineate the boundaries of this political behavior in the cyber political space of organizations. I have tried to do so by providing some preliminary findings that may be beneficial for building a better grounded theory in the field. This theory still needs to be incorporated into current knowledge from two sub-disciplines, the emerging sub-discipline of power, politics, and influence in organizations and the still-to-emerge sub-discipline of virtual team dynamics and performance. Note, however, that my conclusions do not rest on a sufficiently large population, merely on the testimonies of ten team members belonging to only two companies. This limits the predicting power of the findings and leaves much work for future studies. In many respects my view followed Jarvenpaa and Leidner (1998:4) who suggested that effective groups are engaged simultaneously and continuously in three functions: (1) production (problem solving and task performance), (2) member support (member inclusion, participation, loyalty, commitment), and (3) group well-being (interaction, member roles, power, and politics). The chapter focused on aspects of the third function, namely power, politics, and influence, with the expectation that it has the potential to shed more light on other core virtual team dynamics such as production, effectiveness, performance, and even member-support.

NOTE

1. Some parts of this chapter are based on Elron and Vigoda (2003) Influence and Political Processes in Virtual Teams, in C.B. Gibson and S.G. Cohen, *Virtual Teams That Work,* pp. 317–34, San Francisco, Jossey Bass. Copyrights by permission from John Wiley & Sons.

7. Summary and implications: interdisciplinary reflections and new directions

SYNTHESIS

Social scientists attempt to understand the nature of various aspects of human behavior. For the last hundred years the fields of psychology, sociology, political science, and management theory have been recognized as distinct disciplines, each with its own 'scientific autonomy.' However, one of the classic behavior components mentioned by all of them is the human tendency and need to control and influence events in order to advance one's personal agenda. This aspect of people's behavior is generally referred to as 'politics' and when it is expressed in organizations it is referred to as 'organizational politics.'

The cluster of studies included in this volume focuses on the political aspects of the individual's behavior in the workplace. They all take a positivistic view, trying to apply an empirical guided research in various sectors, cultures, and populations. Organizational politics is demonstrated as a central field in management and organization theory, but as suggested in all the chapters it necessarily integrates psychological, sociological, and political theories and approaches. The behavioral approach to the study of organizations is endemic to all of these disciplines and attempts to understand organizational structures, features, and processes through explanations based on elements of human activities and the implications of these activities for the organization, its environment, members, and products.

In his book *Power in and Around Organizations*, Henry Mintzberg, one of the most important researchers in the organizational management and behavior field, refers to power and its influence on organizations and says (Mintzberg, 1983):

> Power is a major factor, one that cannot be ignored by anyone interested in understanding how organizations work and end up doing what they do. If we are to improve the functioning of our organizations from within, and to gain control of them from without to ensure that they act in our best interests, then we must understand the power relationships that surround and infuse them. (pp. 1–2)

Mintzberg refers to power as the main asset that motivates organizations. Similarly, the theory of power is closely related to the concepts underlying organizational politics. Hence it should be clear to organizational theory researchers that politics and power dynamics are inseparable components of work life. Although this component has recently received some research attention, what we know about this topic is still far less than what we do not know. It thus seems that the study of political behavior in organizations has great potential for helping us understand the individual's place within the organization and various aspects of political behavior in general.

It is important to note at the beginning of this closing discussion that the depiction of political structures within different environments through the study of terms such as power, force, and influence and their use in achieving goals had always been at the center of political scientists' attention. Lasswell (1958) defined politics as the process of influence for the purpose of actualizing different interests and argued that political processes are basically meant to decide *who gets what, when, and how* in a given social system. The discussion of asset distribution and goal achievement figures prominently in many academic fields as part of the attempt to formulate overarching theories and guiding principles. Political science researchers use terms such as force, influence, authority, power, etc. in various manners. International relations researchers examine their expression in the international arena among countries. Government theory researchers discuss questions related to the nature of the relations within the country, between its formal and non-formal bodies and among the social groups that try to influence governmental processes. Political philosophers and researchers interpret social reality using ideas dealing with, among other issues, power and influence. Political scientists bring a unique perspective to this discussion. Those who deal with political economics explain the force dynamics within the state using terms borrowed from theories of economics (cost/efficiency, profit/loss, demand/supply). Political sociologists provide social explanations for political phenomena (social functionality/disfunctionality, social strata, socialization, group dynamics). Political psychologists make use of behavioral explanations resulting from the personality of the arena-players and their individual characteristics (personality traits, learning, perceptions, personal attitudes, and tendencies). It seems that this book can be placed within this last field of research, which deals with the aspects of psychological politics within the work sphere.

The main disciplines from which this book draws its terms are, therefore, management, public administration and organizational theory, political science, and political sociology and psychology. I have also tried to demonstrate that management and administration theory are frequently concomitant with political science, especially when public administration organizations are at the center of the discussion. Although management theory and public administration researchers have tried throughout the years to formulate different approaches in order to explain organizational structures and processes (in the private and the public sectors), the use of political terms as part of behavioral theories has surprisingly not been widespread and has not been empirically examined (Ferris et al., 1991). This is remarkable for two main reasons:

1. Many political science departments include management and administration researchers in addition to researchers in the classic fields of the discipline. Naturally a mutual influence among the different research fields, branches, and sub-disciplines takes place. Accordingly one would expect that questions regarding political processes and the employment of force, power, and influence would be raised in the organizational context as well. However, this has not been the case. The significantly small number of empirical studies discussing organizational issues from a political perspective testifies to that.

2. Political factors serve many researchers as tools for explaining various social phenomena. This leads to the question of why these factors are not made wider use of in explaining organizational processes (in the business, private, or public sectors) when it is clear that there, too, power struggles exist. On many occasions organizations function as political bodies par excellence. Analyzing them using political terminology, as has been done in this book, may present phenomena in a new light and open up possibilities for fascinating explanations regarding the mechanisms and implications of internal processes.

Indeed acknowledging the importance of the political factor in work organizations has been a slow but steady process that has finally culminated in its recognition as a key element in research design. For example, Long (1962:110) wrote that people tend to believe that governments are like organizations. The opposite statement that organizations are like governments is also true but has received far less attention. Thirty years later Pfeffer (1992) stated that:

'Organizations, particularly large ones, are like governments in that they are fundamentally political entities. To understand them, one needs to understand organizational politics, just as to understand governments, one needs to understand governmental politics'. (p. 8)

This statement is supported by those who claim that the discussion of political processes goes beyond their use in nations, legislative bodies, and elections. The recognition of the pervasive role that politics plays in every aspect of life implies that it has tremendous importance in the workplace as well (Molm, 1997). The obvious conclusion is that the analysis of the political phenomenon in organizations from an interdisciplinary perspective is worthwhile.

As I have tried to present throughout this book organizational politics express the struggle over different interests in the work environment, a struggle that is very similar to the one that takes place in the governmental and national arenas. Sometimes national players are involved in organizational politics, and this is especially true of public organizations where the state and the politicians representing it have a larger influence. This kind of involvement is expressed particularly in the staff nomination processes and in decision- and policy-making processes. National politics is also involved in the private sector (for example, through regulations and rules or through personal activism) and the degree of involvement changes in accordance with the governing body's character, policy, culture, and its staff's world view. Sometimes the national players do not participate in the political process in the organization. This is especially true when the interests discussed are not social or governmental but organizational, group, or personal interests. Only those closely involved in the daily production process, among whom are employees and managers, and employee committees and internal groups that are formed ad hoc, are usually involved in the interorganizational political game. Frequently, as I have tried to demonstrate throughout this book, those with a direct interest in the nature of the production process, such as the organization's clients, suppliers, or potential competitors, become major parties as they contribute to the formation of politics perceptions in and around the workplace.

It may thus be stated that the political phenomenon and the potential power dynamics within the organization are expressed by the relations between:

1. the management, employees, and employee committees;
2. the employees themselves and among them and their subordinates or superiors;
3. the different groups within the organization;
4. the organization, its clients, its service providers, and other bodies involved with it;
5. the organization and other organizations in its environment;
6. the work organization and the social, economic, and political systems in the country.

Each of the above-mentioned interactions deals with a different stratum of political relations within the work sphere that together form the organizational political process. It is apparent that there are various aspects to this phenomenon, and it is therefore understood that no single research study, as broad based as it may be, can deal with all these strata. The present book has tried to deal theoretically and empirically with a specific and limited aspect of the organizational politics phenomenon, politics on the micro-organizational level as taken from the employees' point of view. These views have shaped the most prevalent concept in organizational politics to date, namely, perceptions of organizational politics. However, this limitation excludes other levels, especially those involving extra-organizational players, from our discussion.

As presented in the various chapters of this book there are many definitions of the (inter)organizational politics phenomenon. Functional and limited definitions state that organizational politics is a tool used by employees and managers as a way to achieve their goals in situations where competition exists (in contrast with situations where co-operation exists). The limited definitions usually claim that organizational politics is an aspect of an informal and illegitimate organizational behavior that in many cases is opposed to the organization's goals. More general definitions refer to organizational politics as a dynamic and complex process of using influence (by members of the organization and its different units) to achieve goals over and above contributions made by formal and direct work performance (for further information see Cropanzano et al., 1997).

Despite the many differences that supposedly exist between the different definitions it seems that the common denominator of all of them lies in the term *influence*. Each member of the organization acts so as to influence and promote certain goals and is in a way an 'organizational political activist' who performs a 'political' behavior. Each individual in the organization has a relative amount of power. Power is thus an asset that promotes the influence activity. Like any other asset, power is unequally divided among the members of the organization and each member makes use of it differently. Thus the level of influence and of political activity of the organization's members varies as well and may be examined on a continuum. A person who has power can influence his or her organizational environment more than a person lacking power. From the moment an organization member actualizes power assets and turns them into operative and intended influence tactics until the moment when it becomes clear whether he has achieved his goals, several different processes and interactions between the members of the organization take place. These interactions shape the results of the political activity in terms of the achievement or non-achievement of specific personal or organizational goals. The person employing influence for the actualization of goals will be rewarded with great satisfaction, a feeling of accomplishment and success, and frequently with other prizes such as economic benefits, improvement of work conditions, and respect and appreciation from colleagues, subordinates, and/or superiors. This activity will similarly result in a general perception of workplace politics that is a core concept of this book. Hence it encouraged us to examine the interorganizational influence processes that express politics in the work environment with greater attention and attempt to evaluate the various reasons for them as well as the various results they have in terms of employees' production. Therefore the definition of organizational politics in this book is based on the influence component that is customary in most other studies and expresses the influence activities that are intentionally employed by the members of the organization for the purpose of achieving specific personal or organizational goals. This definition also makes an extensive use of perceptions of politics as viewed by various organizational members.

SUMMARY AND NEW DIRECTIONS

Aristotle (1962) argued centuries ago that man is a political animal, and few have challenged this claim. Political activities cross social boundaries and take place almost everywhere. We all generally agree that wherever there are people there is a struggle for power, resources, and benefits, and attempts are made to maximize interests and sustain goals by influencing others. Political scientists, sociologists, and psychologists have discussed political behavior in many ways, but in spite of its importance organizational politics has not received enough attention or empirical examination. As Block (1988) noted:

> Politics in organizations is like sex was in the 1950s – we knew it was going on, but nobody would really tell us about it. The same with politics – we know it is woven in the fabric of our work, but to get reliable information about it is next to impossible. (p. 5)

Perhaps some major obstacles to organizational politics studies are:

1. the ambiguity and pervasiveness of the issue;
2. the relatively recent interest in this phenomenon (about twenty years);
3. the methodological difficulties that arise in empirical quantitative research of this kind.

Indeed, data collection on human political activities is quite a complicated process, especially when it takes place in a relatively intimate social unit such as the workplace. People are not enthusiastic to reveal this hidden aspect of their attitudes and behavior toward others. They usually feel that their influence tactics and the way they act to advance self-interests or organizational goals are their own business. Sometimes they even feel threatened by research attempts that, in their opinion, might eventually negatively affect them. Therefore while in fact no one argues about the importance of organizational politics, few studies have been conducted to illuminate the exact role of that phenomenon and its effect on people, processes, and performances at work.

To overcome these obstacles we need more empirical efforts in this direction. Studies need to adopt a sophisticated research design that takes into account employees' concerns. Examples of such approaches might include an emphasis on the independent nature of the study and a guarantee to participants of its confidentiality. It is most important that every study on organizational politics creates a high level of confidence between the researcher and the participants. Such reassurances can be achieved by preliminary meetings with the employees as well as by the support and commitment for the independence of the study of higher levels in the organization. Another way of overcoming obstacles in the study of organizational politics may be the use of interviews or role-playing activities as ways of building greater confidence and openness between the researcher and the participants. In light of this I believe that this book will contribute to our collective understanding of organizational politics in three important ways.

1. It provides a comprehensive summary and review of the theoretical background and different perspectives of current research concerning organizational politics. By doing so, it helps clarify organizational politics' nature and definition, distinguishing it from other similar terms and processes such as power, influence, authority, and conflict.
2. I apply a more balanced perspective toward organizational politics, considering both its negative and positive outcomes. The conceptual advantages of such a perspective are set up in a model that tries to correlate organizational politics and employee performance.
3. Developing Ferris and Kacmar's (1992) suggestion, this book proposes a more explicit theory and accurate measurement for the relationship between organizational politics and employee performance. Very few researchers have discussed organizational outcomes from a political point of view. I hope that the study here has pointed out the advantages of and need for such a discussion.

The book further emphasizes the meaning and centrality of perceptions of organizational politics. This construct of politics is important since it reflects employee attitudes to actual political events that take place around them. I theoretically support the importance given to perceptions of organizational politics by Ferris and Kacmar (1992) and others, but I disagree with the assumption that organizational politics and the perception of organizational politics are synonymous. Therefore I suggest discussing politics in organizations from a broader point of view that includes two separate facets: (1) the specific influence tactics used by all organizational members to promote their interests in the workplace; and (2) the perception of organizational politics by organizational members. I also argued that met expectations and POF (job congruence) have an important effect on the effective use of politics in organizations. High fit improves the probability of attaining desirable results through the implementation of organizational politics. Met expectations is proposed as a useful measurement instrument that gauges the individual's fulfilled interests and goals. Eventually met expectations might have some effect on attitudes toward equity and fairness in the organization and on performance at work.

Finally I suggest that organizational politics is still an evolving field that requires more investigation. Figure 7.1 shows the current knowledge about organizational politics and suggests future directions for its development. More studies are needed to empirically test antecedents to organizational politics as well as its impact on various aspects of work performance. In addition, theorists should clearly integrate the perception of politics with actual political behaviors as expressed through numerous influence tactics. Moreover, follow-ups to recent studies about the role of mediators and moderators should also be undertaken.

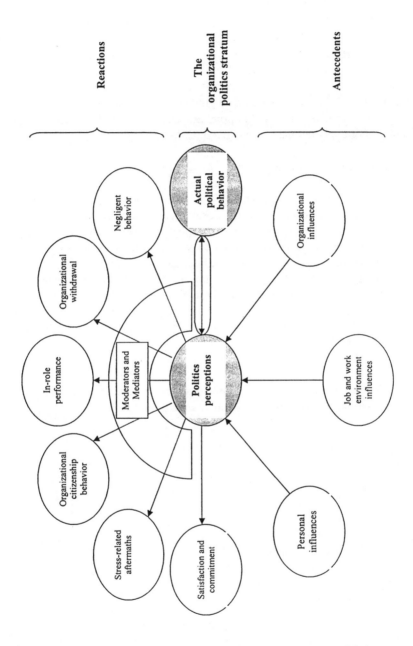

Figure 7.1   The organizational politics landscape: a revised model
and future directions

Thus organizational politics should involve theories from different fields (for example, political science, sociology, psychology) since politics in organizations has much in common with politics and influence in other social systems, governmental institutions, communities, family, interpersonal relationships, and day-to-day life (Peterson, 1990). This field has great potential, and this book has tried to guide the researcher to an understanding of our current knowledge and to point out areas in need of development. The most important issues that deserve our attention are:

1. exploring the elements and antecedents that can contribute to the explanation of politics in organizations;
2. giving additional attention to cross-cultural studies since organizational politics, like general political behavior, changes according to culture, environment and organizational atmosphere (Almond and Verba, 1965);
3. improving the conceptualization of organizational politics by including other behaviors or influence tactics that better define it. I assume that the lack of scientific studies concerning politics in organizations has been due to measurement obstacles. These obstacles still have to be addressed in order to develop some valid and reliable gauges of organizational politics and related behaviors. Kipnis et al.'s (1980) theory may be useful in this regard;
4. rethinking the idea that organizational politics is by definition negative and considering the possibility that under certain circumstances it has some desirable and positive outcomes that are functional and beneficial for employees as well as the entire organizational system.

Appendix 1   Measures used in the studies

STUDIES 1, 2, AND 3   A SURVEY OF LOCAL GOVERNMENT EMPLOYEES AND MANAGERS

Perception of Organizational Politics Scale (POPS)

The variable 'perceptions of organizational politics' was measured by the shorter version of the perceptions of organizational politics scale (POPS) which was first developed by Kacmar and Ferris (1991) and re-examined by Kacmar and Carlson (1994). The above studies, like this one, defined POPS as the degree to which the respondents view their work environment as political, and therefore unjust and unfair. While Kacmar and Ferris's original scale included 40 items I have followed Kacmar and Carlson's study that used the smaller set of only 12 items. The scale ranged from 1 (strongly disagree) to 5 (strongly agree), so that a higher score indicated a higher perception of organizational politics. Reliability of the scale was 0.77, which is quite similar to that reported in other studies (for example, 0.74 in Ferris and Kacmar, 1992; 0.76 in Parker et al., 1995).

Influence Tactics (Actual Organizational Politics)

This variable represents actual political behavior in the work environment and was based on the scale used by Kipnis et al. (1980) and other studies (Block, 1988; Erez and Rim, 1982; Tosi, 1992; Yukl and Tracey, 1992). The measure combined three subscales of 14 items each, totaling 42 items. In line with Kipnis et al. (1980) and Yukl and Tracey (1992) each scale represents influence tactics aimed at a different target: supervisors, co-workers and subordinates. The 14 items of each group were identical to the other two groups except for the target persons to which they referred. Respondents were asked to indicate how frequently they used a given influence tactic in their organization on a 5-point scale ranging from 1 (never or very seldom) to 5 (very frequently or always). The correlation among the three 14-item constructs was very high. Factor analysis likewise showed no meaningful distinction among the three scales, so I decided to combine them into one scale. The coefficient alpha internal consistency of the final 42-item scale was 0.93.

Hierarchical Level

This variable measures the position of an employee in the organization. Following Ferris et al. (1996b) it was measured as a dichotomous variable (0 = employee; 1 = manager).

Participation in Decision Making

This variable was defined as the extent to which staff members participated in setting the goals and policies of the entire organization. It was measured by four items adopted from Aiken and Hage (1968). Respondents were asked how frequently they participated in decisions on the following issues: (1) promotion of any of the professional staff; (2) adoption of new policies; (3) adoption of new programs; and (4) hiring of new staff. The scale ranged from 1 (never) to 5 (always). Reliability of this scale was 0.85.

Job Satisfaction

Respondents were asked to indicate how satisfied they were with six aspects of their job: current job, co-workers, supervisors, current salary, opportunities for promotion, and work in general. The scale for these questions ranged from 1 (very unsatisfied) to 5 (very satisfied). This measure was developed by Schriesheim and Tsui (1980). Note that the reliability in this sample (0.77) is quite similar to that reported by Tsui et al. (1992) in an American sample (0.73).

Organizational Commitment

This variable was measured by the most commonly used measure of organizational commitment, the attitudinal Organizational Commitment Questionnaire (OCQ) introduced by Porter and Smith (1970). The scale, also known as the Porter et al. measure (1974), is the most visible measure of affective commitment [and] has enjoyed widespread acceptance and use'. In its shortened 9-item version the measure reflects the three dimensions of the definition of commitment suggested by Porter et al.: (1) desire to retain membership in the organization; (2) belief in and acceptance of the values and goals of the organization; and (3) willingness to exert effort on behalf of the organization. Mowday et al. (1979) and Mowday et al. (1982) demonstrated the well-proven psychometric properties of this measure. The scale for this measure ranged from 1 (strongly disagree) to 5 (strongly agree) and the reliability was 0.88.

Personal/Control Variables

Gender (0 = male, 1 = female); job status (0 = full-time job, 1 = part-time job on study 1; 0 = tenure, 1 = temporary on study #2; education (measured on a scale from 1 = partial high-school education to 5 = master's or higher degree); income (net values/month) that was also measured on a 5-point scale from 1 (up to NIS 2000 [about $500]: very low salary) to 5 (over NIS 8000 [about $2000]: very high salary); age (a ratio scale).

Met Expectations (ME)

According to Wanous et al. (1992:288) employee's met expectations represents the discrepancy between what a person encounters on the job in the way of positive and negative experiences and what he or she expected to encounter. This variable was measured by a 9-item scale applied by Lee and Mowday (1987). Respondents were asked to describe how well their expectations about their immediate supervisor, kind of work, co-workers, subordinates, physical working conditions, financial rewards, career future and organizational identification, and their overall jobs had been met in recent months. The scale for this measure ranged from 1 (less than expected) to 5 (more than expected). Reliability was 0.83, close to the 0.85 reliability found by Lee and Mowday (1987).

Person–Organization Fit (POF)

A comprehensive 15-item scale for the measurement of POF was suggested by Bretz and Judge (1994:37–8). This scale was proposed to cover four different perspectives of fit. The first assessed the degree to which individual knowledge, skills, and abilities match job requirements. The second determined the degree of congruence between individual needs and the organizational reinforcement system and structure. The third matched patterns of organizational values and patterns of individual values. The fourth perspective concerned individual personality and perceived organizational image as key constructs of POF. I applied all four dimensions of Bretz and Judge's (1994) scale with one exception: the scale here included only 13 items because I decided to omit two items unsuited to a public sector setting.

The scale included two sets of questions, the first asking respondents to indicate how descriptive each statement was of their current organizational environment. The second set asked them to indicate how well each statement described them personally. Naturally, the two sets were quite similar in content. In line with Bretz and Judge (1994) the amount of fit was operationalized as the sum of the differences between responses to corresponding items on the two sets of questions. The scale for each item ranged from 1 (not at all true) to 5 (definitely true). The reliability of this scale was 0.78.

Intentions of Exit and Neglect

Measures of exit and neglect were based on the theoretical conception of Hirschman (1970) and subsequent studies that developed it. According to Farrell and Rusbult (1992:202) the *exit-quitting* category includes job movement both within and across organizational boundaries as well as a variety of cognitive activities that precede leaving. This behavior includes intentions of searching for a different job and thinking about quitting. The *neglect* category includes reactions wherein the employee passively allows conditions to worsen. Such behavior is best described as reduced interest or effort at work, or increased error rate.

Exit
To test for intentions of exit and neglect I used an 11-item scale. Respondents were asked to report how much they agreed with the items. The response scale ranged from 1 (strongly disagree) to 5 (strongly agree). Intentions of exit were measured by a 5-item scale. Sample items are (1) 'I often think about quitting'; (2) 'Next year I will probably look for a new job outside this organization'; and (3) 'Lately I have taken an interest in job offers in the newspaper.'

Neglect
The scale of neglect was reframed and extended by the application of the study by Leck and Saunders (1992). The 6-item scale included such items as (1) 'I sometimes put in less effort in my work than I know I can'; (2) 'Sometimes I postpone important duties for an unlimited period of time'; and (3) 'I work hard on my job' (reversed-scored). Reliability of all the scales was close to the findings of Farrell and Rusbult (1985) (in square brackets) and was 0.84 [0.70] for exit and 0.67 [0.58] for neglect.

In-role Performance

This variable represented employees' adherence to and completion of formal job duties (Katz, 1964). The scale was based on the studies of Williams and Anderson (1991) and Morrison (1994) who separated intra-role (formal) from extra-role (informal) performance. A 7-item scale was completed for each participant by his or her direct supervisor. Evaluations were made on a scale from 1 (never or almost never) to 5 (always or almost always). Supervisors reported the degree to which each subordinate (sample items) (1) 'adequately completes assigned duties'; (2) 'fulfils responsibilities specified in the job description'; and (3) 'meets formal performance requirements of the job.'

Organizational Citizenship Behavior (OCB) and In-role Behaviors

On the basis of suggestions by Williams and Anderson (1991) and Morrison (1994) a mixed scale of OCB and intra-role behaviors was used. This was done to better define the boundaries between the two performance measures that are sometimes difficult to distinguish. Smith et al. (1983) found two fairly clear-cut aspects of OCB. One factor dealt with the quality of altruism, whose component items all concerned helping a specific person, be it the supervisor, a co-worker, or a client. The other factor, at the time labeled general compliance, represented a more impersonal sort of OCB – conscientiousness in attendance, use of work time, and adherence to various rules, but a conscientiousness that far surpassed any enforceable minimum standards. It implied more of a 'good soldier' syndrome of doing things that were 'right and proper,' but doing them for the sake of the system rather than for specific individuals (Smith et al., 1983). Consequently, a 20-item list taken from OCB and the in-role behavior scales developed by Williams and Anderson (1991), Morrison (1994), and Organ and Konovsky (1989) was presented to the supervisors. Twenty-one supervisors completed the list and evaluated each of their employee's behavior over the past year. Each item was measured on a scale ranging from 1 (never) to 5 (always).

Principal component factor analysis with varimax rotation revealed three clear factors. The largest factor included eight items and was labeled OCB altruistic because all of its items referred to helping a specific person, either the supervisor or a co-worker. The resultant Cronbach's alpha for this factor was 0.93. The second factor included five items representing the more impersonal sort of OCB. In accordance with the literature this factor was labeled OCB compliance. All of the items included in this factor indicated conscientiousness and responsibility toward the normal operation of the organization over and above the formal requirements of job duties. A

Cronbach's alpha of 0.80 was achieved. A third factor generated by the analysis included seven items, all of them dealing with formal duties at work, and therefore this factor was labeled in-role performance. Cronbach alpha for this factor was 0.92. Factor analysis showed that the supervisors were able to distinguish intra-role and extra-role performance (the two OCB factors) in their particular setting. Smith et al. (1983) argued that because the two OCB dimensions represent distinct classes of citizenship behavior they should be analyzed separately. Williams and Anderson (1991) and Smith et al. (1983) added that the two OCB dimensions might have different antecedents, as demonstrated in their results. The present study, based on the studies above and on the findings of a confirmatory factor analysis (CFA) that will be presented in the findings section, analyzed the three dimensions as distinct but related constructs.

STUDY 4 A THREE-SAMPLE SURVEY (STUDIES A, B, C) OF EMPLOYEES FROM A GOVERNMENTAL AUTHORITY, A NON-PROFIT ORGANIZATION, AND A HIGH-TECH FIRM

Organizational Politics

Organizational politics was defined in this study as individuals' perceptions of organizational politics in the work environment. The items used in all three samples were the following: (1) 'Favoritism rather than merit determines who gets ahead around here'; (2) 'Rewards come only to those who work hard in this organization' (reversed item); (3) 'There is a group of people in my department who always get things their way because no one wants to challenge them'; (4) 'People in this organization attempt to build themselves up by tearing others down'; (5) 'I have seen changes made in policies here that only serve the purposes of a few individuals, not the work unit or the organization'; and (6) 'There is a no place for yes-men around here: good ideas are desired even when it means disagreeing with superiors' (reversed item). Respondents were asked to report the degree to which they agreed with the items on a scale from 1 (strongly disagree) to 5 (strongly agree). A higher score meant a higher perception of organizational politics. Reliability of the scale was 0.77 in study A, 0.78 in study B and 0.68 in study C. These values were close to those found in other studies (for example, 0.74 in Ferris and Kacmar, 1992; 0.76 in Parker, et al., 1995).

Job Stress

House and Rizzo (1972) devised a scale to measure 'the existence of tensions and pressures growing out of job requirements, including the possible outcomes in terms of feelings or physical symptoms' (p. 481). The original scale was 17 items, and it referred to three types of tension–stress factors: job-induced tension (JIT); somatic tension (ST); and general fatigue and uneasiness (GFU). For reasons of brevity I used only four items, which, however, were representative of the three factors: (1) 'I work under a great deal of tension' (JIT); (2) 'If I had a different job, my health would probably improve' (JIT); (3) 'I get irritated or annoyed over the way things are going here' (ST); and (4) 'I seem to tire quickly' (GFU). Respondents were asked to report the degree to which they agreed with the items on a scale from 1 (strongly disagree) to 5 (strongly agree). A higher score meant a higher level of job stress. Reliabilities were 0.75 in studies A and B and 0.83 in study C.

Burnout

Burnout was measured by a 6-item scale taken from the Maslach Burnout Inventory – MBI (Maslach and Jackson, 1986). Items were: (1) 'I feel emotionally drained by my work'; (2) 'I feel used up at the end of the work day'; (3) 'Working with people all day is really a strain for me'; (4) 'I feel burned out by my work'; (5) 'I feel I'm working too hard on my job'; and (6) 'I feel like I'm at the end of my rope.' Respondents were asked to report the degree to which they agreed with the items on a scale from 1 (strongly disagree) to 5 (strongly agree), and a higher score reflected a higher level of burnout. Reliability of the scale was 0.81 in study B and 0.87 in study C.

Aggressive Behavior

Aggressive behavior was defined following Berkowitz (1993:3) as any form of behavior at work that is intended to injure someone physically or psychologically. To measure employees' aggressive behavior I used a 4-item scale that asked individuals to report whether they were personally involved in any kind of verbal or physical aggressive behavior in their work environment. Items were: (1) 'Lately I have been personally involved in verbal confrontations with other workers'; (2) 'Lately I have been involved in verbal confrontations with clients'; (3) 'Lately I have found myself involved in physical confrontations with others in my organization'; and (4) 'I think that sometimes my behavior toward others at work can be defined as aggressive.' Respondents were asked to report the degree to which they agreed with the items on a scale from 1 (strongly disagree) to 5 (strongly agree), and a higher score indicated greater orientation toward aggressive behavior. Reliability of the scale was 0.76.

Job Satisfaction

This variable was measured by the same scale used in the previous studies. Reliabilities for studies A and B were both 0.70, while for study C reliability reached 0.78.

Organizational Commitment

This variable was measured by a slightly shorter version of the scale used in the previous studies (8 items instead of 9). Reliability was 0.90 in study A, 0.78 in study B and 0.79 in study C.

Control Variables

As in the previous studies three variables were included in this category: age, education, and job status (categorical variable: 0 = tenured employee, 1 = temporary employee).

STUDY 5   A TWO-SAMPLE STUDY OF PUBLIC SECTOR EMPLOYEES FROM ISRAEL AND BRITAIN

Perceptions of Organizational Politics Scale (POPS)

POPS was defined as the degree to which the respondents view their work environment as political, and therefore unjust and unfair. This variable was measured by a 6-item version of POPS first suggested by Kacmar and Ferris (1991). The items used in both samples were the following: (1) 'Favoritism rather than merit determines who gets ahead around here'; (2) 'Rewards come only to those who work hard in this organization' (reversed item); (3) 'There is a group of people in my department who always get things their way because no one wants to challenge them'; (4) 'People in this organization attempt to build themselves up by tearing others down'; (5) 'I have seen changes made in policies here that only serve the purposes of a few individuals, not the work unit or the organization'; (6) 'People here usually don't speak up for fear of retaliation by others.' Respondents were asked to report the degree to which they agreed with the items on a scale from 1 (strongly disagree) to 5 (strongly agree). A higher score meant a higher perception of organizational politics. Reliability of the scale was 0.79 for the Israeli sample and 0.94 for the British sample. Both these values are higher than those reported in other studies (for example, 0.74 in Ferris and Kacmar, 1992; 0.76 in Parker et al., 1995).

Participation in Decision Making

This variable was similar to the one used in study #1. Reliability of this scale was 0.85 for the Israeli sample and 0.89 for the British sample.

Formalization

This variable was defined as the use of rules in an organization. It was measured by a 3-item scale adopted from Aiken and Hage's (1966) formalization inventory. Respondents were asked how true each item was with respect to their job. The scale ranged from 1 (not at all true) to 5 (very true). The items were: (1) 'In this organization, there is no rule manual' (reversed score); (2) 'Whatever situation arises, we have procedures to follow in dealing with it'; and (3) 'The employees are constantly being checked on for rule violations.' Reliability of the scale was 0.65 for the Israeli sample and 0.70 for the British sample.

Job Autonomy

This variable represented the extent to which employees had a say in scheduling their work, selecting the equipment they used, and deciding on procedures to be followed. To measure it I applied a 4-item scale used by Beehr (1976). Respondents were asked how true each item was with respect to their job. The scale ranged from 1 (not at all true) to 5 (very true). The items were: (1) 'I have a lot of say over what happens on my job'; (2) 'I have enough freedom as to how I do my work'; (3) 'My job allows me to make a lot of decisions on my own'; and (4) I have enough freedom as to how I do my work.' Reliability was 0.87 for the Israeli sample and 0.86 for the British sample.

Intention to Leave (Exit)

This variable was similar to the one used in study #2. Reliability was 0.84 in the Israeli sample and 0.94 in the British sample.

Voice

The voice category included informal methods of interest articulation and a formal mechanism for attempting to bring about positive change (Farrel and Rusbult, 1992). This behavior incorporates attempting to solve problems with others, suggesting solutions, and taking steps to improve the quality of work. Voice was measured by a 6-item scale ranging from 1 (strongly disagree) to 5 (strongly agree). Sample items were: (1) 'I am not afraid to "blow the whistle" on things I find wrong with my organization'; and (2) 'I have a great deal of say over what has to be done in my job.' Reliability for this scale was 0.77 in the Israeli sample and 0.84 in the British sample.

Loyalty

Loyalty was defined by Farrel and Rusbult (1992) as a constructive yet passive reaction whereby employees stand by the organization during hard times, waiting for conditions to improve. Loyal employees support the organization, trust it to do the right thing, and generally become 'good soldiers' on whom the managers can rely. Here I applied a 6-item scale taken from Leck and Saunders (1992) and Farrel and Rusbult (1992). The scale ranged from 1 (strongly disagree) to 5 (strongly agree) and sample items were: (1) 'I don't criticize my organization in front of other people'; and (2) 'I usually accept my supervisors' decisions even if I disagree with them.' Reliability of this scale was 0.68 in the Israeli sample and 0.74 in the British sample.

Neglect

This variable was similar to the one measured in the previous studies. Here a reliability of 0.67 was achieved in both samples.

Job Satisfaction

This variable was similar to the one measured in the previous studies. Here reliability in the Israeli sample was 0.77 while in the British sample it was 0.85.

Met Expectations (ME)

This variable was similar to the one measured in the previous studies. Reliability was 0.80 for the Israeli sample and 0.81 for the British sample.

Absenteeism

Employees were asked to report their estimate of the number of days missed from work (during the previous year) for reasons other than sickness (and in the Israeli sample for mandatory reserve military service also). This variable was recorded as a continuous variable.

Personal Variables

Five demographic variables were used, similar to the ones used in the previous studies, namely job hierarchy, job status (full-time/part-time job), age, education, and gender.

Appendix 2   Measuring organizational politics by the Perceptions of Organizational Politics Scale (POPS)[1]

1. Favoritism rather than merit determines who gets ahead around here.
2. There is no place for yes-men around here: good ideas are desired even when it means disagreeing with superiors (reversed score).
3. Employees are encouraged to speak out frankly even when they are critical of well-established ideas (reversed score).
4. There has always been an influential group in this department that no one ever crosses.
5. People here usually don't speak up for fear of retaliation by others.
6. Rewards come only to those who work hard in this organization (reversed score).
7. Promotions in this department generally go to top performers (reversed score).
8. People in this organization attempt to build themselves up by tearing others down.
9. I have seen changes made in policies here that only serve the purposes of a few individuals, not the work unit or the organization.
10. There is a group of people in my department who always get things their way because no one wants to challenge them.
11. I can't remember when a person received a pay increase or a promotion that was inconsistent with the published policies (reversed score).
12. Since I have worked in this department, I have never seen the pay and promotion policies applied politically (reversed score).

NOTE

1. This is a shorter version based on Kacmar and Carlson (1994).

Appendix 3   Measuring organizational politics by influence tactics

GENERAL INSTRUCTIONS

The following questionnaires (Versions A, B, and C) measure the way you tend to use influence tactics toward other individuals in your work environment. Try to remember events in which you were involved during the last year where you had to use any form of influence tactic toward others (subordinates, supervisors, or co-workers). Then indicate how frequently you used each of the following tactics in order to reach your goal. Please be sincere in your answers and answer according to your decision at that time, not as you think you should have acted with the benefit of hindsight.

QUESTIONNAIRE VERSION A (SHORT): SUPERVISORS

Many times and for many reasons we try to influence others in our work environment to make them behave the way we want. Below you will find a list of influence tactics. Please circle a number representing the degree to which you usually use this tactic in your relations with other subordinates.

	Never or almost never	Seldom	Some-times	Usually	Always or almost always
I try to influence subordinates by being friendly or by making them feel important	1	2	3	4	5
I try to influence subordinates using sanctions or treats when necessary	1	2	3	4	5
I offer an exchange to a subordinate if he/she will do what I want	1	2	3	4	5
I make appeals to higher levels in the organization to back up my requests	1	2	3	4	5
I obtain the support of others to back up my requests	1	2	3	4	5

(Continued)

QUESTIONNAIRE VERSION A (SHORT): SUPERVISORS
(Continued)

	Never or almost never	Seldom	Some-times	Usually	Always or almost always
I sophistically maneuver subordinates into doing what I want	1	2	3	4	5
I use personal contacts to influence subordinates	1	2	3	4	5
I use logical and reasoned arguments to influence subordinates	1	2	3	4	5
I politely but determinedly insist that my opinion be accepted	1	2	3	4	5
Sometimes I stop cooperating with subordinates until they do what I want	1	2	3	4	5

QUESTIONNAIRE VERSION B (SHORT): SUBORDINATES

Many times and for many reasons we try to influence others in our work environment to make them behave the way we want. Below you will find a list of influence tactics. Please circle a number representing the degree to which you usually use this tactic in your relations with other subordinates.

	Never or almost never	Seldom	Some-times	Usually	Always or almost always
I try to influence supervisors by being friendly or by making them feel important	1	2	3	4	5
I try to influence supervisors using sanctions or treats when necessary	1	2	3	4	5
I offer an exchange to a supervisor if he/she will do what I want	1	2	3	4	5
I make appeals to higher levels in the organization to back up my requests	1	2	3	4	5
I obtain the support of others to back up my requests	1	2	3	4	5

(Continued)

QUESTIONNAIRE VERSION B (SHORT): SUBORDINATES
(Continued)

	Never or almost never	Seldom	Some-times	Usually	Always or almost always
I sophistically maneuver supervisors into doing what I want	1	2	3	4	5
I use personal contacts to influence supervisors	1	2	3	4	5
I use logical and reasoned arguments to influence supervisors	1	2	3	4	5
I politely but determinedly insist that my opinion be accepted	1	2	3	4	5
Sometimes I stop cooperating with supervisors until they do what I want	1	2	3	4	5

QUESTIONNAIRE VERSION C (SHORT): CO-WORKERS

Many times and for many reasons we try to influence others in our work environment to make them behave the way we want. Below you will find a list of influence tactics. Please circle a number representing the degree to which you usually use this tactic in your relations with other subordinates.

	Never or almost never	Seldom	Some-times	Usually	Always or almost always
I try to influence co-workers by being friendly or by making them feel important	1	2	3	4	5
I try to influence co-workers using sanctions or treats when necessary	1	2	3	4	5
I offer an exchange to a co-worker if he/she will do what I want	1	2	3	4	5
I make appeals to higher levels in the organization to back up my requests	1	2	3	4	5
I obtain the support of others to back up my requests	1	2	3	4	5

(Continued)

QUESTIONNAIRE VERSION C (SHORT): CO-WORKERS
(Continued)

	Never or almost never	Seldom	Some-times	Usually	Always or almost always
I sophistically maneuver co-workers into doing what I want	1	2	3	4	5
I use personal contacts to influence co-workers	1	2	3	4	5
I use logical and reasoned arguments to influence co-workers	1	2	3	4	5
I politely but determinedly insist that my opinion be accepted	1	2	3	4	5
Sometimes I stop cooperating with co-workers until they do what I want	1	2	3	4	5

Bibliography

Aiken, M. and Hage, J. (1966), 'Organizational alienation', *American Sociological Review, 31*, 497–507.

Aiken, M. and Hage, J. (1968), 'Organizational interdependence and intraorganizational structure', *American Sociological Review, 33*, 912–30.

Aiken, L.S. and West, S.G. (1991), *Multiple Regression: Testing and Interpreting Interactions*, London: Sage.

Allen, R.W., Medison, D.L., Porter L.W., Renwick, P.A., and Mayes, B.T. (1979), 'Organizational politics: Tactics and characteristics of political actors', *California Management Review, 22*, 77–83.

Allison, G.T. (1969), 'Conceptual models and the Cuban missile crisis', *American Political Science Review, 63*, 689–718.

Allison, G.T. (1971), *Essence of Decision*, Boston: Little Brown.

Almond, G.A. and Verba, S. (1965), *The Civic Culture: Political Attitudes and Democracy in Five Nations: An Analytic Study*, Boston: Little Brown.

Almond, G.A. and Verba, S. (eds) (1980), *The Civic Culture Revisited*, Boston: Little Brown.

Andersson, L.M. and Pearson, C.M. (1999), 'Tit for tat? The spiraling effect of incivility in the workplace', *Academy of Management Journal, 24*, 452–71.

Aristotle (1962), *The Politics*, Harmondsworth: Penguin.

Asher, H. (1984), *Presidential Elections and American Politics (3rd ed)*, Chicago: Dorsey Press.

Bacharach, S.B. and Lawler, E.J. (1980), *Power and Politics in Organizations*, San Francisco: Jossey-Bass.

Bar-Haim, A. and Berman, G.S. (1991), 'Ideology, solidarity, and work values: The case of the Histadrut enterprises', *Human Relations, 44*, 357–70.

Baron, R.A. (1977), *Human Aggression*, New York: Plenum.

Baron, R.A. (1984), Reducing organizational conflict: An incompatible response approach, *Journal of Applied Psychology, 69*, 272–279.

Baron, R.A. and Kenny, D.A. (1986), 'The moderator–mediator variable distinction in social psychological research: Conceptual, strategic, and statistical considerations', *Journal of Personality and Social Psychology, 6*, 1173–82.

Baron, R.A. and Neuman, J.H. (1996), 'Workplace violence and workplace aggression: evidence on their relative frequency and potential causes', *Aggressive Behavior, 22,* 161–73.

Barzelay, G. (1987), *Democracy in War,* Unpublished doctoral dissertation, The Hebrew University of Jerusalem (Hebrew).

Beehr, T.A. (1976), 'Perceived situational moderators of the relationship between subjective role ambiguity and role strain', *Journal of Applied Psychology, 61,* 35–40.

Beehr, T.A. (1990), 'Stress in the workplace: An overview', in J.W. Jones, B.D. Steffy and D.W. Bary (eds), *Applying Psychology in Business,* Lexington, MA: Lexington Books.

Benson, P.G. and Hornsby, J.S. (1988), 'The politics of pay: The use of influence tactics in job evaluation committees', *Group and Organizational Studies, 13,* 208–24.

Bentler, P.M. (1990), 'Comparative fit indexes in structural models', *Psychological Bulletin, 107,* 238–46.

Bentler, P.M. and Bonett, D.G. (1980), 'Significance tests and goodness-of-fit in the analysis of covariance structures', *Psychological Bulletin, 88,* 588–606.

Berkowitz, L. (1993), *Aggression: Its Causes, Consequences, and Control,* New York: McGraw-Hill.

Blau, G., Linnehan, F., Brooks, A., and Hoover, D.K. (1993), 'Vocational behavior 1990–1992: Personnel practices, organizational behavior, workplace justice, and industrial/organizational measurement issues', *Journal of Vocational Behavior, 43,* 133–97.

Blau, G. (1987), 'Using a person–environment fit model to predict job involvement and organizational commitment', *Journal of Vocational Behavior, 30,* 240–57.

Blau, P. (1964), *Power and Exchange in Social Life,* New York: Wiley.

Block, P. (1988), *The Empowered Manager: Positive Political Skills at Work,* San Francisco: Jossey-Bass.

Bluhm, W.T. (1971), *Theories of the Political System (2nd edition),* Englewood Cliffs, NJ: Prentice Hall.

Bollen, K.A. (1989), *Structural Equation with Latent Variables,* New York: Wiley.

Bottger, P.C. (1984), 'Expertise and air time as bases of actual and perceived influence in problem-solving groups', *Journal of Applied Psychology, 69,* 214–21.

Boudreau, M.C., Loch, K.D., Robey, D., and Straud, D. (1998), 'Going global: using information technology to advance the competitiveness of the virtual transactional organization', *Academy of Management Executive, 12,* 120–28.

Bozeman, D.P., Perrewe, P.L., Kacmar, K.M., Hochwarter, W.A., and Brymer, R.A. (1996), *An examination of reactions to perceptions of organizational politics*, Paper presented at the Southern Management Association Meeting, New Orleans, LA.

Brass, D.J. (1984), 'Being in the right place: A structural analysis of individual influence in an organization', *Administrative Science Quarterly*, *29*, 518–39.

Bretz, R.D. and Judge, T.A. (1994), 'Person–organization fit and the theory of work adjustment: Implications for satisfaction, tenure, and career success', *Journal of Vocational Behavior*, *44*, 32–54.

Brooke, P.P. and Price, J.R. (1989), 'The determinants of employee absenteeism: An empirical test of a causal model', *Journal of Occupational Psychology*, *62*, 1–19.

Browne, M. and Cudeck, R. (1989), 'Single sample cross-validation indices for covariance structure', *Multivariate Behavioral Research*, *24*, 445–55.

Browne, M. and Cudeck, R. (1993), 'Alternative ways of assessing model fit', In K.A. Bollen and J.S. Long (eds), *Testing Structural Equation Models*, Newbury Park, CA: Sage.

Burns, T. (1961), 'Micropolitics: Mechanisms of institutional change', *Administrative Science Quarterly*, *6*, 257–81.

Bycio, P. (1992), 'Job performance and absenteeism: A review and meta–analysis', *Human Relations*, *45*, 193–220.

Campbell, A. (1960), *The American Voter*, New York: John Wiley.

Campbell, A. (1962), 'The passive citizen', *Acta Sociologica*, *6*, 9–21.

Chatman, J.A. (1989), 'Improving interactional organizational research: A model of person–organization fit', *Academy of Management Review*, *14*, 333–49.

Chatman, J.A. (1991), 'Matching people and organizations: Selection and socialization in public accounting firms', *Administrative Science Quarterly*, *36*, 459–84.

Cheng, J.L. (1983), 'Organizational context and upward influence: An experimental study of the use of power tactics', *Group and Organizational Studies*, *8*, 337–55.

Christiansen, N., Villanova, P., and Mikulay, S. (1997), 'Political influence compatibility: Fitting the person to the climate', *Journal of Organizational Behavior*, *18*, 709–30.

Cohen, J. and Cohen, P. (1983), *Applied Multiple Regression/Correlation Analysis for the Behavioral Sciences* (2nd edn), Hillsdale, NJ: Lawrence Erlbaum.

Cohen, A. and Vigoda, E. (1999), 'Politics and the workplace: An empirical examination of the relationship between political behavior and work outcomes', *Public Productivity and Management Review*, *22*, 3, 389–406.

Cohen, A. and Vigoda, E. (2000), 'Do good citizens make good organizational citizens? An empirical examination of the relationship between general citizenship and organizational citizenship behavior in Israel', *Administration and Society*, *32*, 5, 596–624.

Cook, B.B. (1977), 'Public opinion and federal judicial policy', *American Journal of Political Science*, *21*, 567–600.

Cordes, C.L. and Dougherty, T.W. (1993), 'A review and an integration of research on job burnout', *Academy of Management Review*, *18*, 621–56.

Cropanzano, R., Howes, J.C., Grandey, A.A., and Toth, P. (1997), 'The relationship of organizational politics and support to work behaviors, attitudes, and stress', *Journal of Organizational Behavior*, *18*, 159–80.

Cyert, R.M. and March, J.G. (1963), *A Behavioral Theory of the Firm*, Englewood Cliffs, NJ: Prentice Hall.

Dahl, R.A. (1963), *Modern Political Analysis*, Englewood Cliffs, NJ: Prentice Hall.

DeLeon, L. and Ewan, A.J. (1997), 'Multi-source performance appraisals: Employee perceptions of fairness', *Review of Public Personnel Administration*, *17*, 22–36.

Deri, D. (1993), *Political Appointments in Israel,* Tel Aviv: Hakibbutz Hameuhad (Hebrew).

DeSanctis, G. and Monge, P. (1999), 'Introduction to the special issue: Communication processes for virtual organizations', *Organization Science*, *10*, 693–703.

Dierendonck, D.V., Schaufeli, W.B., and Buunk, B.P. (1998), 'The evaluation of an individual burnout intervention program: The role of inequity and social support', *Journal of Applied Psychology*, *83*, 392–407.

Drory, A. (1993), 'Perceived political climate and job attitudes', *Organizational Studies*, *14*, 59–71.

Drory, A. and Beaty, D. (1991), 'Gender differences in the perception of organizational influence tactics', *Journal of Organizational Behavior*, *12*, 249–58.

Drory, A. and Romm, T. (1988), 'Politics in organizations and its perception within the organization', *Organization Studies*, *9*, 165–79.

Drory, A. and Romm, T. (1990), 'The definition of organizational politics: A review', *Human Relations*, *43*, 1133–54.

DuBrin, A.J. (1988), 'Career maturity, organizational rank and political behavior tendencies: A correlational analysis of organizational politics and career experience', *Psychological Reports*, *63*, 531–7.

DuBrin, A.J. (1989), 'Sex differences in endorsement of Influence tactics and political behavior tendencies', *Journal of Business and Psychology*, *4*, 3–14.

Dye, T. (1995), *Understanding Public Policy (8th edition),* Englewood Cliffs, NJ: Prentice Hall.

Edwards, J.R. (1992), 'A cybernetic theory of stress, coping, and well-being in organizations', *Academy of Management Review, 17,* 238–274.

Eisenhardt, K.M. and Bourgeois III, L.J. (1988), 'Politics of strategic decision making in high-velocity environments: Toward a midrange theory', *Academy of Management Journal, 31,* 737–70.

Elchanan, M., Esformes, Y., and Friedland, N. (1994), 'Congruence and differentiation as predictors of worker's occupational stability and job performance', *Journal of Career Assessment, 2,* 40–54.

Elron, E. (1997), 'Top management teams within multinational corporations: effects of cultural heterogeneity', *Leadership Quarterly, 8,* 393–412.

Emerson, R.E. (1962), 'Power-dependence relations', *American Sociological Review, 27,* 31–41.

Emerson, R.E. (1972), 'Exchange theory. Part 1: A psychological basis for social exchange, and Part 2: Exchange relations, exchange networks, and groups as exchange systems', in J. Berger, M. Zelditch and B. Anderson (eds), *Sociological Theories in Progress, 2,* Boston: Houghton Mifflin.

Erez, M. and Rim, Y. (1982), 'The relationship between goals, influence tactics and personal and organizational variables', *Human Relations, 35,* 877–8.

Erez, M., Earley, C.P., and Hulin, L.C. (1985), 'The impact of participation on goal acceptance and performance: A two–step model', *Academy of Management Journal, 28,* 50–66.

Farh, J.L., Podsakoff, P.M., and Organ, D.W. (1990), 'Accounting for organizational citizenship behavior: Leader fairness and task scope versus satisfaction', *Journal of Management, 16,* 705–21.

Farkas, A.J. and Tetrick, L.E. (1989), 'A three-wave longitudinal analysis of the causal ordering of satisfaction and commitment on turnover decisions', *Journal of Applied Psychology, 74,* 855–68.

Farrell, D. and Rusbult, C.E. (1992), 'Exploring the exit, voice, loyalty and neglect typology: The influence of job satisfaction, quality of alternatives, and investment size. Special Issue: Research on Hirschman's Exit, Voice, and Loyalty model', *Employee Responsibilities and Rights Journal, 5,* 201–18.

Ferris, G.R., Fedor, D.B., Chachere, J.G., and Pondy, L.R. (1989a), 'Myths and politics in organizational context', *Group and Organization Studies, 14,* 83–103.

Ferris, G.R., Fedor, D.B., and King, T.R. (1994), 'A political conceptualization of managerial behavior', *Human Resource Management Review, 4,* 1–34.

Ferris, G.R., Frink, D.D., Bhawuk, D.P.S., and Zhou, J. (1996a), 'Reactions of diverse groups to politics in the workplace', *Journal of Management*, *22*, 23–44.

Ferris, G.R., Frink, D.D., Galang, M.C., Zhou, J., Kacmar, M.K., and Howard, J.L. (1996b), 'Perceptions of organizational politics: Prediction, stress-related implications, and outcomes', *Human Relations*, *49*, 233–66.

Ferris, G.R., Frink, D.D., Gilmore, D.C., and Kacmar, K.M. (1994), 'Understanding as an antidote for the dysfunctional consequences of organizational politics as a stressor', *Journal of Applied Social Psychology*, *24*, 1204–20.

Ferris, G.R., Harrell-Cook, G., and Dulebohn, J.H. (1998), 'Organizational Politics: The nature of the relationship between politics perceptions and political behavior', In S.B. Bacharach and E.J. Lawler (eds), *Research in the Sociology of Organizations*, Greenwich, CT: JAI Press.

Ferris, G.R. and Kacmar, K.M. (1992), 'Perceptions of organizational politics', *Journal of Management*, *18*, 93–116.

Ferris, G.R. and King, T.R. (1991), 'Politics in human resources decisions: A walk on the dark side', *Organizational Dynamics*, *20*, 59–71.

Ferris, G.R., King, T.R., Judge, T.A., and Kacmar, K.M. (1991), 'The management of shared meaning in organizations', in R.A. Giacalone and P. Rosenfeld (eds), *Applied Impression Management* (pp. 41–64), Newbury Park, CA: Sage.

Ferris, G.R., Russ, G.S., and Fandt, P.M. (1989), 'Politics in organizations', In R.A. Giacalone and P. Rosenfeld (eds), *Impression Management in the Organization*, Hillsdale, NJ: Lawrence Erlbaum.

Fisher, D. (1993), *Communication in Organizations* (2nd edn), St. Paul, MN: West Publishing Company.

Fitzgerald, L.F. and Rounds, J.B. (1989), 'Vocational behavior, 1988: A critical analysis', *Journal of Vocational Behavior*, *35*, 105–63.

Folger, R., Konovsky, M.A., and Cropanzano, R. (1992), 'A due process metaphor for performance appraisal', In L.L. Cummings and B.M. Staw (eds), *Research in Organizational Behavior*, 14, (pp. 129–77), Greenwich, CT: JAI Press.

Folkman, S. and Lazarus, R.S. (1991), 'Coping and emotion', in A. Monat and R.S. Lazarus (eds), *Stress and Coping: An Anthology* (pp. 207–27), New York: Columbia University Press.

Frank, M.S. (1993), 'The essence of leadership', *Public Personnel Management*, *22*, 381–9.

French, J.R. and Raven, B.H. (1959), 'The bases of social power', in D. Cartwright (ed.), *Studies in Social Power* (pp. 150–67), Ann Arbor: University of Michigan Press.

Frone, M.R., Russell, M., and Cooper, M.L. (1992), 'Antecedents and outcomes of work–family conflict: Testing a model of the work–family interface', *Journal of Applied Psychology, 77*, 65–78.

Frost, P.J. and Egri, C.P. (1991), 'The political process of innovation', *Research in Organizational Behavior, 13*, 229–95.

Gabrielidis, C., Stephan, W.G., Ybarra, O., Pearson, V., and Villareal, L. (1997), 'Preferred styles of conflict resolution', *Journal of Cross-Cultural Psychology, 28*, 661–77.

Gandz, J. and Murray, V.V. (1980), 'The experience of workplace politics', *Academy of Management Journal, 23*, 237–51.

Ganster, D.C. and Schaubroeck, J. (1991), 'Work stress and employee health', *Journal of Management, 17*, 235–71.

Gibson, C.B. and Cohen, S.G., *Virtual Teams That Work,* San Francisco: Jossey Bass.

Gilmore, D.C., Ferris, G.R., Dulebohn, J.H., and Harrell-Cook, G. (1996), 'Organizational politics and employee attendance', *Group and Organizational Management, 21*, 481–94.

Gire, J.T. and Carment, D.W. (1992), 'Dealing with disputes: The influence of individualism–collectivism', *Journal of Social Psychology, 133*, 81–95.

Golembiewski, R.T., Boudreau, R.A., Mounzenrider, R.F., and Luo, H. (1996), *Global Burnout: A Worldwide Pandemic Explored by the Phase Model*, Greenwich, CT: JAI Press.

Golembiewski, R.T. and Mounzenrider, R. (1981), 'Efficacy of three versions of one burn-out measure: MBI as total score, sub-scale scores, or phases?', *Journal of Health and Human Resources Administration, 4*, 228–46.

Golembiewski, R.T. and Mounzenrider, R. (1984), 'An orientation to psychological burnout: Probably something old, definitely something new', *Journal of Health and Human Resources Administration, 7*, 153–61.

Goldenberg, E. and Traugott, M.W. (1984), *Campaigning for Congress*, Washington, DC: Congressional Quarterly Press.

Gray, B. and Ariss, S.S. (1985), 'Politics and strategic change across organizational life cycles', *Academy of Management Review, 10*, 107–23.

Gummer, B. (1990). *The Politics of Social Administration: Managing Organizational Politics in Social Agencies*, New-Jersey: Prentice Hall.

Hardy, C. (ed.) (1995), *Power and Politics in Organizations*, Cambridge, MA: Harvard University Press.

Harvey, E. and Mills, R. (1970), 'Patterns of organizational adaptation: A political perspective', in Mayer Zald (ed.), *Power in Organizations* (pp. 181–213), Nashville, TN: Vanderbilt University Press.

Herzog H. and Shapira, R. (1986), 'Will you sign my autograph book? Using autograph books for a sociohistorical study of youth and social frameworks', *Qualitative Sociology, 9*, 109–25.

Hills, F.S. and Mahoney, T.A. (1978), 'University budgets and organizational decision making', *Administrative Science Quarterly, 23,* 454–65.

Hirschman, A.O. (1970), *Exit, Voice and Loyalty,* Cambridge, MA: Harvard University Press.

Hochwarter, W.A., Witt, L.A., and Kacmar, K.M. (1997), Perceptions of organizational politics as a moderator of the relationship between conscientiousness and job performance. Paper presented at the Southern Management Association Meeting, Atlanta, GA.

Hofstede, G. (1980), *Culture's Consequences: International Differences in Work Related Values,* London: Sage.

Hofstede, G. (1991), *Cultures and Organizations,* London: McGraw Hill.

House, R.J. and Rizzo, J.R. (1972), 'Role conflict and ambiguity as critical variables in a model of organizational behavior', *Organizational Behavior and Human Performance, 7,* 467–505.

Huff, C., Sproull, L., and Kiesler, S. (1989), 'Computer communication and organizational commitment: Tracing the relationship in a city government', *Journal of Applied Social Psychology, 19,* 1371–91.

Hulin, C.L. (1991), Adaptation, persistence, and commitment in organizations, in M.D. Dunnette and L.M. Hough, L.M. (eds), *Handbook of Industrial and Organizational Psychology,* Vol. 2, (2nd ed), (pp. 445–506), Palo Alto, CA: Consulting Psychologists Press.

Huselid, M.A. (1995), 'The impact of human resource management practices on turnover, productivity, and corporate financial performance', *Academy of Management Journal, 38,* 635–72.

Izraeli, D.N. (1975), 'The middle manager and the tactics of power expansion: A case study', *Sloan Management Review, 16,* 57–70.

Izraeli, D.N. (1987), 'Sex effects in the evaluation of influence tactics', *Journal of Occupational Behavior, 8,* 79–86.

Jackson, S.E. and Maslach, C. (1982), 'After-effects of job related stress: Families as victims', *Journal of Occupational Behavior, 3,* 63–77.

James, L.R. and Brett, J.M. (1984), 'Mediators, moderators, and tests for mediation', *Journal of Applied Psychology, 69,* 307–21.

Jarvenpaa, S.L. and Leidner, D.E. (1998), 'Communication and trust in global virtual teams', *Journal of Computer Mediated Communication, 3,* 4. At http://www.ascusc.org/jcmc/vol3/issue4/jarvenpaa.html

Jex, S.M. and Beehr, T.A. (1991), 'Emerging theoretical and methodological issues in the study of work-related stress', in G.R. Ferris and K.M. Rowland (eds), *Research in Organizational Behavior,* Vol 2, (pp. 81–127), Greenwich, CT: JAI Press.

Jex, S.M., Beehr, T.A., and Roberts, C.K. (1992), 'The meaning of occupational stress items to survey respondents', *Journal of Applied Psychology, 77,* 623–8.

Joreskog, K. and Sorbom, D. (1994), *Structural equation modeling with the SIMPLIS command language*, Chicago: Scientific Software International.

Judge, T.A. and Bretz, R.D. (1994), 'Political influence behavior and career success', *Journal of Management, 20*, 43–65.

Kacmar, K.M., Bozeman, D.P., Carlson, D.S., and Anthony, W.P. (1999), 'An examination of the perceptions of organizational politics model: Replication and extension', *Human Relations, 52*, 383–416.

Kacmar, K.M. and Carlson, D.S. (1994), Further validation of the perceptions of politics scale (POPS): A multiple sample investigation. Paper presented at Academy of Management Meeting, Dallas, Texas.

Kacmar, K.M. and Ferris, G.R. (1991), 'Perceptions of organizational politics scale (POPS): development and construct validation', *Educational and Psychological Measurement, 51*, 193–205.

Kanter, R.M. (1979), 'Power failure in management circuits', in J. M. Shafritz and J. S. Ott (eds), *Classics of Organizational Theory* (4th edn), New York: Harcourt Brace and Company.

Kaplan, A. (1964), 'Power in perspective', in R.C. Kahn and E. Boulding (eds), *Power and Conflict in Organization*, London: Tavistock.

Katz, D. (1964), 'The motivational basis of organizational behavior', *Behavior Science, 9*, 131–3.

Katz, D. and Kahn, R.L. (1966), *The Social Psychology of Organizations*, New York: Wiley.

Kaufman, H. (1964), 'Organization theory and political theory', *American Political Science Review, 58*, 5–14.

Kavanagh, D. (1972), *Political culture*, London: Macmillan.

Kavanagh, D. (1980), 'Political culture in Great Britain: The Decline of the civic culture', in G.A. Almond and S. Verba (eds), *The Civic Culture Revisited* (pp. 124–76), Boston: Little Brown.

Kenny, D.A., Kashy, D.A., and Bolder, N. (1998), 'Data analysis in social psychology', in D.T. Gilbert, S.T. Fiske, and G. Lindzey (eds), *The Handbook of Social Psychology*, 1, (4th ed), (pp. 233–65), New York: Oxford University Press.

Kim, U., Triandis, H.C., Kagitcibasi, C., Choi, S.C., and Yoon, G. (1994), *Individualism and Collectivism: Theory, Method, and Applications*, Newbury Park, CA: Sage.

Kipnis, D., Schmidt, S.M., and Wilkinson, I. (1980), 'Intraorganizational influence tactics: exploration in getting one's way', *Journal of Applied Psychology, 65*, 440–52.

Klingner, D.E. (1982), 'Personnel, politics and productivity', *Public Personnel Management, 11*, 277–81.

Konovsky, M.A. and Pugh, S.D. (1994), 'Citizenship behavior and social exchange', *Academy of Management Journal, 37*, 3, 656–69.

Kumar, P. and Ghadially, R. (1989), 'Organizational politics and its effects on members of organizations', *Human Relations*, *42*, 305–14.

Kurland, N.B. and Egan, T.D. (1999), 'Telecommuting: justice and control in the virtual organization', *Organization Science*, *10*, 500–13.

Landau, S.F. (1997), 'Conflict resolution in a highly stressful society: The case of Israel', in D.P. Fry and K. Bjoerkqvist (eds), *Cultural Variation in Conflict Resolution: Alternatives to Violence* (pp. 123–36), Mahwah, NJ: Erlbaum.

Lasswell, H.D. (1958), *Politics: Who Gets What, When, How*, Cleveland: World Publishing.

Latane, B., Liu, J. H., Nowak, A., Bonevento, M., and Zheng, L. (1995), 'Distance matters: Physical space and social impact', *Personality and Social Psychology Bulletin*, *21*, 795–805.

Leck, J.D. and Saunders, D.M. (1992), 'Hirschman's loyalty: Attitude or behavior?', *Employee Responsibilities and Rights Journal*, *5*, 219–29.

Lee, T.W. and Mowday, R.T. (1987), 'Voluntarily leaving an organization: An empirical investigation of Steers and Mowday's model of turnover', *Academy of Management Journal*, *30*, 721–43.

Leiter, M.P. and Maslach, C. (1988), 'The impact of interpersonal environment on burnout and organizational commitment', *Journal of Organizational Behavior*, *9*, 297–308.

Leung, K. and Wu, P. (1990), 'Dispute processing: A cross-cultural analysis', in R.W. Brislin (ed.), *Applied Cross-Cultural Psychology* (pp. 209–31), London: Sage.

Lewin, K. (1936), *Principles of Topological Psychology*, New York: McGraw Hill.

Liden, R.C. and Mitchell, T.R. (1988), 'Ingratiatory behaviors in organizational settings', *Academy of Management Review*, *13*, 572–87.

Long, N. E. (1962), 'The administrative organization as a political system', in S. Mailick and E.H. Van Ness (eds), *Concepts and Issues in Administrative Behavior*, Englewood Cliffs, NJ: Prentice Hall.

Machanic, D. (1962), 'Sources of power lower level participants in complex organizations', *Administrative Science Quarterly*, *7*, 349–64.

Madison, L.M., Allen, R.W., Porter, L.W., Renwick, P.A., and Mayes, B.T. (1980), 'Organizational politics: An exploration of managers' perceptions', *Human Relations*, *33*, 79–100.

Martin, N.H. and Sims, J.H. (1974), 'Power tactics', in D.A. Kolb, I.M. Rubin and J.M. McIntyre (eds), *Organizational Psychology: A Book of Readings* (pp. 177–83), Englewood Cliffs, NJ: Prentice Hall.

Maslach, C. (1978), 'The client role in staff burnout', *Journal of Social Issues*, *34*, 111–24.

Maslach, C. (1982), *Burnout: The Cost of Caring*, Englewood Cliffs, NJ:

Prentice Hall.

Maslach, C. and Jackson, S.E. (1981), 'The measurement of experienced burnout', *Journal of Occupational Behavior*, *2*, 99–113.

Maslach, C. and Jackson, S.E. (1984), 'Burnout in organizational settings', in S. Oskamp (ed.), *Applied Social Psychology Annual: Applications in Organizational Settings*, 5, (pp. 133–53), Beverly Hills, CA: Sage.

Maslach, C. and Jackson, S.E. (1986), *Maslach Burnout Inventory*, Palo Alto, CA: Consulting Psychologists Press.

Maslyn, J.M. and Fedor, D.B. (1998), 'Perceptions of politics: Does measuring different foci matter?', *Journal of Applied Psychology*, *83*, 645–53.

Matteson, M.T. and Ivancevich, J.M. (1987), *Controlling Work Stress*, San Francisco: Jossey-Bass.

Matuszek, P.A., Nelson, D.L., and Quick, J.C. (1995), 'Gender differences in distress: Are we asking all the right questions?', *Journal of Social Behavior and Personality*, *10*, 99–120.

May, R. (1972), *Power and Innocence*, New York: Norton.

Mayes, B.T. and Allen, R.W. (1977), 'Toward a definition of organizational politics', *Academy of Management Review*, *2*, 672–8.

McKenney, J.L., Zack, M.H., and Doherty, V.S. (1992), 'Complementary communication media: A comparison of electronic mail and face-to-face communication in a programming team' in N. Nohria and R. Eccles (eds), *Networks and Organizations: Structure, Form, and Action* (pp. 262–87), Harvard Business School Press, Boston.

McKevitt, D. (1998), *Managing Core Public Services*, Oxford: Blackwell.

Medsker, G.J., Williams, L.J., and Holahan, P.J. (1994), 'A review of current practices for evaluating causal models in organizational behavior and human resources management research', *Journal of Management*, *20*, 239–64.

Meir, E. and Hasson, R. (1982), 'Congruence between personality type and environment type as a predictor of stay in an environment', *Journal of Vocational Behavior*, *21*, 309–17.

Meyer, J.P., Paunonen, S.V., Gellatly, I.R., and Goffin, R.D. (1989), 'Organizational commitment and job performance: It's the nature of the commitment that counts', *Journal of Applied Psychology*, *74*, 152–6.

Milbrath, L.W. (1981), 'Political Participation', in Samuel L.L. (ed.), *Handbook of Political Behavior*, *4*, New York: Plenum.

Milbrath, L.W. and Goel, M.L. (1977), *Political Participation* (2nd edn), Chicago: Rand McNally and Company.

Mills, C.W. (1959), *The Sociological Imagination*, Oxford: Oxford University Press.

Mintzberg, H. (1983), *Power in and Around Organizations*, Englewood Cliffs, NJ: Prentice-Hall.

Mintzberg, H. (1985), 'The organization as political arena', *Journal of Management Studies, 22*, 133–54.

Mintzberg, H. (1989), *Mintzberg on Management*, New York, NY: Free Press.

Molm, L.D. (1997), *Coercive Power in Social Exchange*, Cambridge: Cambridge University Press.

Moorhead, G. and Griffin, R.W. (1989), *Organizational Behavior*, Boston: Houghton Mifflin.

Moorman, R.H. (1991), 'Relationship between organizational justice and organizational citizenship behaviors: Do fairness perceptions influence employee citizenship?', *Journal of Applied Psychology, 76*, 6, 845–55.

Morrison, E.W. (1994), 'Role definitions and organizational citizenship behavior: The importance of the employee's perspective', *Academy of Management Journal, 37*, 1543–67.

Morrow, P.C., Mullen, E.J., and McElroy, J.C. (1990), 'Vocational behavior 1989: The year in review', *Journal of Vocational Behavior, 37*, 121–95.

Mossholder, K.W., Bedeian, A.G., Norris, D.R., Giles, W.F., and Field, H.S. (1988), 'Job performance and turnover decisions: Two field studies', *Journal of Management, 14*, 403–14.

Mowday, R.T., Porter, L.M., and Steers, R.M. (1982), 'Employee–Organization Linkages: The Psychology of Commitment', *Absenteeism and Turnover*, New York, NY: Academic Press.

Mowday, R.T., Steers, R.M., and Porter, L.M. (1979), 'The measurement of organizational commitment', *Journal of Vocational Behavior, 14*, 224–47.

Murray, M.A. (1975), 'Comparing public and private management – an exploratory essay', *Public Administration Review, 35*, 364–71.

Nachmias, D. (1991), 'Israel's bureaucratic elite: Social structure and patronage', *Public Administration Review, 51*, 413–20.

Namboodiri, N.K., Carter, L.F., and Blalock, H.M. (1975), *Applied Multivariate Analysis and Experimental Design*, New York: McGraw Hill.

Near, J.P., Rice, R.W., and Hunt, R.G. (1987), 'Job satisfaction and life satisfaction: A profile analysis', *Social Indicators Research, 19*, 383–401.

Netemeyer, R.G., Johnston, M.W., and Burton, S. (1990), 'Analysis of role conflict and role ambiguity in a structural equation framework', *Journal of Applied Psychology, 75*, 148–57.

Nie, N.H., Verba, S., and Petrocik, J. (1979), *The Changing American Voter*, Cambridge, MA: Harvard University Press.

Niehoff, B.F. and Moorman, R.H. (1993), 'Justice as mediator of the relationship between methods of monitoring and organizational citizenship behavior', *Academy of Management Journal, 36*, 3, 527–56.

Nilles, J.M. (1994), *Making Telecommunication Happen*, New York: Van
Nostrand Reinhold.
Nohria, N. and Eccles, R. (1992), 'Face-to-face: making network
organizations work', in N. Nohria and R. Eccles (eds), *Networks and
Organizations: Structure, Form, and Action* (pp. 288–308), Boston:
Harvard Business School Press.
Northwestern National Life Insurance Company (1993), 'Fear and Violence
in the Workplace', *Research Report*, Minneapolis, MN.
Ohbuchi, K.I., Fukushima, O., and Tedeschi, J.T. (1999), 'Cultural values in
conflict management: Goal orientation, goal attainment, and tactical
decision', *Journal of Cross-Cultural Psychology*, *30*, 51–71.
O'Leary-Kelly, A.M., Paetzold, R.L., and Griffin, R.W. (2000), 'Sexual
Harassment as aggressive behavior: An actor-based perspective', *Academy
of Management Review*, *25*, 372–88.
O'Reilly, C.A., Chatman, J., and Caldwell, D.F. (1991), 'People and
organizational culture: A profile comparison approach to assessing person–
organization fit', *Academy of Management Journal*, *34*, 487–516.
Organ, D.W. (1988), *O.C.B.: The Good Soldier Syndrome*, Lexington, MA:
Lexington Books.
Organ, D.W. and Konovsky, M. (1989), 'Cognitive versus affective
determinants of organizational citizenship behavior', *Journal of Applied
Psychology*, *74*, 157–64.
Organ, D.W. and Ryan, K. (1995), 'A meta-analytic review of attitudinal and
dispositional predictors of organizational citizenship behavior. Special
issue: Theory and literature', *Personnel Psychology*, *48*, 775–802.
Pandarus, A. (1973), 'One's own primer of academic politics', *American
Scholar*, *42*, 569–92.
Papa, M.J. and Canary, D.J. (1995), 'Conflict in organizations: A competence–
based approach', in A.M. Nicotera (ed.), *Conflict and Organizations:
Communicative Processes* (pp. 153–79), New York: State University of
New York.
Parker, C.P., Dipboye, R.L., and Jackson, S.L. (1995), 'Perceptions of
organizational politics: an investigation of antecedents and consequences',
Journal of Management, *21*, 891–912.
Pateman, C. (1970), *Participation and Democratic Theory*, London:
Cambridge University Press.
Pavett, C.M. and Lau, A.W. (1983), 'Managerial work: The influence of
hierarchical level and functional speciality', *Academy of Management
Journal*, *26*, 170–77.
Perrow, L.R. (1979), *Complex Organizations*, Glenview, IL: Scott, Foresman.
Peterson, S.A. (1990), *Political Behavior*, Newbury Park, CA: Sage.

Pettigrew, A. (1973), *The Politics of Organizational Decision-Making*, London: Tavistock.

Pettigrew, A.M. (1979), 'On studying organizational cultures', *Administrative Science Quarterly*, 24, 570–81.

Pettigrew, A.M. (1990), 'Organizational climate and culture: Two constructs in search of a role', in B. Schneider (ed.), *Organizational Climate and Culture* (pp. 413–34), San Francisco: Jossey Bass.

Pfeffer, J. (1981), *Power in Organizations*, Marshfield, MA: Pitman Publishing.

Pfeffer, J. (1991), 'Organization theory and structural perspectives on management', *Journal of Management*, 17, 789–803.

Pfeffer, J. (1992), *Management With Power*, Boston: Harvard Business School Press.

Pfeffer, J. and Moore, W.B. (1980), 'Average tenure of academic department heads: The effects of paradigm, size and department demography', *Administrative Science Quarterly*, 25, 487–506.

Pfeffer, J. and Salancik, G., (1974), 'Organizational decision making as a political process: The case of the university budget', *Administrative Science Quarterly*, 19, 135–51.

Pines, A. and Maslach, C. (1980), 'Combating staff burn-out in a day care center: A case study', *Child Care Quarterly*, 9, 5–16.

Pollitt, C. (1988), 'Bringing consumers into performance measurement', *Policy and Politics*, 16, 77–87.

Pollitt, C. (1990), 'Performance indicators, root and branch', in M. Cave, M. Kogan, and R. Smith (eds), *Output and Performance Measurement in Government: The State of the Art* (pp. 167–78), London: Jessica Kingsley.

Porter, L.W. and Smith, F.J. (1970), The etiology of organizational commitment. Unpublished paper, University of California, Irvine.

Porter, L.W. and Steers, R.M. (1973), 'Organizational, work, and personal factors in employee turnover and absenteeism', *Psychological Bulletin*, 80, 151–76.

Porter, L.W., Steers, R.M., Mowday, R.T., and Boulian, P.V. (1974), 'Organizational commitment, job satisfaction and turnover among psychiatric technicians', *Journal of Applied Psychology*, 59, 603–9.

Putnam, L.L. (1995), 'Formal negotiations: The productive side of organizational conflict', in A.M. Nicotera (ed.), *Conflict and Organizations* (pp. 183–200), NY: State University of New York.

Rainey, H.G. (1991), *Understanding and Managing Public Organizations*, San Francisco; Jossey-Bass.

Ralston, D.A., Giacalone, R.A., and Terpstra, R.H. (1994), 'Ethical perceptions of organizational politics: A comparative evaluation of

American and Hong Kong managers', *Journal of Business Ethics*, *13*, 989–99.

Randall, M.L., Cropanzano, R., Borman, C.A., and Birjulin, A. (1999), 'Organizational politics and organizational support as predictors of work attitudes, job performance, and organizational citizenship behavior', *Journal of Organizational Behavior*, *20*, 159–74.

Randolph, W.A. (1985), *Understanding and Managing Organizational Behavior*, Homewood, IL: Richard D. Irwin.

Rao, A., Hashimoto, K., and Rao, A. (1997), 'Universal and culturally specific aspects of managerial influence: A study of Japanese managers', *Leadership Quarterly*, *8*, 295–312.

Reykowski, J. (1994), 'Collectivism and individualism as dimensions of social change', In U. Kim, H.C. Triandis, C. Kagitcibasi, S.C. Choi, and G. Yoon (eds), *Individualism and Collectivism* (pp. 276–92), London: Sage.

Rollinson, D., Broadfield, A., and Edwards, D.J. (1998), *Organizational Behavior and Analysis*, New York: Addison Wesley Longman.

Romano, C. (1994), 'Workplace violence takes a deadly turn', *Management Review*, *83*, 5.

Romm, T. and Drory, A. (1988), 'Political behavior in organizations: A cross-cultural comparison', *International Journal of Value Based Management*, *1*, 97–113.

Rusbult, C. and Lowery, D. (1985), 'When bureaucrats get the blues: Responses to dissatisfaction among federal employees', *Journal of Applied Social Psychology*, *15*, 80–103.

Russell, B. (1938), *Power: A New Social Analysis*, London: George Allen and Unwin.

Ryan, A. (1977), 'How free are we?', *New Society*, *42*, 454–7.

Ryan, M. (1989), 'Political behavior and management development. Special issue: Politics and management development', *Management Education and Development*, *20*, 238–53.

Sagy, S., Orr, E., and Bar-On, D. (1999), 'Individualism and collectivism in Israeli society: Comparing religious and secular high-school students', *Human Relations*, *52*, 327–48.

Salancik, G.R. and Pffefer, J. (1974), 'The bases and uses of power in organizational decision making: The case of a university', *Administrative Science Quarterly*, *19*, 453–73.

Samuel, Y. (1990), *Organizations*, Haifa: Haifa University Press (Hebrew).

Sato, T. and Cameron, J.E. (1999), 'The relationship between collective self-esteem and self-construal in Japan and Canada', *The Journal of Social Psychology*, *139*, 426–35.

Scandura, T.A. (1997), 'Mentoring and organizational justice: An empirical investigation', *Journal of Vocational Behavior, 51*, 58–69.

Schein, E.H. (1968), 'Organizational socialization and the profession of management', *Industrial Management Review, 2*, 59–77.

Schein, E. (1978), *Career Dynamics: Matching individual and organizational needs*, Reading, MA: Addison Wesley.

Schilit, W.K. and Locke, E.A. (1982), 'A study of upward influence in organizations, *Administrative Science Quarterly, 27*, 304–16.

Schnake, M. (1991), 'Organizational citizenship: A review, proposed model, and research agenda', *Human Relations, 44*, 735–59.

Schneider, B. (ed.) (1990), *Organizational Climate and Culture*, San Francisco: Jossey-Bass.

Schriesheim, C. and Tsui, A.S. (1980), Development and validation of a short satisfaction instrument for use in survey feedback interventions, Paper presented at the Western Academy of Management Meeting, Phoenix, AZ.

Schwartz, D.C. (1974), 'Toward a more relevant and rigorous political science', *Journal of Politics, 36*, 103–37.

Schwartz, S.H. (1990),' Individualism–collectivism: Critique and proposed refinements', *Journal of Cross-Cultural Psychology, 21*, 139–57.

Schwartz, S.H. (1992), 'Universals in the content and structure of values: Theoretical advances and empirical tests in 20 countries', in M. Zanna (ed.), *Advances in Experimental Social Psychology, 25*, (pp. 1–66), New York: Academic Press.

Selye, H. (1975), *Stress without Distress*, New York: Signet.

Shaker, Z. (1987), 'Organizational politics and the strategic process', *Journal of Business Ethics, 6*, 579–87.

Shirom, A. (1989), 'Burnout in work organization', in C.L. Cooper and I. Robertson (eds), *International Review of Industrial and Organizational Psychology*, (pp. 25–48), New York: Wiley.

Shore, L.M. and Martin, H.J. (1989), 'Job satisfaction and organizational commitment in relation to work performance and turnover intentions', *Human Relations, 42*, 625–38.

Smart, J.C., Elton, C.F., and McLaughlin, G.W. (1986), 'Person–environment congruence and job satisfaction', *Journal of Vocational Behavior, 29*, 216–25.

Smith, C.A., Organ, D.W., and Near, J.P. (1983), 'Organizational citizenship behavior: Its nature and antecedents', *Journal of Applied Psychology, 68*, 653–63.

Sobel, R. (1993), 'From occupational involvement to political participation: An exploratory analysis', *Political Behavior, 15*, 339–53.

Spector, P.E. (1986), 'Perceived control by employees: A meta-analysis of studies concerning autonomy and participation at work', *Human Relations*, *39*, 1005–16.

Sprinzak, E. and Diamond, L.J. (eds) (1993), *Israeli Democracy under Stress*, Boulder, CO: Lynne Rienner.

Spokane, A. (1985), 'A review of research on person–environment congruence in Holland's theory of careers', *Journal of Vocational Behavior*, *26*, 306–43.

Steiger, J.H. (1990), 'Structural models evaluation and modification: An interval estimation approach, *Multivariate Behavioral Research*, *25*, 173–80.

Tan, D.S.K. and Akhtar, S. (1998), 'Organizational commitment and experienced burnout: an exploratory study from Chinese cultural perspective', *International Journal of Organizational Analysis*, *6*, 310–33.

Tansky, J.W. (1993), 'Justice and organizational citizenship behavior: What is the relationship?', *Employees Responsibilities and Rights Journal*, *6*, 195–207.

Tharenou, P. (1993), 'A test of reciprocal causality for absenteeism', *Journal of Organizational Behavior*, *14*, 269–87.

Tosi, H. (1992), *The Environment/Organization/Person Contingency Model: A Meso Approach to the Study of Organizations*, Greenwich, CT: JAI Press.

Triandis, H. (1989), 'Self and social behavior in differing cultural contexts', *Psychological Review*, *96*, 269–89.

Triandis, H. (1994), *Culture and Social Behavior*, New York: McGraw Hill.

Triandis, H. (1995), *Individualism and Collectivism*, Boulder, CO: Westview.

Tziner, A., Latham, G.P., Price, B.S., and Haccoun, R. (1996), 'Development and validation of questionnaires for measuring perceived political considerations in performance appraisal', *Journal of Organizational Behavior*, *17*, 179–90.

Valle, M. and Perrewe, P.L. (2000), 'Do politics perceptions relate to political behaviors? Tests of an implicit assumption and expanded model', *Human Relations*, *53*, 359–86.

Valocchi, S. (1989), 'The relative autonomy of the state and the origins of British welfare policy', *Sociological Forum*, *4*, 349–65.

Van den Berg, A., Masi, A.C., Smith, M.R., and Smucker, J. (1998), 'To cut or not to cut: A cross-national comparison of attitudes toward wage flexibility', *Work and Occupations*, *25*, 49–73.

Vardi, Y. and Wiener, Y. (1996), 'Misbehavior in organizations: A motivational framework', *Organization Study*, *7*, 151–65.

Verba, S. and Nie, N.H. (1972), *Participation in America*, New York: Harper and Row.

Verba, S., Schlozman, K.L., and Brady, H. (1995), *Voice and Equality*, London: Harvard University Press.

Vigoda, E. (2000), 'Internal politics in public administration systems: An empirical examination of its relationship with job congruence, organizational citizenship behavior and in–role performances', *Public Personnel Management, 26*, 185-210.

Vigoda, E. (2000a), 'The relationship between organizational politics, job attitudes, and work outcomes: Exploration and implications for the public sector', *Journal of Vocational Behavior, 57*, 326–47.

Vigoda, E. (2001), 'Reactions to organizational politics: A cross-cultural examination in Israel and Britain', *Human Relations, 54*, 1483–518.

Vigoda, E., (2002), 'Stress-related aftermaths to workplace politics: An empirical assessment of the relationship among organizational politics, job stress, burnout, and aggressive behavior', *Journal of Organizational Behavior, 23*, 571–91.

Vigoda, E. and Cohen, A. (1998), 'Organizational politics and employee performances: A review and theoretical model', *Journal of Management Systems, 10*, 3, 59–72.

Vigoda, E. and Cohen, A. (2002), 'Influence tactics and perceptions of organizational politics: A longitudinal study', *Journal of Business Research, 55*, 4, 311–24.

Vigoda, E. and Elron, E. (2003), 'Influence and political processes in virtual teams', in S.G. Cohen and C.B. Gibson (eds), *Creating Conditions for Effective Virtual Teams,* (pp. 317–34), San Francisco: Jossey-Bass.

Voyer, J.J. (1994), 'Coercive organizational politics and organizational outcomes: An interpretive study', *Organizational Science, 5*, 72–85.

Vroom, V.H. (1964), *Work and Motivation*, New York: Wiley.

Wagner, J.A. and Gooding, R.Z. (1987), 'Shared influence and organizational behavior: A meta-analysis of situational variables expected to moderate participation–outcome relationship', *Academy of Management Journal, 30*, 524–41.

Wallace, M. and Szilagyi, A. (1982), *Managing Behavior in Organizations*, Glenview, IL: Scott, Foresman.

Wanous, J.P., Poland, T.D., Premack, S.L., and Davis, K.S. (1992), 'The effect of met expectations on newcomer attitudes and behaviors: A review and meta-analysis', *Journal of Applied Psychology, 77*, 288–97.

Wayne, S.J. and Ferris, G.R. (1990), 'Influence tactics, affect, and exchange quality in supervisor-subordinate interactions: a laboratory experiment and a field study', *Journal of Applied Psychology, 75*, 487–99.

Wayne, S.J. and Green, S.A. (1993), 'The effects of leader–member exchange on employee citizenship and impression management behavior', *Human Relations, 46,* 1431–440.

Wayne, S.J., Liden, R.C., Graf, I.K., and Ferris, G.R. (1997), 'The role of upward influence tactics in human resource decision', *Personnel Psychology, 50,* 979–1006.

Weber, M. (1947), *The Theory of Social and Economic Organizations,* New York: Free Press.

Welsh, M.A. and Slusher, E.A. (1986), 'Organizational design as a context of political activity', *Administrative Science Quarterly, 31,* 389–402.

Whetten, D.A. and Cameron, K.S. (1991), *Developing Management Skills,* New York: Harper Collins Publishers Inc.

Wiesenfeld, B., Raghuram, S., and Garud, R. (1999), 'Communication patterns as determinants of organizational identification in a virtual organization', *Organization Science, 10,* 777-90.

Wildavsky, A. (1966), 'The political economy of efficiency: Cost–benefit analysis, systems analysis, and program budgeting', *Public Administration Review, 26,* 292–310.

Wildavsky, A. (1989), 'Frames of reference come from culture: A predictive theory', in M. Freilich (ed.), *The Relevance of Culture.* New York: Bergin and Garvey.

Williams, L.J. and Anderson, S.E. (1991), 'Job satisfaction and organizational commitment as predictors of organizational citizenship and in-role behaviors', *Journal of Management, 17,* 601–17.

Witt, L.A. (1998), 'Enhancing organizational goal congruence: A solution to organizational politics', *Journal of Applied Psychology, 83,* 666–74.

Witt, L.A., Andrews, M.C., and Kacmar, M. (2000), 'The role of participation in decision-making in the organizational politics–job satisfaction relationship', *Human Relations, 53,* 341–58.

Wolpin, J., Burke, R.J., and Greenglass, E.R. (1991), 'Is job satisfaction an antecedent or a consequence of psychological burnout?', *Human Relations, 44,* 193–219.

Wright, T.A. and Cropanzano, R. (1998), 'Emotional exhaustion as a predictor of job performance and voluntary turnover', *Journal of Applied Psychology, 83,* 486–93.

Wrong, D.H. (1979), *Power: Its Forms, Bases and Uses,* Oxford: Basil Blackwell.

Yukl, G. and Tracey, J.B. (1992), 'Consequences of influence tactics used with subordinates, peers, and the boss', *Journal of Applied Psychology, 77,* 525–35.

Zaleznik, A. (1970), 'Power and politics in Organizational Life', *Harvard Business Review, 48,* 47–60.

Zhou, J. and Ferris, G.R. (1995), 'The dimensions and consequences of organizational politics perceptions: A confirmatory analysis', *Journal of Applied Social Psychology*, *25*, 1747–64.

Index of Authors

Index of Contents